Lady of the Two Lands

Lady of

FIVE QUEENS

the Two Lands

OF ANCIENT EGYPT

Leonard Cottrell

THE BOBBS-MERRILL COMPANY, INC.

A Subsidiary of Howard W. Sams & Co., Inc., Publishers

INDIANAPOLIS / KANSAS CITY / NEW YORK

For Diana

Acknowledgements

For permission to quote from books and articles mentioned in the text, the author and publishers are grateful to the following:

Journal of Egyptian Archaeology; University of Chicago Press; Charles Scribner's Sons; New York Graphic Society; University Books, Inc.; Oxford University Press; British Museum; Egypt Exploration Society; Princeton University Press.

Contents

Illustrations

Plates 1 to 26 following page 118

Plates 27 to 47 following page 150

*A family tree of the Amarnan royal family
will be found at the end of the text, page 227.*

Lady of the Two Lands

Introduction

THE WOMEN OF THE ANCIENT WORLD ARE EVEN MORE ENIG-
matic than their modern counterparts because whereas
today women can (and do) speak for themselves, in novels,
plays, television and the press, those of the remote past—with
few exceptions—owe their immortality to what men have written about them.

Nevertheless, their lineaments are clear and recognisable.
In the literature of Greece and Rome, especially, the familiar
stereotypes are paraded for our view; the innocent and not-so-
innocent virgin, the devoted housewife and mother, the terma-
gant, the shrew, the scold, the 'femme fatale,' the courtesan and
her poor relation the trollop. We have the ultra-feminine women
whom men profess to admire but often find boring, and, in the
Messalinas and Clytemnestras, the power-loving female who, in
the words of Noel Coward, 'uses sex like a shrimping-net.'

We also find that even more formidable creature, the
woman with a male mind in a female body. Zenobia of Palmyra
defied the armies of Rome and gave the Emperor Aurelian—

poor man—a great deal to explain to the Senate when they accused him of 'making war on a woman.' The Empress Theodora, formerly a circus performer, can claim at least equal status with Justinian in moulding the Byzantine Empire.

Turning to Ancient Egypt one finds that, although the Pharaohs ruled, their Queens were given high honour, and, like the wives of the nobles depicted in the tombs, shared in the lives of their husbands to an extent which would have been unthinkable among the classical Greeks (though not among the Mycenaeans). Although this belief has been recently challenged in some quarters, it is generally accepted that in Ancient Egypt, inheritance was through the female line and not the male; usually a Pharaoh could not establish his right to rule unless he married the heiress of the preceding King. And Petrie points out in his *Social Life in Ancient Egypt* that 'The ancestors are always traced farther back in the female than the male line. The father was only the holder of office; the mother was the family link. The same in respect of property; that goes through the *nebt per*, the mistress of the house; we never find a *neb per* or master of the house.'

This would account for the custom of brother-sister marriages, even in Graeco-Roman times. 'You may go half-way in Athens,' said the Romans, referring to the fact that Greeks permitted marriage with half-sisters, 'the whole way in Alexandria.' The purpose was to keep inheritance within the family and prevent interlopers gaining power or property (or both) by marrying an heiress.

Why was this? Why was it that in Ancient Egypt women, though nominally subordinate to men, enjoyed these rights and privileges, as apparently did Minoan and Mycenaean women before the Dorian Greeks entered with their predominantly male gods and male-orientated society? Could it be a distant survival of a period when Woman, as the giver of life, was more important than Man who, apart from his necessary functions as hunter and warrior, was merely a fertilising agent? And if one goes far enough back in time, one finds a period when the sexual act was not, in the eyes of primitive people, necessarily associated with childbirth. Women might be fertilised by the winds, or by a spirit; anthropologists have occasionally encountered modern primitives who had so far failed to observe the relationship between coitus and procreation.

Such fascinating speculations inevitably arise in the mind of any author contemplating a book on women of the ancient world, and they enter into this one. But they are not its main *raison d'être*. It is essentially a crystallisation of many impressions and experiences stretching back to 1946, when I first visited Egypt. Since that year I have revisited the land of the Pharaohs again and again, written five books on the subject, accumulated a mass of notebooks, photographs and memories. For a long time I have contemplated a book on some of the most notable Egyptian Queens but have hesitated for what seems to me a very good reason. With the exception of Cleopatra (who was not Egyptian anyway) very little is known about their personal lives. Of the others, the forceful Hashepsowe (Hatshepsut) alone has left a record of her achievements, though her personality remains shadowy; of the lives of Tiye, Ankhesnamun, Nefertiti and Nefertari, one can only say, as Arnold says of Shakespeare:

> *Others abide our question, thou art free.*
> *We ask and ask; thou smilest, and art still.*

How frustrating it is! For of all the great civilisations of the ancient world, not one has left so many alluring portraits of women. How one would have liked to have known Nefertiti, whose beauty has survived more than 3,000 years, or Nefertari, the favourite wife of the great Ramesses II; the slim, elegant little Queen standing between the knees of her husband's colossus in the Karnak temple, or sculpted in sinuous relief in the lovely temple of Hathor which he had carved for her at Abu Simbel, is enchanting. So, evidently, was Tiye, wife of the uxorious, luxury-loving Amenophis III. A woman whose royal husband could create a huge lake purely so that she could go boating, and issue a special scarab to commemorate the event, must have had extraordinary fascination, particularly as Ameno-phis was evidently a connoisseur of women. (The Amarna letters reveal how assiduous he was in regularly re-stocking the royal harem with Syrian and other foreign princesses.)

As for the formidable Hashepsowe—the only Queen of Egypt to rule as a divine Pharaoh in her own right, even to wearing the male dress and adopting the full Pharaonic titles—there is another enigma. Every student of Egyptology is familiar with the story of how she prevented her young co-regent Tuth-mosis from gaining any real power until he was long past his majority; and of how, after her death, he appears to have taken revenge by defacing her great monuments and the tomb of her favourite, Sen-en-mut. I had always imagined Hashepsowe with a hard-jawed face hewn out of granite, a masculine woman. Yet when, some years ago, I visited the Metropolitan Museum of Art in New York, I was astonished to discover that the features of this Queen, far from being hard, were soft and feminine. Yet it was a face of decided character.

How did she attain power? How did she contrive to re-strain her redoubtable nephew and stepson for those many years, and how, in a predominantly male society, did she make all Egypt 'bow the head,' as one chronicler puts it? There are so many things one would like to have known; of her relationship with Sen-en-mut, a man of lowly birth who was not only her Minister of Works and possibly the architect of her great temple, but also the tutor of her daughter by her husband Tuthmosis II. Was Sen-en-mut more than her favourite and Minister?

Then there is the child-Queen Ankhesnamun, wife of Tut-ankhamun, himself little more than a boy. Of these minor royal-ties, the last of a dying dynasty, practically nothing is known save what was discovered in Tutankhamun's gorgeously-fur-nished tomb. Yet there exists a group of letters, sent by Ank-hesnamun to the Hittite king after her husband's death, which are dramatically moving.

However, I must state at the outset that this is a deliber-

ately discursive book; discursive, that is, in the way that Herodotus, in his great history of the Graeco-Persian war, makes
wide sweeps into interesting local terrain while always returning
to the main highway. I hasten to add that this is not to compare
my modest efforts with those of that revered master, but when
planning the book it seemed to me that his method was admi-
rably suited to my subject. The reasons for this are that the hard
facts concerning each of the five Queens whose lives I have
attempted to describe would hardly fill one brief chapter.

No knowledgeable student of Ancient Egypt expects to
find it well documented. Egyptian history is 'a thing of shreds
and patches.' There is no Livy, Polybius, Suetonius or Tacitus
to provide us with professionally-written history. Scattered,
fragmented papyri, a few formal and usually uninformative inscriptions on tombs and temples are all that we can depend on;
these plus the marvellous collection of well-preserved remains
in the form of temples, tombs, furniture, ornaments and domestic objects which give the Egyptologist a unique advantage over
most archaeologists.

In dealing with the lives of my five Queens I was faced
with two alternatives: either to use the few scanty facts but pad
them out with woolly speculation, a popular method but one
which I dislike, or only give what is authentically known about
the lives of the Queens but also show the fascinating process by
which this knowledge has been obtained and is being supple-
mented. In seeking the truth about Ancient Egyptian civilisation
the archaeologist and philologist are like detectives. From a
few scattered clues they must piece together a plausible, often
hypothetical, reconstruction of what may have happened. It is
by these circuitous paths that I have approached the heroines
of my story.

The calm, lovely faces, remote and yet warmly human,
beckon and bewitch. And not only the faces of the Queens.
Gradually, over the years, reading and re-reading Ancient Egyptian inscriptions and papyri, gazing yet again at the bas-reliefs
and painted frescoes in the now familiar tombs of the nobles—

those of Sennufer, Ramose, Rekhmire, Nakht, Men-na—or the temple reliefs at Karnak, Luxor and Abydos, the women of Ancient Egypt have returned ever more frequently to my mind. Thousands of their sculpted or painted portraits survive, and, in the burning sunlight of Egypt, seem more alive than, say, the prim matrons of Rome, or even the marble nymphs and goddesses of classical Greece. And it was this which finally decided me to embark on this book.

But it is not only about five Queens.

One might compare the book's pattern with an Egyptian frieze, in which the tall figures of the Great Ones, dignified but static, are contrasted with the smaller, but more animated portraits of the lesser women who were their subjects. Of these one can learn a considerable amount, not only from their tomb-paintings and the hieroglyphic inscriptions which accompany them, but from Ancient Egyptian stories and poems in which women appear, from the love-songs which were sung to them, and about them, at royal and noble feasts, and from the innumerable objects of feminine use which archaeologists have discovered. We can see and handle the exquisite jewellery which adorned their bodies, their hand-mirrors, their cosmetic and perfume jars, the chairs on which they sat and the beds they slept in.

Even the wives and daughters of the common folk are remembered in the tomb-paintings of their masters and mistresses. There are paintings, and realistic models which show them at work, kneading dough, brewing beer, spinning, weaving, reaping corn, or dancing and singing at some princely festivity, in that eternal prolongation of earthly affluence which was the Egyptian nobleman's conception of Paradise.

They are not always behaving discreetly, these high-born dames. 'I wish to drink until I am drunk!' exclaims one elegantly-gowned lady. 'My inside is like a straw!' Smilingly, their less-fortunate sisters, the serving-girls, hand them wine with the exhortation to 'spend a festive day!' And they do, to judge from a portrait in one tomb which shows one of the female guests, overcome by her potations, being quietly sick into a bowl.

Naturally, as with modern women, the Egyptians existed

not in isolation but in close association with their menfolk; and thanks to the fact that Egyptian society was more liberal to women than that of Greece or Rome, we often see them sharing in the social life of their husbands. Even the activities which they did not share, such as warfare and politics, must have affected them deeply, so in this book I have tried to show the kind of men who were their fathers, lovers, husbands, brothers and sons. Sometimes we see a man through a woman's eyes, as in this lovely poem, which dates between 1300 and 1100 BC:

> *The voice of the swallow speaks and says*
> *'The land has brightened—What is thy road?'**
>
> *Thou shalt not, O bird, disturb me!*
> *I have found my beloved in his bed*
> *And my heart is still more glad*
> *(When he) said to me:*
> *'I shall not go afar off.*
> *My hand is in thy hand,*
> *I shall stroll about,*
> *And I shall be with thee in every pleasant place.'*
> *He makes me the foremost of maidens.*
> *He injures not my heart.*[1]

So this book, which includes all that I have been able to glean about five of the Queens of Egypt, has been broadened to embrace their lesser sisters who, though not entitled to wear the royal serpent on their head-dress, or sleep in the Valley of the Queens, were not unlike those who enjoyed such privileges. Nor, judging from such information as we have, were they totally unlike the women of today. If you doubt this, look at their faces.

LEONARD COTTRELL
February, 1966

---

* i.e. 'Where are you walking in the early morning?'
[1] Pritchard, J. B. *Ancient Near Eastern Texts,* Princeton University Press, 1958

1

The World They Lived In

IMAGINE SOME FUTURE HISTORIAN BEING ASKED TO DESCRIBE THE women of Britain at any time between AD 300 and 1966. Apart from their femininity, is there anything which links the wife of a Romano-British chieftain of the third century with that of a British businessman of the mid-twentieth? A similar problem faces a writer attempting to portray the women of Ancient Egypt, a civilisation which extended over twice the period of time which separates us from Roman Britain.

Fortunately for the social historian, the civilisation of Egypt was far more static and conservative than ours. Religion, social customs, political organisation changed far less in three millennia than ours have changed in three centuries. A woman in 2700 BC at the time of the pyramid-builders lived a life not very dissimilar to that of a woman of the same rank born under the Ptolemies, some 2,400 years later. Both spoke basically the same language, worshipped similar gods, wore similar dress and observed similar customs. There were differences, of course. An educated Egyptian lady living in 300 BC would have had a wider horizon than her remote ancestress living in the time of Cheops. As part of the Hellenistic world, she would possibly speak Greek as well as Egyptian, and be aware of the Mediterranean world of culture which existed beyond the frontiers of Egypt. She would have been influenced by Greek art, Greek literature and Greek fashion. But it is fairly safe to say that at any time between 3000 and 1000 BC the Egyptian woman would have regarded Egypt as the world. What lay beyond was little known, and, in general, feared.

South lay the hinterland of Africa, penetrated to some extent by the Pharaoh's armies, which had established fortresses and trading-stations along the Upper Nile. But the source of the great river which gave birth to, and sustained, Egyptian civilisation remained a mystery.

West lay the uncharted Sahara, the home of the desert-dwelling Libyans whose raids occasionally troubled the Pharaohs, though rarely seriously. More serious was the threat from the north-east, the 'High Lands,' as the Egyptians called this mountainous region, wherein lived the 'vile Asiatics' in what are now the Lebanon, Jordan, and Syria. Some of the earliest Pharaohs had sent trading-ships along these coasts, bringing back the famous 'cedars of Lebanon,' a necessary commodity in a country which had no tall trees from which to make ships' masts. Later Pharaohs conquered and colonised these lands, and established governors and garrisons in many of their cities. These colonies served more than one purpose. They were a source of wealth through trade and tribute, but equally important, they acted as a buffer and 'advanced warning system' against the encroachments of the greater Asiatic powers to the north, such as the Hittites of Asia Minor who occasionally threatened Egypt.

At one time certain Asiatic tribes, among whom may have been the ancestors of the Hebrews, actually occupied the Nile Delta and established a loose control over Egypt which lasted for some 150 years. Eventually the strong princes of Thebes, in Upper Egypt, drove the intruders out, and then the great warrior-Pharaoh Tuthmosis I, father of Hashepsowe, pursued them deep into their homelands. So did her stepson and successor Tuthmosis III, who carried Egypt's triumphs beyond the Euphrates. The period which followed was that of Egypt's greatest wealth and glory, her Imperial Age. Those were the days when the Asiatic kings sent emissaries to the Egyptian capital at Thebes, fawning for the Pharaoh's favour.

They sent Syrian princesses to Thebes, as wives and concubines for the King and his great ministers; they sent the rare products of their countries and introduced new and sometimes unwelcome ideas to the conservative Egyptian court. In return the Pharaohs sent them gold by the bushel, for, as the King of Mitanni wrote to Amenophis III, 'in thy land gold is but as dust.'

To most Egyptian women, save perhaps the Queens, these political and diplomatic manoeuvres were probably only a faint, distant background to their lives. They themselves never visited these far-off lands, but their husbands and sons did, and brought back stories about them. However, being women and loving novelty, they would know that from Nubia and the 'land of Kush' came ivory, ebony and exotic animals—even, occasionally, a 'dancing-dwarf' (pigmy) to entertain the Court. From the 'land of Punt,' probably Somaliland (now mostly Somali Republic), came perfumes and incense; from Asia came spices, precious woods and exotic foreign plants, which were welcome, and exotic foreign women, who were not.

To the north and north-west, beyond the Nile mouth, lay the 'Great Green Sea' which most Egyptians did not like; but from its islands came bronzed, slim-waisted sailors and merchants from 'Keftiu' (probably Crete) bringing as trade-goods the lovely manufactured products of their land—bronze, gold-inlaid swords and daggers; vases, cups and other drinking-vessels of gold, silver and bronze; and exquisite ceramics of egg-shell thickness adorned with intricate painted decoration—octopuses, dolphins and sea-urchins, creatures unfamiliar to the land-bound Egyptian.

I suppose that if an Ancient Egyptian woman of rank

and wealth were to be given the opportunity of choosing the period in which she was to spend her life it would probably be this one—roughly between 1550 and 1200 BC, when Egyptian wealth, power and security reached their peak, and before the subsequent decline began. On the other hand a serving-girl, a field-labourer, a drudge working in a brewery, bakery, or at the loom or spinning-wheel, could hardly have minded in which period she lived. Her life was little more than an endless round of labour, beginning at dawn and only ending at sunset. There would be no golden jewellery for her, no fine garments of gauffered linen, no rich food and wine, no hunting-expeditions on the Nile, and no parties, save those she may have attended in the capacity of servant, musician or dancing-girl. And at the end there would be no fine tomb and the promise of eternal life, only a nameless grave.

But as almost every woman would like to have been a Cleopatra, and as every woman knows how she would use wealth if she had it, I make no apology for concentrating most of my attention on the New Kingdom, and on the Queens and great ladies of that period when the Pharaohs ruled, from Thebes, over the richest and most powerful empire on earth. In addition to the Queens, the wives and mothers of the divine Pharaohs, we shall also meet the lesser Queens and concubines who made up the sumptuous harem of the Pharaoh; we shall meet some of the wives and daughters of the great officials who attended His Majesty, some of whom were related to the Royal Family, and many more who would have liked that privilege. Through their eyes we may also glimpse, occasionally, their less fortunate or less respectable sisters: the wives and daughters of merchants, sailors, tradesmen, labourers, and the courtesans, harlots and entertainers.

For those who are not already familiar with Ancient Egypt, however, a few facts may be useful to set the scene against which these women lived. People who first encounter the world of more than 3,000 years ago are apt, when they find some common human link with the past, to exclaim 'how like us they were!' From this it is easy to make the fatal error of seeing the world of the twentieth century BC through the eyes of the twentieth century AD, as too many plays and novels testify.

With a little imagination it is not too difficult to make the transition from a mechanised, technological society to one in which the fastest form of land transport was a horse-drawn vehicle, and the swiftest ships were propelled by oars and sails. Little more than a century and a half ago we were in the same position. As for medicine and surgery, in which we take so much justifiable pride, the patient of an Egyptian physician of 2000 BC was probably no worse off than we would have been in the hands of a seventeenth-century doctor. The Ancient Egyptians had a considerable knowledge of medicine and surgery, as their famous 'Medical Papyrus' proves; they understood the nature and treatment of many diseases, and some of the drugs they prescribed are still in use today. If she had the luck to enjoy reasonable health a wealthy woman of the New Kingdom was probably as physically happy and content as her modern equivalent. And Egypt, as Herodotus commented, was a very wealthy country, thanks to its climate.

'Next to the Libyans they are the healthiest people in the world,' he writes. 'I should put this down to the absence of changes in the climate; for change, and especially change of weather, is the prime cause of disease.'

An exaggeration, of course, because the Ancient Egyptians did suffer from diseases which are still endemic in Egypt today, such as trachoma and schistosomiasis; the mummies prove this, as do the medical papyri. But so far as the upper classes were concerned they were a cleanly people, given to frequent washing and changes of linen. The poorer quarters of their towns probably appeared as filthy as those of today, but even there appearances can be deceptive. In the dry climate of Egypt, as any modern traveller can testify, dirt does not stick as it does in more humid climates; it brushes off easily. And the burning heat of the sun, though it can 'breed maggots in a dead dog,' is also a powerful antiseptic. It also acts like a perpetual Turkish

Bath; one sweats, but sweats only water. A garment soaked in perspiration, after drying out in the sun, surprisingly doesn't smell.

The most enervating disease, then as now, was probably schistosomiasis (Bilharzia), transmitted by a snail which breeds in the irrigation canals in which the Egyptian fellah has to work. Organisms called *cercariae*—fork-tailed larvae—to which the snails act as hosts, penetrate the skin and enter the blood-stream, eventually attacking the liver and intestines. Infection spreads because of the diseased fellah's habit of defecating in or near the canals, and so the cycle continues. But obviously only the female field-workers would be likely to contract this disease. Their more fortunate sisters would be largely unaffected.

None the less it is ironical to reflect that the gorgeous gold and jewelled head-dress worn by the Queens of Egypt was ultimately derived, as Petrie suggested, from the headband worn by the field-workers of primitive times to keep their hair in place.

This simple fact—the connection between the Queens of Egypt and their remote ancestors who created Egyptian civilisation from the mud of the Nile—symbolises the difference between their world and ours. They were, it is true, in many ways just like us. The difference lay in this: civilisation, such as we know it, has existed for less than 6,000 years anywhere on earth. And the Ancient Egyptians were more than 3,000 years nearer the primitive than we are. This accounts for a number of features of Egyptian civilisation which we find strange and bizarre, though superficially there are startling similarities between the New Kingdom and the modern world.

For instance, an Egyptian lady of birth and fortune (or merely with fortune) in 1500 BC took infinite care over her hairstyle, her make-up, her scent, her gown and jewellery. She painted her eyelids with green eye-shadow. She delicately outlined her eyebrows, and used, not a lipstick, but a lip-brush. Her necklaces, bracelets and ear-rings, of gold, lapis-lazuli and carnelian, were of such sophisticated design and craftsmanship as to send modern western women into frenzies of envy and emulation. Thousands of Cairo jewellers, busily manufacturing reproductions, have reason to thank their predecessors of 3,000 years ago. The 'modernity' of Egyptian women of the Eighteenth Dynasty was such that, if Nefertiti were to return and could be induced to wear a Dior gown, she could walk into a fashionable hotel without causing any comment save that due to her beauty. Even her make-up would be in fashion.

By contrast, Aspasia would have looked archaic, Messalina overdressed, and Octavia (almost certainly) a frump. Cleopatra, being Cleopatra, would probably have got away with it —just. But she would have not looked like Elizabeth Taylor, with whom Nefertiti would have had more in common, superficially.

Meryet, wife of Rekhmire, the most powerful minister in Egypt under Tuthmosis III, gave parties for her husband's distinguished friends, just like any modern hostess. And, like them, she wears exactly the same frozen smile of welcome, only partly concealing her grinding boredom, as she stands in her elegant off-the-shoulder gown to greet her husband's guests. She has stood thus, in one of the painted frescoes of Rekhmire's tomb, for more than thirty centuries, evoking sighs of sympathy from all hostesses, from Graeco-Roman to modern times, who have had to face a similar situation.

All around, in similar rock-cut sepulchres, the vividly-painted portraits of her friends and enemies, wives and daughters of other great officials, stand in similar attitudes. If they are not presiding at parties they are perched unsteadily in fast skiffs, holding on to their menfolk's legs as they spear fish or hurl their throwing-sticks at the startled wildfowl. For Egyptian women shared at least in some of their husbands' peaceful activities. How contemporary it all seems!

And yet those same ladies could not—with rare exceptions —read or write (they did not need to; scribes did it for them). They could not enter any profession. There were no women doctors, barristers, engineers, civil servants. When their menfolk went abroad they stayed behind. And though they shared in some of their husbands' social activities they also had to share their love, for not only kings and princes, but any man of wealth maintained a harem.

These facts might or might not astonish western women, depending on how much they valued education, literacy and independence; millions of Oriental women would not find them strange or unfamiliar. But they are not the most important difference between the Ancient Egyptian world and ours; this is that basically, Egyptian society and its whole hierarchy of government rested on *religious* assumptions which are foreign to us. The first of these assumptions was the divinity of the king. He was the 'son of Re' (the sun-god) and though born of an earthly mother he would, after death, join his fellow-deities and become as immortal as they. Like most Egyptian myths this one was not well-formulated or consistent—at least to our way of thinking. For instance, although the Pharaoh was the 'son of Re' he was also recognised—except in a few cases—as the son of his earthly father too.

During the period of the New Kingdom the older god, Re, had been conjoined with Amun, originally a mere local Theban god in the days before Thebes became the capital. Thus the name of the principal deity became Amun-Re, and his temples at Karnak are of an immensity which still staggers the eye and mind.

The Queen also qualified for immortality, though she was not buried in her husband's tomb in the Valley of the Kings. She had her own independent sepulchre some distance away, usually in the Valley of the Queens. This Egyptian obsession with preparations for the After-Life is another characteristic of their civilisation which divides it from ours. It was not, as many people imagine, an obsession with death, but with its opposite. Egyptian funerary customs, like the religious beliefs of which they were an expression, are extremely complex and puzzling to the modern mind. But as the Egyptian woman took them as much for granted as we take atomic energy we must try to do the same.

The Ancient Egyptians lavished more care and wealth on their tombs and temples than on their homes, elegant though the latter were. But whereas royal and princely palaces and the villas of the nobility were built of mud-brick, tombs and temples were either built of enduring stone or hewn out of rock. The word 'tomb' in fact gives a false impression. The Egyptian name for it was 'House of Eternity,' which was what it was intended to be, and such sepulchres were built during the owner's lifetime. Those of the kings were of enormous size, particularly if the monarch enjoyed a long reign. They were tunnelled for hundreds of feet into the Theban hills on the west bank of the Nile opposite the city of the living. Even the tombs of the nobles and other men of rank were elaborately constructed, usually with a forecourt, a chapel for offerings, and behind that a deep pit in which the two sarcophagi lay. For the wife of a nobleman shared his tomb, and the delightful paintings which adorned its chapel-walls depict the couple and their children taking part in all the activities which they had enjoyed in life, and which they hoped to continue enjoying in the After-Life.

This was the essential idea underlying the elaborate burial arrangements. Far from being death-obsessed, the Ancient Egyptians enjoyed life on earth so much that they could think of nothing better in life to come: there the great minister would continue to serve his royal master as he had done in life; there the general would still command his army, the admiral his navy. Sports and pastimes would be the same—eternal hunting, eternal fishing and wild-fowling, and gay parties and feasts enjoyed with one's family and friends.

But although the Egyptians subscribed to these beliefs, and acted upon them, it does not follow that they were all passionately devout. That they had doubts is certain—some of their songs and poems prove it. There was, underlying conventional religious beliefs, a strain of scepticism and pessimism. But they were essentially a practical people who believed in insurance. Many of them were probably a little like Soames Forsyte who, though a sceptic, went to Church occasionally 'just in case.' But whereas to the Forsytes and their like, an occasional show of devotion was all that was necessary, the Ancient Egyptian was forced, by the nature of his religious traditions, to go to much more trouble and expense.

The Egyptian woman was taught from childhood that, though she had been born with a spirit or *ka* which would survive her physical death, that spirit could not continue to exist in the After-Life unless the body was preserved from corruption and the *ka* was provided in perpetuity with physical sustenance in the form of food offerings. It would also need many of the appurtenances of earthly life—clothing, furniture, jewellery, and servants to carry out the menial tasks. In fact, the earliest Queens of Egypt, who reigned about 3000 BC, long before the first pyramids were built, had their servants killed and buried around their tombs. These have been discovered by Professor Emery at North Sakkara, and I myself remember seeing one of the mastaba-tombs he had excavated, surrounded by little cubicles each containing a heap of human bones. With these pathetic relics lay the tools of the dead servant's calling; her carpenter had his tools, her pottery-maker his, her female servants had their domestic equipment. It says much for the humanity of the Egyptians that, unlike other peoples, they abandoned this barbarous custom before 2800 BC, more than 1,200 years before the period of which I am writing.

Perhaps it was not only humanity which prompted this change, for the Egyptians were a practical folk, and such customs obviously wasted skilled man-power. So, from an early date, they substituted little statuettes, usually made of *faience* (glazed clay), each of which represented a diminutive human figure which, by process of *magic,* became a living servant in the After-Life. Also, from the pyramid period onwards, the chapels of the noble tombs were adorned with delicately sculptured reliefs, usually painted, depicting the servants of the dead man and woman carrying out their tasks of reaping corn, driving cattle, or cutting up joints of meat, baking bread and brewing beer, pressing grapes and making wine, doing everything, in fact, required to maintain the spirit of the deceased official and his wife in the state of life they had enjoyed on earth.

Similar scenes were depicted on the walls of tomb-chapels of the New Kingdom, though they were usually painted rather than sculpted. The purpose was functional, not decorative; they are all evidence of a belief in magic, yet another characteristic of Egyptian civilisation and that of other ancient peoples. These pictures were never intended to be seen by human eyes, except occasionally by the relatives or descendants of the dead, or priests appointed by them, when they came to offer food at the tomb. But if such offerings ceased to be made the *ka* would still not perish, always provided that the representations of the servants and food offerings were permitted to remain on the walls of the sepulchre. For the Egyptians, like some modern primitives, believed, or were taught to believe, that by a process of sympathetic magic, the thing represented could become the thing itself. Belief in magical spells and incantations, amulets and love-potions was widespread, and continued to be held right down to Greek and Roman times.

Another concept which the modern mind finds difficult to grasp is Egyptian polytheism. Today we may, or may not, believe in *a* God; but to imagine more than 2,000 separate deities, all roughly organised into an elaborate pantheon, is more difficult, especially when many of these gods and goddesses appear to us so grotesque. Some, such as Amun-Re, Osiris, god of death and resurrection, Isis his sister-wife, and Hathor, goddess of love and beauty, were usually represented in human or part-human form, though Amun is sometimes shown with a ram's head, Osiris is wrapped in mummy-bandages, and Hathor has cow's ears. But when we look at the paintings of Thoueris, a repellent, fat-bellied crocodile with human breasts, at Sekhmet, a beautiful girl's body with the head of a lioness, or Anubis, with the head of a jackal, and Thoth, who has a human body with the head of an ibis, one is bewildered.

The answer lies, surely, in the fact pointed out earlier in this chapter, that the Ancient Egyptians were more than 3,000 years nearer uncivilised, or sub-civilised, man than we are. Today, though we may recognise animals—especially mammals —as distinctly kin to ourselves, we have no doubt that they are inferior to us, despite the fact that birds can fly unaided, whereas we cannot, that the lion is stronger than we are, the jaguar swifter and more agile. We kill them for sport or for food, we study them and keep them in zoos, but we do not revere them. Primitive man did—even though he also killed them for food—because he was awed by those very qualities, strength, swiftness, agility, the power of flight, which they possessed but which he did not.

So it was with the Ancient Egyptians, even after they had been civilised for more than 3,000 years. No doubt many of the more thoughtful among them questioned these traditional beliefs, and one Pharaoh at least—Akhenaten, the husband of Nefertiti—attempted to overthrow them, but he failed. He was bound to fail because of the very nature of Egyptian society, which was conservative and tradition-bound beyond any known culture save, perhaps, that of pre-revolutionary China. This blind respect for tradition was both Egypt's strength and her weakness. It gave her a stability which enabled her civilisation to endure longer than any other, but it inhibited art, rejected innovation, and put blinkers on men's minds. The repository of tradition was the priesthood, which was often as powerful as the throne, and on several occasions even more powerful.

The temples were also the schools and universities of Egypt. There was no such thing as a secular education; the priests were the equivalent of the modern engineers and technologists and they guarded the precious secret of the writings. Only through literacy could a man rise from low rank to a position of authority; only the scribes, freed from taxation and manual labour, could run the complex administrative system through which the Pharaohs ruled Egypt. And few women, even Queens and Princesses, learned to read and write.

If this long preamble has emphasised the peculiar characteristics of Egyptian society, this is because, in my opinion, we can only begin to understand the Queens and other women of Egypt if we first absorb and accept these characteristics as the women of the Nile Valley accepted them. Only then can we observe and enjoy the way in which the Egyptian woman resembled her modern counterpart.

2

The Mystery of Hashepsowe

ONE OF THE FASCINATIONS OF EGYPTOLOGY IS THE SIGNIFICANCE —or possible significance—of minute detail. It might be thought that because the Ancient Egyptians covered the walls of their tombs and temples with scenes and written inscriptions, and because they have left for our examination more of their personal possessions than any other people, they tell us more about themselves. This, alas, is not true. They tell us only what they want us to know, and little more. The scenes and inscriptions are 'official history,' or, more often than not, propaganda. The Egyptologist might be compared with the probing journalist trying to penetrate behind the P.R.O.'s 'hand-out,' or the detective who, on examining the apparently tidy room, observes some tiny detail which suggests that its occupant did not, as he states, spend the previous evening quietly watching television.

We will take, as an example, the case of Queen Hashepsowe, who reigned over Egypt more than 3,400 years ago. Apart from Cleopatra, we know more about Hashepsowe than any other Egyptian Queen. Her life is described in every history of Egypt, and more than one writer has attempted a brief biography of her. Reading these, one after the other, is like listening to a Theme and Variations. The theme comes from the bare official records, mostly from inscriptions on the monuments set up by the Queen and her contemporaries, eked out by some archaeological research. The variations exist only in the mental attitude of the writer, and in which elements of the official records he or she wishes to stress. The late Dr. Margaret Murray, in an essay written some thirty years ago, presents Hashepsowe as if she were an emancipated Edwardian female, freeing herself from male tyranny, taking on a man's job and doing it better than he could, abhorring war and devoted to the arts of peace. Much more recently, Mrs. Barbara Mertz takes a similar, if somewhat more sophisticated, view of the great Queen, though in her version one feels that Hashepsowe, had she lived today, might have been a worthy product of Vassar.

Mrs. Mertz's fellow-countryman, the late Dr. William Hayes of the Metropolitan Museum of Art, New York, did not think much of Hashepsowe, and said so. The late Sir Alan Gardiner, with scholarly caution and detachment, gave the facts, admitted that 'no events in Egyptian history have given rise to so much controversy' and left the reader to make up his own mind. Gardiner, whose knowledge of all the known inscriptions was encyclopaedic, had advantages not always possessed by some other writers, and, being far more up-to-date in this respect than Dr. Murray, his version of the story makes hers seem somewhat naïve. If I rely on Gardiner for the facts (and for the rendering of the Queen's name, which is usually given as *Hat-shep-sut*) this is only because he is perhaps the most knowledgeable. The interpretation is necessarily my own, and could well be wrong.

But I think it would be more interesting to the reader if, instead of reading yet another re-hashing of the inscriptional evidence, he or she could step into the Egyptologist's shoes and look at the original material—or some of it.

If any scribe wrote a biography of Hashepsowe on a papyrus-scroll it has not survived. Our sources of written information, as with nearly all Ancient Egyptian monarchs, are as follows: (a) various 'king-lists' which give the names of the monarchs, their reign-lengths, and occasionally a few sparse details concerning their achievements, (b) inscriptions about Hashepsowe on the tombs and monuments of her subjects, (c) inscriptions which the Queen herself caused to be made in her own monuments, notably her great funerary temple at Deir el Bahri. Additional information concerning her predecessors and successors can be obtained from their monuments.

We can dismiss (a) immediately since her name does not appear on the 'king-lists,' which may in itself be significant. In these lists the name of her father, Tuthmosis I, is followed first by Tuthmosis II and then by Tuthmosis III. So far as these chronicles are concerned, the Queen did not even exist.

Under category (b) there are a number of references to Hashepsowe, her predecessors and successors. For instance there was a certain official named Ineni whose career, as inscribed in his tomb, spanned the reigns of Tuthmosis I, Tuthmosis II, Hashepsowe and Tuthmosis III. He outlived the first two monarchs, but not, it appears, the latter two. His references to Tuthmosis I are useful, since they give us an idea of the character and achievement of Hashepsowe's father, and show us the kind of man he was.

Tuthmosis I was born in about 1528 BC. He himself was of non-royal stock, but he married a Theban princess of high parentage named Ahmose, and through her gained his right to the throne. He was the third king of the Eighteenth Dynasty (c. 1575–1308 BC), the period when Egypt's power reached its greatest extent. But his capital city, Thebes, had not yet attained the magnificence which it was to achieve. When Tuthmosis came to the throne there must still have been men living who remembered the heroic years during which the fighting Pharaohs of the late Seventeenth and early Eighteenth Dynasties threw the hated Asiatics (the *Hyksos*) out of Egypt and then pursued them deep into their homeland. There had been Sekenre, whose battered body had been rescued from the battlefield and piously buried in his royal tomb. Even today his mummified body survives, the skull gashed with hideous wounds. There had been Kamose, and Ahmose (who bore the same name as Tuthmosis's Queen) and Amenophis I, all warriors.

Of Tuthmosis I, Ineni wrote:

> ... the Good God [i.e. the Pharaoh] who smites the Nubians, lord of might, who overthrows the Asiatics. He made his boundary as far as the Horns of the Earth, and the marshes in Kebeh. . . . The sand-dwellers bore their tribute like the impost of the South and North; his majesty forwarded them to Thebes, for his father Amun, each year. . . .[1]

This brief passage indicates that not only did Hashepsowe's father defeat Egypt's traditional southern enemies, the Nubians, but led his armies as far as the Euphrates—'the marshes in Kebeh' to the north-east. There is an even more striking passage in the tomb of another of the King's followers, also confusingly called Ahmose, at a place called El Kab. For clarity we will call him 'Ahmose of El Kab.'

> I sailed the King . . . triumphant, when he ascended the river to Khenthenofer, in order to cast out violence in the highlands, in order to suppress the raidings of the hill region. I showed bravery in his presence in the bad water, in the passage of the ship by the bend. He appointed me chief of the sailors.

After describing how the King 'raged like a panther' at the destruction wrought by his foe, Ahmose tells how—

> his majesty cast his first lance, which remained in the body of that fallen one. . . . This was . . . powerless before his flaming uraeus [the gold serpent the king wore in his helmet] made so in an instant of destruction; their people were brought off as living prisoners.

And of the King's Asiatic campaign he writes:

> His majesty arrived at Naharin. His majesty found that foe was planning destruction; his majesty made a great slaughter

among them. Numberless were living prisoners, which his majesty brought off from his victories. Meanwhile I was at the head of our troops, and his majesty beheld my bravery. I brought off a chariot, its horses, and him who was upon it as a living prisoner. . . .[2]

It was in this militant, adventurous atmosphere that Hashepsowe was brought up. Thebes must have been an exciting city to live in. Less than a century before it had been merely an important provincial town (though some of the kings of the Twelfth Dynasty had been buried there), owing allegiance to a hated foreign ruler who lived at Avaris, far to the north. Now it was the thriving, expanding capital of a dynamic, rejuvenescent Egypt, its streets echoing to the tramp of soldiers, its pillared halls often thronged with the 'Followers of His Majesty,' the gay young officers of chariotry, freshly returned from campaigning, with fascinating stories of foreign lands, and no doubt rich gifts for their womenfolk. Not all the loot, one may be sure, went into the treasury of the god Amun-Re.

For those who have visited the ruins of Thebes, or those who are yet to visit them, it may be well to describe the city as it appeared at this time. On the east bank of the Nile rose the royal palace and the villas of the noble families and court officials, set in walled gardens bright with flowers and rare plants brought from Asia. The buildings were mainly of mud-brick, covered with plaster, smoothed and decorated. Stone was rarely used except for temples and other monuments, but in the perpetual sunshine of Egypt mud-brick is an ideal building material; even today there survive huge mud-brick tombs built 5,000 years ago.

On the east bank also would be the wharves for the numerous ships, from warships and glittering royal and princely barges to merchant vessels of many sizes and shapes; also small, elegant private yachts for travel and pleasure. Roads were few in Ancient Egypt, for the Nile provided easy transport from one end of the kingdom to the other. Some distance from the residences of the great was the mercantile and manufacturing quarter, small houses, also of mud-brick, huddled together and threaded by narrow lanes.

Although the Pharaoh and the richer of his high officials kept harems, the word should not mislead one into imagining that the women lived in seclusion. Far from it; though not, perhaps, on terms of complete equality with their men, they shared in many of their social activities. In tomb-paintings of the period we see them sitting at feasts, their arms affectionately round their husbands' waists, or sailing with them on the Nile when they fished or hunted wildfowl. The river banks must have been more attractive than they are today. Masses of tall papyrus-reeds rose from the marshy banks, and there were many wild flowers. In one painting there is a charming scene of a nobleman standing in his hunting-skiff hurling a throwing-stick at the wildfowl, while one of his daughters leans over the side plucking water-plants. Egyptian women loved flowers, and there is rarely a banqueting scene without some of the guests holding lotus-blooms in their hands, and flowers were often worn in the hair.

The huge hypostyle hall of the Karnak temple with its forest of gigantic pillars did not then exist. There was a temple, but by comparison it was much smaller and parts of it dated from the far-off days of the Twelfth Dynasty—four hundred years earlier. But the Eighteenth Dynasty Pharaohs had already begun extensions and rebuilding. The Queens were represented there, too. The Great Royal Wife of the Pharaoh acted as High Priestess at certain ceremonies, and his lovely daughters are depicted participating in sacred dances, or shaking the systrum —the sacred rattle which gave out a rhythmic jingling sound.

On the western bank of the Nile, opposite the city of the living, lay the city of the dead; in fact the Ancient Egyptian name for the dead was 'the westerners' and on dying one literally 'went west,' i.e. was buried in a rock-cut tomb hollowed out of the sandy cliffs which rose starkly beyond the green of the cultivated land. But when Hashepsowe lived in the palace of her royal father there was no 'Valley of the Kings.' The valley existed, of course, on the far side of the cliffs, but it did not then contain a single body. However, our friend Ineni, whose offices included that of Chief Architect of the King, was already tunnelling out the first royal tomb for his master. He tells us so in the inscription within his own sepulchre.

'It was a great work which I did there, no-one seeing, no-one hearing . . . it was a work such the ancestors had not done which I was obliged to do there. . . . I shall be praised because of my wisdom after years, by those who shall imitate that which I have done.'[3]

From this and the preceding inscriptions it will be noted that Ancient Egyptian officials were not troubled by false modesty. They were proud of their achievements and said so, not only to the living but to the gods of the Underworld. In this same inscription, Ineni informs us that he was as much in favour with Tuthmosis II as he had been with Tuthmosis I. He outlived them both, recording the death of the first in these charming words:

The king rested from life, going forth to heaven, having completed his years in gladness of heart.

Tuthmosis II, who was Hashepsowe's half-brother, being the son of Tuthmosis I by another wife, appears to have married his half-sister, since she was the heiress and the royal inheritance passed through her. His reign was not especially distinguished and lasted about twenty years. He campaigned in Nubia where 'he raged like a panther' (just like his father, as Gardiner comments) and Ahmose of El Kab accompanied him on an expedition to Palestine. The proof that he was married to Hashepsowe exists in a stela (inscribed stone) probably from Heliopolis which shows him with the widowed Queen of Tuthmosis I, Ahmose, and with Hashepsowe who is merely described as 'the king's great (i.e. principal) wife.'

Now we come to one of the crucial points of the story. According to the later 'king-lists' Tuthmosis II was succeeded by Tuthmosis III, but Ineni, in his tomb inscription, has this tactful but illuminating comment:

Having ascended into heaven, he [Tuthmosis II] became united with the gods, and his son, being arisen in his place as king of the Two Lands, ruled upon the throne of his begetter, *while his sister, the god's wife Hashepsowe governed the land and the Two Lands were under her control; people worked for her, and Egypt bowed the head.*[4] [our italics]

The young monarch who, according to Ineni, 'ruled on the throne of his begetter' was the son of Tuthmosis II, not by Hashepsowe but by an obscure concubine named Ese (Isis). Hashepsowe was therefore his stepmother, and at the time of his father's death he was only a boy. It would be natural, therefore, that the royal widow and heiress, Hashepsowe, should govern Egypt as regent until her stepson was old enough to assume control himself. Natural, that is, if the Queen was one content to follow established custom, and *if she believed that the young Tuthmosis had a greater claim to the throne than she had.*

But had he? Are there any inscriptions which can inform us? There are, and each gives a diametrically opposite point of view. But as both represent 'official history' we had better read them.

One appears on the great funerary temple which Hashepsowe had built for herself at Deir el Bahri. It describes how Tuthmosis I summoned his court and 'there was a sitting of the king himself, in the audience-hall of the right of the court, while these people prostrated themselves in the court.'

Said his majesty before them; 'This is my daughter, Khnemet-Amun, Hashepsowe, who liveth, and I have appointed her . . . she is my successor upon my throne, she it assuredly is who shall sit upon my wonderful seat. She shall command the people in every place of the palace; she it is who shall lead you . . .'[5]

The other inscription appears on one of the walls of the

Karnak temple built in the reign of Tuthmosis III. The King himself is speaking.

> I am his son, whom he commanded that I should be upon his throne, while I was one dwelling in his nest, he begat me in uprightness of heart . . . there is no lie therein; since my majesty was a stripling, while I was a youth in his temple, before occurred my installation to be prophet . . . my majesty. I was in the capacity of the 'Pillar of his Mother' like the youth Horus in Khemnis. . .

Then follows a description of how the youth Tuthmosis, a 'mere stripling,' a 'youth in his temple,' was taking part, no doubt as a priest, in the great ceremony when the sacred barque of the god Amun-Re was carried in solemn procession round the hall.

> . . . (the god) made the circuit of the hypostyle on both sides of it, the heart of those who were in front did not comprehend his actions, while searching for my majesty in every place. On recognizing me, lo, he halted. . . . (I threw myself on) the pavement, I prostrated myself in his presence. He set me before his majesty, I was stationed at 'the Station of the King' . . .[6]

The 'Station of the King' was evidently the spot on which the reigning Pharaoh stood during the ceremony. Thus the god, by this act, was recognising the young prince as King.

These two ringing statements, one trumpeted from Hashepsowe's splendid temple on the west, the other from her stepson's not-quite-so-splendid building on the east bank, have at least two factors in common. Both were almost certainly lies. And both were inscribed long after the events they purport to describe. But they stand as fitting symbols of the great power-struggle which must have riven Egypt's ruling class, the famous 'feud of the Tuthmosids' about which so much has been written but of which so little is really known.

One fact is quite certain. Hashepsowe *did* reign as Pharaoh long after her frustrated and gifted stepson was old enough to reign himself. Only twice before in fifteen centuries of Egyptian history had a Queen usurped the kingship. It is known that, much as the Egyptians honoured their Queens, they did not like them as sole rulers. But the iron-willed daughter of Tuthmosis I went even further. Not only did she adopt the full royal titles of a King but she had herself represented wearing Pharaonic dress, the historic kilt, pectoral, and Double Crown which had been the ceremonial dress of the kings of Egypt since the earliest Dynasties.

So she is shown in her funerary temple, together with other inscriptions which reveal how she wished to be known to posterity. The 'public face' of Hashepsowe is absorbing in itself, as we shall see in the next chapter. But can anything be known of how she gained and maintained her unique position? She could not have attained it alone. Archaeologists can tell us a little more, thanks to their attention to those tiny, significant details which they are trained to observe and interpret.

[1] Breasted, J. H., *Ancient Records of Egypt,* Volume II, Chicago University Press, 1906-07; 1927

[2] Breasted, J. H., op. cit.

[3] Breasted, J. H., op. cit.

[4] Gardiner, Sir Alan, *Egypt of the Pharaohs,* Oxford University Press, New York, 1961

[5] Breasted, J. H., op. cit.

[6] Breasted, J. H., op. cit.

3

Hail, King... Female Sun!

O N THE WEST BANK OF THE NILE OPPOSITE LUXOR, A SEMI-circle of precipitous cliffs soars into the hot blue sky. At dawn they merge from russet to warm gold, at sunset from deep purple to an ominous black. But at midday, when the sandy plateau at their feet scorches the soles of the stumbling, sun-weary visitors, the glare from that ochreous wall of rock is like that of live coals.

On this, the most dramatic site in the Theban Necropolis, just where the plateau meets the cliff, stands what many regard as the most beautiful temple in Egypt, Hashepsowe's splendid funerary monument which she began building shortly after her reign (or co-regency) began. Though it has suffered grievously, first by deliberate, savage mutilation and then by over 3,000 years of neglect, it has been rescued and partly restored by a succession of distinguished archaeologists. Today it is her chief memorial, in that it tells us practically all that she wished us to know about herself.

We approach it, as she did, from a road which leads from

the west bank of the Nile, across the green of the cultivated land, to the point where, quite suddenly, the desert begins. The cliffs, beyond which lies the Valley of the Kings, loom even nearer, until, as we pass into the first forecourt, they dwarf us. But they do not dwarf the building which rises, terrace upon terrace, until it unites with them. For the architect, a man of genius, seized his opportunity. If he had designed a conventional temple, in which the height was greater than the width, it would have been absorbed by the vigorous verticality of the deep fissures which score the cliff-face. Instead he created a building in which the main emphasis is horizontal, and above which the cliffs rise like a tremendous back-drop.

The first and largest courtyard is rectangular, just a huge walled enclosure with nothing in it save a broad central avenue, originally lined with sphinxes—each with the head of Hashepsowe—leading to the second terrace, which is supported by a broad, columned portico, broken only at the centre by a gently-sloping ramp. Before ascending this we will seek the shade of the first colonnade and examine the painted and sculpted reliefs on its inner walls.

At first, after the outer glare, one sees very little. Then, as our eyes grow accustomed to the comparative—but only comparative—dimness, rich colours begin to glow from the walls, which are of pale yellow limestone. Everywhere there are figures, the men's skins always of the conventional terracotta to indicate their sex, while the women have paler skins. This was purely a convention; in reality the Egyptians, though a dark people, were probably no darker than the average Spaniard today. The men, most of whom spent more of their time out of doors, would be more tanned, but that was the only difference.

The first thing one notices is that in many places certain figures and inscriptions have been deliberately erased, though the outline can be seen under the marks of the destroyers' chisels. Usually it is the largest of the figures, the tall, majestic shape of a Pharaoh wearing the traditional kilt, the breast bare save for golden ornaments, and above this the outline of a regal face, wearing the false beard (used on ceremonial occasions) and high, cylindrical crown. The face, in every case, was that of Hashepsowe.

The reliefs on the walls to the right of the approach-ramp depict scenes from the life of the Queen, from her birth to her coronation. They are arranged in horizontal bands or 'registers,' one above the other. One series of scenes and inscriptions describes how her father, Tuthmosis I, informed the court that she was to be his legitimate successor. Of these once-lovely reliefs, only the handsome figure of the great Queen Ahmose, wife of Tuthmosis I and mother of Hashepsowe, remains unspoiled. She has a face of great dignity and nobility.

The register below this appears to contradict the first, since it purports to show that Hashepsowe, far from being merely the daughter of Tuthmosis I, was the daughter of the god Amun-Re himself. But this inconsistency did not worry the Ancient Egyptians, whose tortuous minds were capable of accepting two mutually contradictory sets of beliefs. The unfolding of this story, which closely resembles the Greek legend of Zeus and Alcmene, wife of Amphitrion, is fascinating, both pictorially and verbally. We see Amun, who has taken the form of Tuthmosis I, sitting with Ahmose 'upon the heavens,' supported by two female divinities.

'He found her,' says the accompanying text, 'as she slept in the beauty of her palace. She waked at the fragrance of the god, which she smelled in the presence of his majesty. He went to her immediately . . . he imposed his desire upon her, he caused that she should see him in his form of a god. When he came before her she rejoiced at the sight of his beauty, his love passed into her limbs, which the fragrance of the god flooded; all his odours were from Punt' (the land of perfumes).[1]

Queen Ahmose replies:

'How great is thy fame! It is splendid to see thy front; thou hast united my majesty with thy favours, thy dew is in all my limbs.'

'After this,' the text continues, 'the majesty of this god did all that he desired of her.'

Moving further along the lofty, columned corridor we see, in succession, Amun summoning the creator-god, Khnum, to whom he says 'Go, to make her, together with her *ka* (spirit) from these limbs which are in me; go, to fashion her better than all gods; shape for me this my daughter whom I have begotten.' Then Khnum is seen seated at his potter's wheel fashioning two *male* children, the Queen and her *ka*. Next we see Ahmose saluted by Thoth, god of wisdom; then she is led, between Thoth and another deity, Heket, to her confinement. The sculptor has made it quite clear that the Queen is pregnant, and has depicted her with a delightful smile.

The next scene is immediately after the birth; the Queen is seated, holding the child, while in front of her four goddesses, the arms outstretched to her, have evidently acted as midwives. Later Hathor, goddess of love, presents the infant Hashepsowe to Amun, who joyfully exclaims, 'Glorious part which has come forth from me; king, taking the Two Lands, upon the Horus-throne forever.'

In this, and perhaps only this scene, the Ancient Egyptians seem to anticipate the attitude of the Ancient Greeks to their gods. The immortal deities have become human, and even the great sun-god himself, creator of all life, expresses the joy of love and parenthood. In this the artist, sculptor and writer have transcended the paltry political manoeuvre which was the scene's *raison d'être*.

It is only when one reads what Hashepsowe wrote of herself that one's sense of the ridiculous returns.

Her majesty became more important than anyone else. What was within her was godlike; godlike was everything she did; her spirit was godlike. Her majesty became a beautiful maiden, blossoming out. The goddess Uto, at this moment, applauded her divine shapeliness. She is a woman of distinguished appearance.

Even allowing for the superlatives which the Pharaohs were accustomed to bestow on themselves, this, one feels, is going rather far.

Was she beautiful? The reader may judge from Plates 2 and 3. These statues, which once adorned Hashepsowe's temple, among scores of others, had been smashed into small fragments by her enemies after her death. The bits, found dumped in a nearby quarry, were painstakingly rejoined by the Metropolitan Museum of Art, New York, which mounted a number of archaeological digs at Deir el Bahri and its environs. The life-size seated statue, in Pharaonic dress and in the typical Pharaonic attitude, is probably idealised, but it is indubitably feminine, and not unattractive. The resemblance to her parents and the other Tuthmosis is obvious. The other portrait is probably more like the real Hashepsowe. The ruthlessness, strength and intelligence stamped on its features chime with the known facts of her career. Some of the highlights of that career are illustrated in the reliefs which adorn the colonnade fronting the second, higher courtyard which we approach after climbing the central ramp.

As we cross the wide space, the sunlight, reverberating from that stupendous wall of rock, stabs our eyes. It is a relief once again to enter the shade of the many-columned portico where more colours glow from the smooth walls of yellow limestone. This time we are not in the unreal world of gods, goddesses and divine births, but the living world of Ancient Egypt, 3,500 years ago.

The scenes, which form a pictorial sequence like those in the lower colonnade, depict a trading expedition which Hashepsowe sent to the 'land of Punt.' The expedition was organised in order to collect incense and incense-bearing trees; the Egyptians used incense in large quantities, and Punt, 'the land of perfumes,' was its principal source. 'Punt' was a land held in high estimation by the Egyptians. They sometimes refer to it as 'divine Punt.' They saw it differently from the land of their traditional enemies, the Nubians and the Asiatics, and some archaeologists have argued that the Egyptians regarded it as the home of their remote ancestors. All we know is that it lay to the east, and bordered on the Red Sea. It probably lay in what is now French Somaliland, although some authorities have argued that 'the land of Punt' embraces both sides of the Red Sea, i.e. that it included the coast of Arabia.

Professor Breasted rightly comments that:

> These are the most interesting series of reliefs in Egypt. . . . They are as beautiful in execution as they are important in content. They record an important expedition of the queen thither, which was successfully concluded before her ninth [regnal] year.

After the monotonously-repeated battle-scenes in which the Pharaoh is invariably triumphant over his enemies—always depicted in the same way, from 3000 BC onwards for more than 2,000 years—one's mind is refreshed and delighted by these peaceful scenes which the great Queen represented in such vivid and absorbing detail. I feel that the Ancient Egyptian artists, condemned by religious tradition to an endless repetition of the same subjects, must have relished this opportunity. Some of them were evidently sent on the expedition in order to capture the authentic atmosphere of Punt, rather like the 'war artists' of the First and Second World Wars.

Every detail is included. In the first scene we see the Egyptian fleet, moored at some Red Sea port, preparing to set sail. 'Steer to port!' shouts the commander of the last vessel, as recorded in the hieroglyphs. Nearby is a small boat lashed to a tree, above which appear the words: 'An offering for the life, prosperity and health of her majesty, to Hathor, mistress of Punt . . . that she may bring wind.'

The ships are delineated in such detail that modern naval experts have recognised the constructional features which fitted them for sea-going voyages. It is important to remember that most Egyptian ships were river-craft; also that, owing to the absence of tall trees in Egypt, they had to import their masts

from the Lebanon, and build the hulls of their ships from short
planks which were all that native Egyptian trees could provide.
As Herodotus, who toured Egypt in about 540 BC, comments,
'they cut short planks, about three feet long ... and the method
of construction is to lay them together like bricks and through-
fasten them with long spikes set close together.'

The vessels of Hashepsowe's fleet were, however, sea-going
ships of deeper draught and stouter construction. But as their
design followed that of the Nile vessels with their high, up-
curving prows and sterns, these were tied together with a rope
which, according to one modern naval authority, must have
been 'the width of a man's waist,' thus ensuring rigidity and
preventing the vessel's bending its timber in the heavy seas. The
method was used until recently in sailing ships, and is called
'hog-trussing.'

The next scene shows the fleet at sea. Below the ships the
ocean is depicted, conventionally, by wavy lines, in which appear
various species of fish which live in the Red Sea but not in the
Nile. The inscription reads:

> Sailing in the sea, beginning the goodly way towards
> God's Land, journeying in peace to the land of Punt, by the
> army of the Lord of the Two Lands, according to the command
> of the Lord of Gods, Amun, Lord of Thebes, presider over
> Karnak, in order to bring for him the marvels of every country,
> because he so much loves the King of Upper and Lower Egypt,
> Makere (Hashepsowe) for his father Amun-Re, lord of earth,
> more than the other kings who have been in the land forever.

A scene obviously copied by the temple sculptors and
painters from the sketches brought back from Punt by their
fortunate colleagues shows the arrival of the fleet at a harbour
in Punt, probably a river-mouth. One would have hoped that
such an independent-minded monarch as Hashepsowe would
have defied convention and accompanied the fleet herself, but
no; we see only her deputy, the 'King's messenger' advancing
at the head of his troops. From the left advances the chief of the

Puntites, one Perehu, and the two meet. Between them lies a pile of 'trade-goods,' hatchets, necklaces, daggers, and so on, the same kind of cheap trash with which European traders lured African natives in the nineteenth century.

The inscriptions read:

> The arrival of the King's Messenger in God's Land, together with the army which is behind him, before the chiefs of Punt; dispatched with every good thing from the court . . .

The dialogue which follows is fascinating. Did it ever take place? Did the visitors include not only artists but reporters, or did some Egyptian scribe, who had never left Egypt, indulge his imagination, as writers will, when he makes the chief of the Puntites say:

> Why have ye come hither? Why have ye come hither unto this land, which the people know not? Did ye come down upon the ways of heaven, or did ye sail upon the waters, upon the sea of God's Land? [Punt.] Have ye trodden the ways of Re? Lo, as for the King of Egypt, is there no way to his Majesty, that we may live by the breath which he gives?

Personally I feel that this was a true report, if only because it is reminiscent of the ecstatic response of nineteenth-century African chiefs on being informed that their visitors have been sent by the Great White Queen (Victoria) from far across the seas. The appeal of royalty is irresistible to the primitive mind, especially when the royalty is female.

The response, in this case, was immediate. In subsequent scenes we see two vessels heavily laden with myrrh trees, sacks of myrrh, ivory, wood and apes. The sailors are climbing the gang-planks carrying sacks and whole trees, while their officers shout 'Look to your feet! Behold, the load is heavy!'

And another inscription reads:

> The loading of the ships very heavily with marvels of the country of Punt; all goodly fragrant woods of God's Land,

heaps of myrrh-resin, with fresh myrrh-trees, with ebony and pure ivory, with green gold of Emu, with cinnamon wood . . . eye-cosmetic, with apes, monkeys, dogs and with skins of the southern panther. . . . Never was brought the like for any king who has been since the beginning. . . .

But never is one allowed to forget the great lady for whom this highly-successful expedition was planned . . .

'Prosperity be with us,' cry the sailors, 'for the sake of the myrrh-tree in the midst of God's-Land, heaps of myrrh-resin, with fresh myrrh-leaves, for the sake of Amun; there is the place where it shall be made to grow for Makere (Hashepsowe) in (his) temple, according to command.'

For any visitor tempted to believe that this was an ego-centric fantasy there is an immediate answer. Let him retrace his steps, down the ramps to the lower forecourt, and he will see, to this day, stumps of the actual myrrh-trees which Ha-shepsowe ordered to be brought back for the adornment of her temple. They were found by the archaeologists, still packed around with the earth which was to sustain their roots. But a time came when there was no one to bring them water from the Nile, and they withered and died.

The next scenes illustrate the fleet, in full sail, sailing northwards up the Red Sea to its port of disembarkation, from which the precious goods would have to be transported over-land to the Nile Valley, probably via the Wadi Hamamat, op-posite Koptos.

Sailing, arriving in peace, journeying to Thebes with joy of heart, by the army of the Lord of the Two Lands (Hashep-sowe) with the chiefs of this country [i.e. Punt] behind them. They have brought that, the like of which was not brought for other kings, being marvels of Punt . . .

Afterwards we see Hashepsowe meeting two lines of kneeling chiefs from the land of Punt, and behind them come the Egyptians with their myrrh-trees and other offerings.

Kissing the earth to (Hashepsowe) by the chiefs of Punt
. . . doing obeisance with bowed head, bearing their tribute to
the place where her majesty is head . . . lord of Thebes who has
set all the lands beneath her sandals, living forever!

Beyond the second forecourt another ramp leads to the holiest part of the temple, built into the cliffs themselves. In the centre is the sanctuary of Amun-Re, below which Hashepsowe intended to excavate her burial chamber, connected by a long tunnel to her tomb-entrance in the Royal Valley on the western side of the mountain. To its left is the shrine of Hathor, goddess of beauty and love, the Egyptian Aphrodite. Typically, Hashepsowe had her own features carved in the image of the goddess. To the right of Amun's sanctuary lies that of Anubis, the jackal-headed god of the cemeteries and of embalmment. Here the Queen had planned a funerary chapel in which offerings would be made not only to her but to her father Tuthmosis I.

The ruthlessness and egocentricity to which her monuments bear witness is particularly apparent in her treatment of her father's bones. She asserts that she was his daughter, that he appointed her as his successor. Not only did she create a shrine for him in her temple, but, when she built her second great tomb in the Valley of the Kings, where his body already lay in the sepulchre prepared by Ineni, she had two sarcophagi made, one for herself and the other for her father. Both were found in the burial chamber of this deep-delved tomb, excavated by Howard Carter in 1916-17, the largest in the Royal Valley. Presumably she intended to remove her father's mummy from his own tomb and bury it beside hers. Whether or not this was ever done is not certain. Howard Carter, in his excavation report, states that a few scraps of funerary furniture, bearing her name and that of her father, were found in the burial chamber. But the tomb contained no sculptured reliefs and paintings such as adorned those of other Pharaohs. It was manifestly left unfinished, and no one can be certain that Hashepsowe, 'the female Sun' as she is described in the Punt reliefs, together with the proud appellation 'King' which no Queen had borne from the beginnings of Egyptian civilisation, was ever buried in the Valley of the Kings.

Looking at her portraits, and reading the inscriptions which she had placed in her funerary temple, in her tomb, and on her granite obelisks at Karnak, one wonders if her publicly-avowed love for the supreme god, Amun, was really what modern psychiatrists call a 'transference' from her own earthly father. In one of her temple reliefs, on the walls of the lowest colonnade, we see two gigantic granite obelisks, hewn from the quarries at Assuan, resting, base to base, on an enormous raft which is transporting them northward to Thebes.

The raft is some 300 feet long, and is towed by three rows of ships, nine in a row, with a total complement of over 800 oarsmen. Such a demonstration of power had rarely been seen in Egypt, and the Queen was proud of it. She could not, as her father had done, lead great armies into Nubia and Syria; she could not extend the frontiers of the Egyptian Empire, because, as a woman, she could not command armies or fight in battle. Her much-vaunted 'peaceful' achievements, which endeared her to feminists and pacifists of the late nineteenth and early twentieth centuries, may have been merely a substitute for what she would liked to have done.

But to this day there stands, in the Karnak temple east of the Nile, a gigantic obelisk of granite erected by Hashepsowe. It bears an inscription, in hieroglyphs as clear and sharply-cut as on the day they were carved. In it she boasts how this colossal monument, weighing nearly 1,000 tons, was quarried, transported, inscribed and raised in *seven months*. And she adds this message for us:

> And you who after long years shall see these monuments, who shall speak of what I have done, you will say 'we do not know how they can have made a whole monument of gold as if it were an ordinary task' [the obelisks were originally plated with pure gold]. To gild them I have given gold measured by

the bushel, as though it were sacks of grain. And when my majesty had said the amount it was more than the whole of the Two Lands [i.e. Egypt] had ever seen ... When you shall hear this, do not say that this is an idle boast, but 'How like her this was, worthy of her father! ...'

But which father? The great god Amun, or the virile, energetic, restless man whom she remembered, in the royal palace of Thebes, when she was a mere child? She had watched him driving out of Thebes in his golden war-chariot at the head of his army. She had heard of how he sailed up-river to smite the rebellious Nubians, and how his first spear pierced the breast of the enemy chief, who was brought hanging head-downwards from the prow of her father's warship. She may have known that he had extended his empire as far as the 'Horns of the Earth,' that even the people from the 'marshes of Kebeh' (the Euphrates) had been forced to accept the domination of Egypt.

If she had been a conventionally feminine woman she would, no doubt, have accepted these triumphs as a purely male prerogative. But she may have been one of those rare women who would rather have been a man. Of these Chaucer has an apposite story in *The Canterbury Tales*. An old woman is entreated by a young man to answer the question 'What is it that women most desireth?' After hedging for a considerable time the old dame finally comes out with the answer: 'Dominion over men.'

---

[1] The quotations in this chapter are from *Ancient Records of Egypt,* Volume II, by J. H. Breasted, Chicago University Press, 1906-07; 1927

4

The Revenge of Tuthmosis

THE FACTS ABOUT HASHEPSOWE GIVEN IN THE TWO PRECEDING chapters have been known for at least seventy years. The distinguished Swiss archaeologist Naville, who cleared much of the debris from the Queen's funerary temple and began its restoration, wrote about her at the turn of the century. The American amateur archaeologist Mr. Theodore Davis who, with Mr. Howard Carter, cleared Hashepsowe's great tomb in the Valley of the Kings, published a sumptuous volume about it in 1906, including a biography of the Queen by Monsieur Naville. Ten years later Carter, who was then working in collaboration with Lord Carnarvon, discovered yet another, earlier tomb of the Queen, which was never used; the entrance was half-way up a precipitous cliff wall in an even more remote valley called the *Wady e' Taqa e Zeide*. This discovery, too, was published in 1917. Carter had to have himself hauled on a rope 150 feet up the cliff-face in order to investigate the tomb, which also contained a sarcophagus inscribed with the Queen's name.

Much of the work of clearing and partially restoring the

Deir el Bahri temple was carried out by Herbert Winlock of the Metropolitan Museum of Art, New York; he began the Museum's long period of excavation in the area of Deir el Bahri which continued from 1911 until 1931. Among his successors were Professor W. C. Hayes, later Curator of the Egyptian Department of the Museum, and Mr. Ambrose Lansing, both of whom were responsible for some interesting new discoveries.

One day the archaeologists were examining the tomb of a Theban official of the Eighteenth Dynasty, not far from Hashepsowe's temple. Like nearly every one of the hundreds of noblemen's tombs in which the Theban Necropolis abounds, this one had been plundered in antiquity. Whatever rich furnishings its inner chambers had once contained had vanished long ago. But the tomb was of a most unusual type for a non-royal sepulchre, consisting of a long, steeply sloping rock-cut corridor which plunged deep under the temple itself, ending in a burial-chamber and adjoining rooms. In fact it was not unlike that of Hashepsowe herself, not surprisingly since its owner, Sen-en-mut, had been the Queen's most powerful minister and adviser.

In 1931 the Museum acquired a small object which was known to have been found near the entrance to this tomb. It was a flat fragment of limestone, on one side of which was painted the two portraits illustrated (Plate 7). It shows two profile heads of a man with a prominent, arched nose, nervously pursed lips, a well-shaped brow, and deep lines around the mouth and chin. The archaeologists recognised the face immediately. It was that of Sen-en-mut.

Such limestone fragments, called ostraca, are often found near Egyptian tombs, lying among heaps of stone chippings and fragments thrown out by the ancient quarrymen. They are 'test-pieces' on which the artist had made a preliminary sketch of the subject he was going to draw on the plastered walls of the sepulchre. These tomb-paintings, like the inscriptions which accompany them, represent 'official history,' and the workmen, who were usually strictly controlled, had to obey a rigid artistic convention in whatever they drew, and the subjects were almost invariably the same—scenes of the funerary procession, scenes on the nobleman's estates, scenes of him hunting, fishing, and holding feasts. When, however, these artists were not being supervised, but idly sketching on scraps of limestone which they threw away, the result was often more lively, varied and realistic, as in this example. Also, when the foreman was not watching, they could and did indulge their taste for caricature, their victims usually being the Great Ones.

The Egyptologists were particularly interested in Sen-en-mut because of his close association with Hashepsowe. Like all Egyptian officials he was careful to describe the offices and titles he held, which were numerous. One of the most grandiloquent of these titularies is inscribed on a statue which shows Sen-en-mut, kneeling and offering a votive systrum to the goddess Mūt, consort of Amun. In it he makes an offering-prayer to the deity, whose name was incorporated in his.

That she may give glory in heaven and on earth to the spirit of the *Chief Steward of the King, Sen-en-mut;* that she may give the offerings which are in the Southland to the spirit of the *Magnate of the Tens of Upper and Lower Egypt, Sen-en-mut;* that she may give the food which is in the Northland to the spirit of the greatest of the great, the noblest of the nobles, the *Chief of the Mansion of the Red Crown, Sen-en-mut;* that she may give everything which comes forth from her offering-table in 'Most-Select-of-Places' (Karnak) and in (the temple, of the gods of Upper and Lower Egypt) to the spirit of the *Privy Councillor, Sen-en-mut;* that she may give evocations of bread and beer, beef and fowl and a drinking of water at the flood, to the *Chief Steward of Amun, Sen-en-mut* who filled the store-houses and enriched the granaries, the *Overseer of the Double Granary of Amun, Sen-en-mut,* the justified, engendered of the worthy Ramose, the justified, and born of Hat-nufer . . .[1]

These six offices, which he skilfully incorporates in his offering-prayer, by no means exhaust his list of titles. *In addition* he held, at various times, the posts of:

> *Overseer of Works*
> *Overseer of the Fields*
> *Overseer of the Double Gold House*
> *Overseer of the Garden of Amun*
> *Controller of Works*
> *Overseer of the Administrative Office of the Mansion*
> *Conductor of Festivals*
> *Overseer of the Cattle of Amun*
> *Steward of the King's Daughter Nefru-Re.*

The aforementioned statue was, he boasts 'given as a favour of the King's bounty to the *Hereditary Prince and Count* (another title) *Sen-en-mut,* the confidant of the Female Horus (Hashepsowe), the trusted one of the Horus Kha-em-Wast, who executed their eternal monuments and remained in favour with them every day.'

That he was the 'confidant of the female Horus' is without doubt true, for it must be she who loaded him with so many honourable titles and offices. Certainly he walked the 'corridors of power' but the words 'the trusted one of the Horus *Kha-em-Wast*' were probably born out of hope rather than conviction. For *Kha-em-Wast** was Tuthmosis III, Hashepsowe's young and frustrated stepson whom she and her advisers withheld from effective power throughout twenty years of his nominal reign.

As in Ineni's inscription, the names of both Hashepsowe and Tuthmosis are tactfully associated; both are given the title Horus, only borne by Pharaohs, but there is no indication of who was in fact the ruler. But the phrase 'confidant of the Female Horus' is significant, especially as there are several statues of Sen-en-mut which show him with the Queen's only daughter, Nefru-Re, on his knee. He was in fact the Princess's guardian

---

* Each of the Pharaohs bore several names.

(Steward) and tutor; of the ten statues of Sen-en-mut known to exist six show him with Nefru-Re.

At this point I should remind the lay 'Egyptologist-detective' of two important facts. The first is that this is basically a story of power, and in Ancient Egypt it was not enough to seize and hold power; one had to prove one's right to it. Hence the monotonous reiteration of offices held and deeds accomplished. Second, the only way, legitimately, to become Pharaoh was by marrying the royal heiress, and Nefru-Re was the daughter of Hashepsowe and Tuthmosis II, and the grand-daughter of Tuthmosis I.

Was she ever married to Tuthmosis III? It seems extremely unlikely. Professor Hayes, who with Mr. Ambrose Lansing has done so much valuable work at Deir el Bahri, comments:

> The name [of the Princess] occurs in our collection [Metropolitan Museum of Art] on four scarabs of green-glazed steatite and on two marked linen sheets from the wrappings of the mummy of Sen-en-mut's father Ramose. On the linen sheets the name Nefru-Re is written by itself in black ink. On the scarabs it is twice accompanied by the title 'the God's Wife' ... Three of the scarabs (a scarab is a model beetle, one of the forms of the Sun-God and used as an amulet) are from the Deir el Bahri temple or its vicinity but the fourth was found tied to the hand of an old woman buried in the chip-heaps in the front of the tomb of Sen-en-mut.

Hayes goes on to say that Nefru-Re, who seems to have died while still a young girl, is known from a few sculptures, including one:

> where her slender, youthful figure, loaded with royal attributes, is seen standing behind the much larger figures of her mother and half-brother. In this scene, carved near the end of her short life, she bears the titles 'King's Daughter' (of his body whom he loves), Lady of the Two Lands, Mistress of Upper and Lower Egypt, Wife of the God and Holy (Image) of Amun; but neither here nor elsewhere is she called a King's Wife—a

fact which leaves us in some doubt as to whether she was ever actually married to Tuthmosis III.[2]

I have quoted these observations at some length if only to demonstrate the slender threads of evidence on which Egyptologists have to hang their theories. In this case the life of Hashepsowe's royal daughter, the heiress in whose 'slender youthful body' lay all the potentialities of Pharaonic power (for whoever married her) is represented by a few statues, a handful of scarabs, and, most strangely, some linen sheets wrapped round the body of Sen-en-mut's father, Ramose.

Obviously if Tuthmosis III had married his half-sister his claim to the throne would have been much stronger, for Nefru-Re was the daughter of two royal personages, whereas his own mother was a mere concubine. Her youth would have been no objection, since the Pharaohs often married when they were children. Why, then, was he not married to her? We do not know.

We do know quite a lot about Tuthmosis III, however. We know that when at last, after Hashepsowe's death, he was sole ruler, he became the greatest Pharaoh Egypt has ever known, a brilliant general, a wise administrator, and a fighting soldier whose prowess was proved again and again on the battlefield. How did he spend those twenty years during which his stepmother and her satellites controlled the kingdom? Almost certainly in the Army, because we have records which show that he was renowned for his skill as a horseman, charioteer, archer and swordsman. He would not have learned such skills idling in the royal palace, nor, one feels, would he have cared much for the company of Sen-en-mut, Hapi-soneb and the rest of his stepmother's friends.

That this is not speculation will be shown later. Meanwhile we will return to Deir el Bahri and observe Hayes and Lansing searching for further clues to this mystery. Besides Sen-en-mut's great tomb with its 300-foot corridor plunging beneath the temple, he had another, earlier one hewn out of the hill-side above the village of Sheikh abd el Gournah. This he had evidently prepared in the days before he became the most powerful official in the realm. It had been plundered and badly damaged in antiquity, but the archaeologists carefully studied the surviving inscriptions and then concentrated their attention on its environs.

They were rewarded by finding, nearby, the intact tomb of Sen-en-mut's father and mother. The mummies and funerary equipment—which were not rich or elaborate—were intact, and on the mummy of Sen-en-mut's father were linen sheets bearing the name of the royal heiress Nefru-Re. How they came to be there is anybody's guess. A frivolous answer would be that the old man asked his rich and influential son to obtain some of the royal bed-linen for his personal use, and later this was used to wrap the mummy. My own belief is that anything bearing the royal name conferred some kind of protection in the world beyond the grave.

But what interested Hayes most was the discovery that neither of the old people had any claim to distinction. Ramose, the father of the 'noblest of the nobles,' is merely described as 'the worthy,' and Hat-nufer, Sen-en-mut's mother, bore the undistinguished title of 'Lady of the House.'

Hashepsowe's favourite was evidently devoted to his family. In a fragment of the reliefs which had once covered the inner walls of his battered sepulchre there is an inscription referring to 'his beloved sister, Ahotep, the justified,' and the body of an unknown woman found in an anthropoid coffin in a little shelter built of chunks of limestone may, Hayes thinks, be that of this lady. On the same hill-slope near the main tomb were found buried other members of Sen-en-mut's family and household, including a young man named Amunhotep, who may have been a younger brother; a minstrel named Har-mose, with his lute lying beside his coffin; another young man, probably a servant, buried in a reed mat, and a very old woman, also presumably a family servant, encased in a cheap rectangular coffin, but 'wearing tied to one of her fingers a handsome scarab inscribed for the "God's Wife, Nefru-Re." '

The Theban Necropolis, those tumbled heaps of sand and yellow rock where desolation reigns and not a blade of grass grows, still, after 3,000 years of plundering, occasionally yields its secrets. Nowadays the finding of an intact noble tomb is a rare miracle, yet little scraps of funerary equipment, a wooden statuette, a few inscribed scarabs, some fragments of an inscription, may yet provide significant detail. For instance, beneath the terrace of his great tomb Sen-en-mut had buried one of his horses, a little mare only about twelve and a half hands high; this, too, was encased in a rectangular coffin and provided with food in pottery bowls. Near by lay one of his pets, a cynocephalus ape, also swathed in linen bandages and enclosed in a coffin.

Nor should it be imagined that these servants and animals were slain to accompany their master, a barbarous custom which the Ancient Egyptians abandoned in 2800 BC, some fourteen centuries before the time of which we are writing. They must have been buried there long before their master died, since, as we know, he later built himself a much larger tomb near the temple of his royal mistress.

As one sits on a rock above that desiccated hill-side, looking down towards Hashepsowe's many-columned terraces rising towards the sun-bright cliffs, fact and imagination battle in one's mind. The bare outline of the story is there, but if only one could clothe it with warm human detail! All around lie the rifled, empty tombs, painted with pictures of men and women who lived in the time of Hashepsowe, who knew Sen-en-mut and might have told us what they were like. But their voices are 'choked in dust' and there is no sound but the desert wind, and the distant cries of children playing in the village of El Gournah.

The principal actors are the Queen, her stepson, and Sen-en-mut. There were other officials, of course, who played their parts, but their tombs tell us little save their names and titles.

There was Hapi-soneb, the Vizier, who held higher rank even than Sen-en-mut, for the Vizier was the Prime Minister. Yet though his other titles included those of Hereditary Prince and Count, Treasurer of the King of Lower Egypt, First Prophet (i.e. High Priest) of Amun, and Overseer of All Works of the King, his effective power must have been far less than his great rival. It was he, incidentally, who supervised the making of Hashepsowe's enormous tomb in the Royal Valley.

Other officials favoured by Hashepsowe were the Chancellor Nehesy (who led the expedition to the Land of Punt); the Treasurer, Thuty; the Viceroy of Nubia, Inebny; and the Second Prophet of Amun, Puy-em-Re. It must have been men such as these who helped the Queen to retain power, for they held the key positions in the complex administrative system; through them she ruled Egypt.

But Sen-en-mut, a man who had risen from obscurity, was clearly her favourite and most trusted minister, on whom she heaped honours and dignities. Was their relationship closer than that of monarch and adviser, as more than one writer has speculated? Again, we do not know. But two facts may be highly significant: that she entrusted him with the tutelage of her daughter, heiress to the throne, and that not only was he permitted to build a magnificent tomb under her own funerary temple—an unheard-of honour—but, within that temple itself he had his own figure carved, very small and in obscure places where it would not normally be seen.

For instance, in the Holy of Holies, the sanctuary of Amun himself, cut out of the rock-wall, are small recesses like cupboards which were probably used for storing the holy vessels. These recesses were closed by wooden doors which, when they opened (inwards), hid the walls behind them. Today the dragomans showing visitors the sanctuary crouch, candle in hand, point to a tiny kneeling figure carved on the wall. 'Sen-en-mut,' they say, usually with a knowing smile . . .

Of this fact Sir Alan Gardiner comments:

It was no unheard-of thing for a Pharaoh to commemorate his leading officials on the walls of his funerary monument. Pepi II had done this at south Sakkara and Hashepsowe did the same at Deir el Bahri. But it was an unparalleled step for a court favourite, however powerful, to use his sovereign's temple for his own devotional purposes.[3]

If, as some had speculated, Sen-en-mut was Hashepsowe's lover, what was it that attracted her to him? The sculptured portraits reveal an alert, intelligent face, but by no means handsome, and the famous kneeling statue inscribed with his many titles and offices merely shows a rather smooth, soft body on which rolls of flesh around the midriff speak of a sedentary life made pleasant by ease and affluence. He looks, in fact, what he was, a scribe who had 'made good.' Born of humble parents he had by diligence, political astuteness, and not a little cunning, risen to become the highest in the land next to his royal mistress. Her fierce, rebellious stepson, for all his royal ancestry and military bearing, was helpless against the combination of a shrewd feminine mind and an indomitable will, allied with an administrative genius who held all or most of the keys of power. Hashepsowe, brought up in the warlike atmosphere of her father's household, married to another warrior Pharaoh, with a stepson who seemed determined to follow in their footsteps, may have grown weary of war. And Sen-en-mut may have had charm as well as high intelligence.

Here, of course, one is straying into mere speculation. But it is commonplace that women of dominant character tend to prefer gentle men, and Sen-en-mut may well have been gentle. One is reminded of the famous 'Admonition to a Scribe' which Egyptian schoolboys learning the secret of the writings had to write in their exercise-books. Here is part of it in Sir Alan Gardiner's translation:

Be a scribe, that thy limbs may be sleek, and thy hands become soft, that thou mayst go forth in white attire, honour done to thee, and that the courtiers may salute thee. A man of value is sought and thou art found. One does not recognize a little one, but one finds the man that is skilled, and he rises step by step until he has reached (the position) of magistrate, in praise corresponding to his good character.[4]

Sen-en-mut may well have taken that as his text when he was a schoolboy, poring over his writing-tablet in one of the scribal schools, occasionally glancing out of the window as the chariot and retinue of some great nobleman clattered by; or wondering, perhaps, how soon he could eat the lunch packed for him by his mother Hat-nufer. It was very rare for a man of humble birth to rise high within the rigid hierarchy of the Egyptian state. But it had happened once or twice. Might it, perhaps, happen to him?

We do not know what befell Sen-en-mut in the end. It is certain, however, that no more is heard of him after the sixteenth year of the joint reign of Hashepsowe and Tuthmosis III. It is also certain that the Queen lived on for at least another five years, but we do not know whether she died a natural death or by violence. She may have been buried in her great tomb hewn out of the Theban cliffs; her empty sarcophagus was found there, together with another which she had brought there to contain the body of her father Tuthmosis I. The tomb had been robbed in remote antiquity, and though some fragments of funerary furniture were found by Carter, the Queen's mummy has never been discovered. It is just possible that one of the unidentified female mummies found in the famous burial cache at Deir el Bahri, which contained the bodies of some of the greatest Pharaohs of the New Kingdom, may be hers.

Not long after he had become sole ruler, Tuthmosis III began to expunge the name of his hated stepmother wherever it could be found. His workmen descended on her funerary temple, and amid the crash of hammers and scraping of chisels her rows of great statues were overthrown and then pounded into fragments. Not one was spared, and those which we see in the

Cairo Museum, and in the Metropolitan Museum of Art, were reassembled from the thousands of pieces which Winlock found, either lying around the site or dumped in a nearby quarry where the agents of the King had left them. The destruction was thorough and deliberate. First the statue was thrown from its base, then its eyes were hacked out, and the uraeus, the sacred serpent, was struck from the brow. After that the hammers and mauls got to work and the colossi splintered into heaps of rubble.

Within the colonnades other workmen were chipping out the figure of the Queen wherever it appeared; others hacked out her cartouches bearing the royal name and substituted those of Tuthmosis I or Tuthmosis II. The true order of succession was to be restored; the Queen had not existed.

What happened to the surviving favourites of Hashepsowe one can only guess, but a few apparently survived to serve under Tuthmosis. Apart from this outburst of rage he appears to have been a humane and tolerant man. But in pursuit of his old enemies, the men who had helped his stepmother to withhold him from power long after he was old enough to reign, his determination was inflexible, and his vengeance followed them even into their tombs.

This was not the pointless act of petulance which it now appears to be. For the Ancient Egyptians believed that a human being could die twice. The first death was the one suffered by all mortals. The second would only occur if the spirit of the dead man or woman was denied access to the means of eternal life, i.e. the food offerings made at the funerary chapels, or if the magical pictures on the walls which did duty for them were destroyed or mutilated. It was not even necessary completely to destroy the pictures. You could blind a man by removing the eyes from his portrait, or, by cutting the wrist which holds his throwing-stick, prevent him bringing down the wildfowl on the celestial Nile. Thus disabled, the spirit, deprived of its offering and unable to hunt for its food, would starve to death. And that second death was final. This example of 'selective mutilation' can be seen in the well-known tomb of Men-na, in the Theban Necropolis, though, as it happens, it was not carried out by the agents of Tuthmosis III but by some other enemy.

Among those whose tombs suffered the king's vengeance were Thuty, who had been Hashepsowe's Overseer of the Treasury, and Hapi-soneb, her Vizier. In these and other sepulchres the faces of the officials and that of the Queen have been obliterated. It is not known whether the mummies which lay in deep burial shafts behind the chapels were respected, but it seems unlikely. In any case all the tombs were plundered. But the most fanatical destruction was wrought upon the tombs and monuments of Sen-en-mut. The great tomb he had excavated under the temple at Deir el Bahri was never completed or occupied. Nevertheless, Tuthmosis III's agents mutilated its sculptured reliefs, which included a most beautiful ceiling, some of which has happily survived, and which has a map of the night sky with the constellations, the zodiacal signs, and a list of festivals. It is, writes Hayes:

> ... the earliest and one of the finest astronomical ceilings ever known—a great chart of the heavens ... drawn by some skilful penman of the mid-Eighteenth Dynasty.[5]

It is in the antechamber, approached by a rock-cut corridor over one hundred yards long. Here, too, the *ghaffir* shows you, with lifted candle, a tiny figure of the great official which the destroyers missed.

Sen-en-mut was apparently buried in the original tomb he had built for himself near the modern village of Sheikh abd el Gournah, surrounded by graves of his family and staff. Foreseeing what would happen after his death, he had two complete sets of tomb frescoes painted, one above the other with a layer of plaster between. Thus he hoped to escape the vengeance of his enemies who might, he thought, only mutilate the top layer of pictures, not realising that there were others hidden underneath.

He was mistaken. Both layers were discovered and both

were mutilated. It was a forlorn hope, anyway, since the upper layer of plaster, once chipped, would surely reveal that underneath. In the burial chamber the archaeologists found the shattered remains of a once-magnificent quartzite sarcophagus. Scattered on the hill-side around the sepulchre were hundreds more bits: 1,200 separate pieces were collected and pieced together so that two-thirds of the sarcophagus has now been reconstituted. The great oblong chest, seven feet eight inches in length and rounded at both ends, was carved with the names and titles of Sen-en-mut and with funerary texts.

Other workmen sought out and mutilated the tiny figures of Hashepsowe's favourite wherever they found it carved in her temple. The few examples which they overlooked, such as those in the small recesses opening off the sanctuary, are only a small percentage of those which once existed. Originally there were over one hundred, and this fact, together with Sen-en-mut's statement that he 'executed the eternal monuments' of the Queen and her stepson, has led some authorities to believe that he was the architect of this superb building. But there is no proof of this, although he almost certainly supervised the work.

Has Deir el Bahri now yielded all its secrets? By no means. As recently as 1961 the Polish architect Leszek Dabrowski was sent by his government to assist the Egyptian Department of Antiquities in the further reconstruction of Hashepsowe's temple. Behind the shrine of Hathor he came upon the foundations of an even larger temple. Work is still proceeding, but already it is clear that this hitherto-unknown building was raised after Hashepsowe's death, to the south of and at a higher level than her temple. Its builder? Need one ask? Here is yet another example of what one might call 'Tuthmosmanship.'

His main work, however, was concentrated at Karnak, immediately opposite Deir el Bahri on the eastern bank of the Nile. Unwilling or unable to destroy the Queen's obelisks, he had them walled up so that her proud inscriptions could not be seen. In so doing he defeated his own ends, because the walls, which have long since perished, preserved the inscriptions which now stand, sharp-etched by the Egyptian sun, as perfectly as on the day they were carved.

It was at Karnak that Tuthmosis caused to be inscribed the story of how, when a mere 'stripling' in the temple priesthood, the god Amun stopped before him and set him in the Place of the King. This, of course, was intended as counter-propaganda to the story of Hashepsowe's 'divine birth' and may have as little foundation in truth. However, it is just possible that some such event took place, carefully stage-managed by members of the priesthood who favoured the young prince.

So much for the known facts. Their interpretation depends on how one chooses to view Hashepsowe and Sen-en-mut. Those sympathetic to the Queen, such as the late Dr. Margaret Murray and, more recently, Mrs. Barbara Mertz, suggest that she was essentially a feminine woman, though of strong character, who revolted against her warlike ancestors and devoted her reign to the arts of peace and the establishment of peaceful trading relationships. They see Sen-en-mut as a faithful minister whom she raised to high honour because he was able and willing to carry out her plans. Those who take the opposite view, to which I incline, see Hashepsowe as a highly-intelligent, able, but un-scrupulous woman who so loved power that she would go to almost any length to achieve it. With the help of Sen-en-mut and other like-minded ministers she succeeded in preventing the ablest Pharaoh Egypt ever knew from achieving effective rule until long after he had reached maturity.

I have often wondered if her affection for Sen-en-mut was so great that she even planned he might marry her daughter Nefru-Re and so become Pharaoh and the founder of a new Dynasty after her death. If this was so, and Tuthmosis was aware of it, this would account for the fury which he unleashed when at last he gained the right to reign as sole king. His acts of posthumous vengeance against his stepmother and her friends are not in keeping with his known character.

As for Sen-en-mut, there may or may not be significance in the picture which was found drawn on the reverse side of the ostracon discovered near the mouth of his tomb, and which was evidently the work of the same artist who drew the pictures of Sen-en-mut on the other side. It is illustrated in Plate 8 and depicts, in the words of Professor Hayes, 'a lean, hairy rat with prodigiously long whiskers.'

---

[1] Hayes, W. C., *The Scepter of Egypt,* Vol. II, New York Graphic Society for the Metropolitan Museum of Art, Greenwich, Conn., 1959

[2] Hayes, W. C., op. cit.

[3] Gardiner, Sir Alan, *Egypt of the Pharaohs,* Oxford University Press, New York, 1961

[4] Gardiner, Sir Alan, *Hieratic Papyri in the British Museum,* Volume 1, Third Series, The British Museum, 1935

[5] Hayes, W. C., op. cit.

5

Old Gods and New Concepts

Tuthmosis III, who for twenty years had been subordinate to his determined stepmother, reigned as sole King for a further thirty-four years. Short, powerfully built, and chubby-faced, this long-lived Pharaoh has been rightly described as 'the Napoleon of Ancient Egypt,' a military genius under whose rule she attained the peak of her power. But, indirectly, those same conquests, and those of the King's successors, introduced Asiatic influences which had a profound effect on Egyptian society, and even on her traditional religious beliefs.

It is not difficult to represent Hashepsowe as a peace-loving ruler whose pacific foreign policy provided a blessed interregnum between the aggressively militant careers of her father and stepson. This would certainly be an over-simplification of the truth. The two tranquil decades which she and her subjects enjoyed had been purchased with the blood shed on the battle-fields of Nubia and Asia by her fighting ancestors. After twenty years of peace the emergent powers of western Asia, notably the Mitannians and the Hittites, were threatening war and suborning the vassal-states whose rulers owed nominal allegiance to Egypt.

Tuthmosis III, who must have spent much of his youth training with the Army, excelled even his grandfather, and in seventeen campaigns raised Egypt's military glory to its highest point. He subdued the Nubians of the south, the Libyans of the west, and the Asiatics of the north and east. He crossed the Euphrates, as Tuthmosis I had done, but extended his conquests even further. Under his energetic leadership in war, and the wise administration of his great Vizier, Rekhmire, Egypt became the richest and mightiest power in the world, and Thebes approached the period of its greatest magnificence.

The riches which poured into the capital as a result of these conquests enabled the Pharaoh to enlarge and beautify its temples and monuments, especially the temple of Amun-Re at Karnak. The battle-hymn which Tuthmosis caused to be inscribed on one of its walls is one of the finest examples of Egyptian dramatic poetry. In it the god addresses the Pharaoh, his victorious son, in these words;

I have come, causing thee to smite the princes of Zahi,
I have hurled them beneath thy feet among their highlands.
I have caused them to see thy majesty as lord of radiance,
So that thou hast shone in their faces like my image.
I have come, causing thee to smite the Asiatics,
Thou hast made captive the heads of the Asiatics of Retenu.
I have caused them to see thy majesty equipped with thy adornment,
When thou takest the weapons of war in the chariot. . . .

And another passage reads:

I have caused them to see thy majesty as a young bull,
Firm of heart, ready-horned, irresistible . . .

which, coming immediately after the line 'Keftiu and Cyprus are in terror' arouses an intriguing, though doubtful, possibility. For 'Keftiu' was the island of Crete where, as we now know, the cult of the bull was predominant. Admittedly one of the conventional titles of a Pharaoh was 'Mighty Bull' but it seems odd that this reference to 'a young bull, firm of heart' comes immediately after the line about Crete, particularly as the following passage—

I have come, causing thee to smite those who are in their marshes,
The lands of Mitanni tremble under fear of thee

is succeeded by—

> *I have caused them to see thy majesty as a crocodile,*
> *Lord of fear in the water, irresistible . . .*

Mitanni was on the Euphrates, where there must have been many crocodiles, just as Libya was noted for its lions, and the passage describing Tuthmosis's conquest of the Libyans (the 'Tehenu') reads:

> *I have caused them to see thy majesty as a fierce-eyed lion,*
> *Thou makest them corpses in their valleys.*[1]

It may merely be a poetic conceit, of course, and certainly the Egyptians, who were not a seafaring people, would not have dared attack Crete, which controlled the most powerful fleet in the Mediterranean. But Tuthmosis certainly accomplished the other victories of which he boasts, and in so doing he brought the Egyptians into contact with lands of which they had hitherto known nothing, and peoples who worshipped gods who were unknown in the Nile Valley. This had tremendous repercussions in the centuries which followed, as we shall see. In this period conflict shifted from the military to the political and religio-political spheres, and two of the Queens whom we are to describe played essential parts in the drama.

In order to understand this conflict, therefore, it is necessary to know a little more about Egyptian religious beliefs, which were extremely complex. Although Amun-Re had now become the state god, a deity of war and power, there were at least 2,000 other gods and goddesses. The reason for their survival lies in Egyptian conservatism. More than 1,500 years before Tuthmosis

III was born, the primitive ancestors of the Ancient Egyptians lived in separate tribal communities scattered along the length of the Nile, from the Delta to the frontier at Assuan. Each of these tribes had its own local deities. Some were fetiches, such as sacred trees (the hieroglyphic sign called the *Djed-pillar*, the symbol of stability, and which looks rather like a telegraph-pole, was originally a sacred tree). Others were deified animals, such as the jackal-headed Anubis, guardian of the cemetery; the dog Wepwawet, 'opener of the ways'; Wadjet, the serpent goddess of Buto, one of the twin insignia of royalty which the Pharaohs wore in their crowns, the lioness-headed goddess Sekhmet, the crocodile god Sobek, and many others. Even Amun had once worn the head of a ram, and was often depicted thus.

Then there were deities of the elements, and these were very ancient. There was Geb, god of the earth, Shu, god of the atmosphere, and Nūt, goddess of the sky. These primal deities were depicted on the coffins and sarcophagi of the dead Pharaohs, with inscriptions in which they welcomed the deified King (or Queen) to the Underworld and eternal life. When Howard Carter explored the lonely rock-cut tomb of Hashepsowe, high up in a cliff face above the *Wady e' Taqa e Zeide*, he found the sarcophagus of the Queen, inscribed with these welcoming speeches. The earth-god Geb says:

> *O wife of the god, great wife of the king, Hashepsowe, raise thee to thy mother Nūt, that she may take hold of thee and embrace thee. O King's Sister, Hashepsowe, I stand up as one who tendeth thee.*

And Hashepsowe herself is represented as saying:

> *O my mother Nūt, stretch thyself over me, that thou mayst place me among the stars imperishable that are in thee, and that I may not die.*

The two other goddesses, Isis and Nephthys, greet the Queen with the words:

> *O King's Daughter, Hashepsowe, we come that we may raise*

*thee, that thy heart may live . . . O King's Sister, Hashepsowe,
we embrace thy flesh, we command thy limbs to live, and thou
diest not.*

These prayers are moving enough in themselves, but even
more so in the setting which Carter describes:

> The tomb faces west, and the setting October sun throws
> its last beams right into the mouth of the tomb. From this sort
> of raven's nest one gains a magnificent view of the river and the
> plain winding away southward.[2]

These texts occur not only on coffins of the Eighteenth
Dynasty but as far back as the Pyramid Period, thirteen hundred
years before Hashepsowe. They typify the religious conservatism
of the Egyptians who, like congenital hoarders, threw nothing
away. Thus religious beliefs which dated from the beginnings
of their history, and which no longer had any validity, were
retained, and the priests had to try to fit this bewildering variety
of gods and goddesses into an all-embracing pantheon; and they
failed.

Some gods, however, became more important than others.
Besides Amun-Re, his divine consort Mūt and their son Khonsu,
there was Ptah, the artificer-god, corresponding to the Greek
Hephaestos and the Roman Vulcan; Hathor, the Egyptian
Aphrodite, goddess of love and beauty; Thoth, god of wisdom
(represented with the head of an ibis); and Horus, the falcon-
god, emblem of kingly power. But next to Amun-Re the most
popular deity was undoubtedly Osiris, whose myth went through
many transformations. He is always shown as a mummified
figure, wearing the false beard which was one of the insignia
of the Pharaohs from early times, and clasping in each hand
another royal emblem. One was the shepherd's crook; the other,
a short rod with three trailing strings attached to it, is often
described as a flail, or even a whip.

In fact one glance at the V-shaped end from which the
strings hang proves that this emblem could never have been a

whip, nor a flail. Twenty years ago the late Professor Newberry suggested to me that it was an implement called a *ladanesterion*, and I am glad to see that other Egyptologists, e.g. Professor Hayes, have come to accept this theory, which links Osiris logically with a much earlier god called Anzety. Anzety was a goat-god or a deity of goatherds, hence the beard. The three-stringed implement is still used to this day in the Middle East for gathering an aromatic gum called ladanum, by trailing it through the bushes which exude this gum. If the ladanum-gatherers were also goatherds the goats' beards would be matted by the gum, and this is how the Pharaonic false beard looks.

Over a period of more than 2,000 years this god took on the characteristics of others. At Memphis he assimilated the attributes of Sokar, a god of the Underworld; at Abydos he superseded Khentamentiu, the god of the dead. He also acquired a sister-wife, Isis, and a son, Horus (originally the falcon-god). By the time of Tuthmosis III the myth of Isis and Osiris had taken on the form which it retained for the rest of Egyptian history; with the mass of the Egyptians these two deities were far more popular than Amun-Re and his consort, and they retained their hold on the imagination of the people down to Roman times. The reason was their basic humanity; Osiris became the type of the ideal king and father, Isis the perfect wife, Horus the loyal son. And because Isis throws light on the Egyptian ideal of womanhood the myth is worth repeating.

Osiris was the son of the earth-god Geb and the sky-goddess Nūt. He had two sisters, Isis and Nephthys, and a brother, Seth. He was born to be king of all the earth, and shortly after his reign began he 'raised the Egyptian people from their miserable and barbarous existence, caused them to learn about the fruits of the earth, gave them laws and taught them to respect the gods.' These are Plutarch's words. In short Osiris gave the Egyptians their civilisation, and, in one version of the story, induced them to give up cannibalism.

In accordance to Pharaonic custom he married his sister Isis. But the brother Seth grew to hate Osiris and plotted to kill him. The plot was ingenious. He caused a magnificent coffer to be made which exactly fitted the body of Osiris. Then Seth gave a feast, to which he invited his brother, together with a large number of guests, of whom seventy-two were accomplices of Seth. When the coffer was brought in it was greatly admired, and Seth jokingly suggested that whoever fitted it exactly could become its owner. Several of the accomplices tried, but they were either too short or too tall. Then Osiris was invited to try. The moment he lay down in the coffer the friends of Seth rushed forward, sealed it with nails and molten lead, then threw it into the Nile.

Isis and Nephthys then went in search of their brother's body, and after many months located it, washed up at the port of Byblos, in the Lebanon. After numerous adventures they brought the body back to Egypt, but Seth found this out, and cut the corpse into small pieces, which he distributed throughout Egypt. But the penis he threw into the Nile at Oxyrhyncus, where it was eaten by fish.

Undeterred, the faithful Isis travelled the length and breadth of the country, searching for the dismembered remains of her husband's body; eventually she found them all, and put them together. Then, with the help of Nephthys, who fluttered her wings over the head of Osiris, she breathed life into the body. Another version of the tale has it that Re took pity on Isis and sent Thoth, the god of wisdom, with a book of magical spells, to assist her.

So Osiris was reanimated, but as the organ of generation could not be retrieved he could not create life. He therefore became King of the Underworld, and judge of souls. Every dead man or woman, including the Pharaohs and their Queens, had to appear before Osiris. In fact every dead man or woman became an 'Osiris,' which is why the coffins of the Eighteenth Dynasty and later were made in the form of the mummified god.

He was also the god of resurrection, associated with the return of spring and the burgeoning of the crops. In many tombs examples have been found of the 'corn-Osiris,' wooden trays in the shape of the god, containing earth and set with seeds of corn or other cereal.

Before her husband's death Isis had conceived, and bore a son, Horus, and thousands of miniature statues exist showing her suckling the infant. When Horus grew up he revenged himself on his uncle, and on certain temples, notably that at Edfou, sculptured reliefs depict the battle between Horus and Seth, in which the evil uncle is represented as a crocodile and Horus as a harpooner. It is possible that this drama was re-enacted at the spring festivals by the priests of the temple, and that the King and Queen took the parts of Osiris and Isis. Professor Fairman, who has published the translation of these lengthy inscriptions, believes that the ritual was cast in dramatic form, and that this was the world's earliest known example of a Passion-play.

But Osiris, Isis, Horus, Ptah, Sekhmet, etc. had no relevance for the peoples of Asia which the armies of Egypt had entered and whose conquered kings sent their daughters to Thebes as wives and concubines of the Pharaohs. These foreign princesses, and the princes who were also sent to the Pharaoh's court for their education, introduced new and unfamiliar conceptions to the conservative Egyptian mind. Egyptian civilisation, already more than 1,500 years old, had grown up in comparative isolation, protected from invasion by the sterile deserts to east and west, with unknown—or largely unknown—Africa to the south and the 'Great Green Sea' to the north. Egypt was open to invasion only from the north-east, via the Sinai Peninsula, which the hated Hyksos had crossed.

They had driven the invaders out, and in pursuing them into their homeland had encountered lands totally unlike Egypt, lands where there were high mountains, where there was, in their own words 'a Nile in the sky,' i.e. crops were moistened by heavy rainfall and not by a mighty river. Even when they had found a river, the Euphrates, it confused them, because, unlike the Nile, which flowed northward as they thought all rivers should, this one flowed southward. So, in order to describe the

Euphrates the scribes had to invent a cumbersome name which could be translated 'the-river-which-in-flowing-southwards-flows-northwards.'

Tuthmosis III died in the fifty-fourth year of his reign and, like his father and grandfather, was buried in the Valley of the Kings. He was succeeded by Amenophis II (1436–1413 BC), his son by his chief wife, who bore the name Hashepsowe-Meryetre. (To avoid confusion we will call her simply Meryetre.) Amenophis also was a man of extraordinary muscular strength. It is said that he could 'shoot at a metal target of one palm's thickness and pierce it in such a way that his arrow would stick out on the other side.'

A similar story is told of his father, but there are others which carry more conviction. When still a youth, he was sent by his father to the dockyards of Peru-nufe near Memphis, to supervise deliveries of wood. His oarsmanship, it is stated, was such that, using an oar 20 cubits long he was the equal of 200 men, and could row for six times as long without tiring. Allowing for the inevitable exaggeration this anecdote has the individual ring of truth; likewise the statement that his father had such confidence in his horsemanship that he entrusted him with the finest steeds in the royal stables. These, the chroniclers state, he trained in such a way that they could cover great distances 'without sweating.'

His prowess on the battlefield reminds one of his grandfather. An inscription at Karnak, duplicated at Memphis, contains this passage:

His Majesty crossed the Orontes over the water turbulent like the god Rashaph. Then he turned around to look after the rear of his army and saw some Asiatics who had come surreptitiously from the town of Katna to attack the king's army. His Majesty was equipped with the weapons of warfare and His Majesty pounced upon their back like a falcon, and they gave way, their hearts fainting, each one fallen upon his fellow, including their captain. There was none with His Majesty save himself and his strong right arm. His Majesty slew them with a shot.[3]

The atmosphere of the court had again become military, and those who did not enjoy it must have looked back nostalgically to those two peaceful decades under Hashepsowe. Of Queen Meryetre we know practically nothing; such records of this period as exist are taken up almost entirely with war and conquest, of towns taken by storm and siege, and prisoners carried off. But a glance at these prisoner-lists is illuminating. One, recording part of the King's first campaign, reads as follows:

> Arrival of His Majesty at Memphis with joyful heart like a victorious bull. Amount of this plunder; Maryannu, 550; their wives, 240; Canaanites 640; children of princes, 232; female children of princes 323; female musicians of the princes of every land, 270, together with their instruments of silver and gold. Total 2,214. Now the god's wife, king's wife and king's daughter saw the victories of His Majesty.[4]

The effect of this continuing influx of foreign prisoners, especially women for the royal and princely harems, must have been considerable. Gradually one begins to notice Asiatic names among the wives of the nobility, and Asiatic faces in the sculpture and painting of the period. It has sometimes been suggested that these foreign captives may have included the ancestors of the Hebrews, and a word which can be transliterated as 'Apiru' appears in the long lists of conquered tribes. But this identification is now denied by all but a few scholars. Sir Alan Gardiner comments:

> . . . it is, however, generally accepted that they are to be equated with the Habiru (better Hapiru) of the Amarna tablets, apparently a generic term for 'outcasts' or 'bandits' belonging to no fixed ethnic groups; in Egyptian texts they appear as Asiatic prisoners employed in the stone quarries.[5]

Amenophis II, 'ruler of rulers, raging lion in every country,' died after reigning twenty-three years, and was buried in the Royal Valley, the only Pharaoh—apart from Tutankhamun—to remain lying in his own burial place down to the end of the nineteenth century AD. When M. Loret opened the tomb in 1898 there lay, beside the King's body, the great bow which he boasted that only he could draw. His son, also called Tuthmosis, had an undistinguished reign of only nine years. When he died the last faint echoes of battle died away, and Egypt entered a period of tranquil ease and magnificence such as she had never known in her long, long history.

Now we no longer hear the 'noise of the whip, and the rattling wheels' . . . 'the thunder of the captains, and the shouting.' The reigns of Amenophis III and his son Amenophis IV are marked by elegance, by new ideas, the flowering of a new and delicate art, and the influence of two of the most fascinating Queens who ever ruled the Two Lands.

---

[1] Breasted, J. H., *Ancient Records of Egypt,* Volume II, Chicago University Press, 1906-07; 1927

[2] Carter, Howard, *Journal of Egyptian Archaeology,* Volume IV, 1917

[3] Gardiner, Sir Alan, *Egypt of the Pharaohs,* Oxford University Press, New York, 1961

[4] Gardiner, Sir Alan, op. cit.

[5] Gardiner, Sir Alan, op. cit.

6

The Female Encroachment

THERE COULD HARDLY BE A GREATER CONTRAST THAN THAT BE-
tween the Tuthmosid warrior-kings and the two remarkable Pharaohs who succeeded them; or between Hashepsowe,
who tried to rule as a man, and Queens Tiye and Nefertiti, whose
feminine power was exercised *through* men. Why this was so
is difficult to determine, but it was almost certainly connected
with the influx of Asiatic women to the Theban court.

We must not, however, exaggerate this influence which in
any case was only indirect. And though one is tempted to weave
romantic fantasies around those two alluring women, Tiye and
Nefertiti, I shall try, as far as I am able, to stick to the known
facts. No Ancient Egyptian has left us a character-study of them,
nor have they left a single written statement by themselves. As
with Hashepsowe and the Tuthmosids our only sources of information are inscriptions set up by the Pharaohs and their
nobles, paintings and statuary, objects bearing their names, such
as scarabs, and archaeological research. In addition to these

purely Egyptian sources there are a few letters written by Asiatic kings and princes to the Pharaohs which add a few clues.

That some Asiatic women of high rank—daughters of chieftains, even of kings—entered the royal harem has been proved in a number of cases. One of the most intriguing was the discovery in a lonely valley some two miles west of Deir el Bahri of a tomb which had contained the bodies of three Queens of Tuthmosis III.

Unfortunately for archaeology, the tomb had been discovered in modern times by the redoubtable villagers of Sheikh abd el Gournah, whose skill and determination as tomb-robbers equal those of their remote ancestors. Usually they are lucky to find only a few saleable objects, but this time they came upon three sets of magnificent jewellery, together with gold-mounted cosmetic jars, gold-mounted mirrors and other objects. Some of these bore the name of Tuthmosis III, or 'Menkheperre' as he was also known, and others the personal names of the three ladies, which were Menhet, Menwi and Merti.

These are non-Egyptian names and the three women are thought to have been the daughters of Syrian chieftains. Their lovely jewellery and toilet articles, instead of being kept together, were fed on to the antiquities market by the discoverers, and were bought by various dealers and collectors. Gradually the Metropolitan Museum of Art acquired most of the objects, but others are missing, and some of the more delicate jewellery, which had been damaged by rough handling has had to be repaired and restored.

Some of them are illustrated (Plates 11, 12 and 15 and 16) and give a slight idea of the luxury and beauty to which even a minor Queen of the Eighteenth Dynasty was accustomed. For each of these women bore the title 'King's Wife,' but not 'Great Wife of the King,' which was reserved for the chief Queen. The most beautiful jewellery consisted of inlaid gold head-dresses made up of tiny rosettes, and evidently intended to be worn over a wig. Another head-dress, or gold circlet, had two graceful gazelle-heads mounted on the brow, where the sacred serpent, the insignia of royalty, was normally worn. Not being 'Great Wives,' Menhet, Menwi and Merti were not allowed to wear this. Mr. H. E. Winlock in his *Treasure of Three Egyptian Princesses* charmingly suggests that the gazelles symbolised the graceful movements of the harem ladies, who also wore bead armlets of gold and semi-precious stones, necklaces made up of concentric semi-circles of interlacing gold wire arranged in formal patterns; their slim waists were encircled by girdles of gold plaques in the form of tiny fish, separated by beads of red carnelian and blue lapis-lazuli. They also wore, on occasion, 'cheap' costume jewellery, such as blue faience rings and matching strings of blue lenticular beads. Such trinkets were, we know, presented as favours to guests at banquets.

Some of the golden girdles had clasps, others not. These, Mr. Winlock suggests, were 'long enough for a girl to slip over her shoulders and let fall around her hips,' a feat which I find difficult to imagine, unless the girls were contortionists or had unusually broad hips. All this jewellery shows marked Asiatic influence, and lacks the elegance of, for example, the royal regalia of Princess Sith-Hathor-Unet, found by Petrie in a Twelfth-Dynasty pyramid at Lahun. When Professor Hayes allowed me to examine this lovely trinket some years ago I was intrigued to discover that each of the hollow gold lion-heads of which it is composed contained tiny pellets. The Princess must have tinkled when she walked.

The jewellery of Menhet, Menwi and Merti had evidently been worn during their lifetimes. It was not funerary equipment but strongly constructed with practical fastenings which worked. Many of them were rubbed smooth by wear. For their dressing-tables in the After-Life they had silver mirrors with gold-plated handles (Plate 15), and sets of tableware in gold, silver, and gold-mounted glass and alabaster (Plate 16).

Tuthmosis iv also certainly married a princess from Asia. It was a diplomatic marriage with the daughter of the King of Mitanni, that powerful kingdom on the upper Euphrates with which Tuthmosis III had been at war. Unfortunately we do not know the princess's name and at one time some scholars identified her with his 'Great Wife' Mutemwiya, the mother of Amenophis III. But there is insufficient evidence to prove this.

The young Amenophis III was a strikingly handsome man, better-looking than his Tuthmosid forebears if less rugged. He was already married to Tiye, a lady of non-royal stock who, because of the un-Egyptian cast of her features, was at one time also believed Asiatic. It is more likely, however, that she had Nubian blood. Though not classically beautiful she must have been a woman of great charm and intelligence, of whom her husband was so enamoured that, from the beginning of his reign, he flouted precedent and had her name set beside his on all important inscriptions and documents. Far from attempting to conceal her non-royal birth he advertised it. On an inscribed scarab, which he had made in large numbers early in his reign, and distributed throughout the provinces like a news-letter, he gives her name, together with those of her untitled parents Yuya and Thuya, but adds, however, that *she is now the wife of a mighty king* whose dominion extends from Karoy in the northern Sudan to Naharin in western Asia.

The illustrations give some idea of her appearance; most evocative is the fragment of statue of polished jasper which, although only the chin and mouth remain, has a pouting sensuality that speaks volumes. (See book-jacket.) Everything we know about Amenophis points to his having been an extremely sensual man to whom the pleasures of the bedroom and the banqueting-table appealed more strongly than the ardours of the battlefield.

This seems as good a point as any at which to digress upon the sexual behaviour of the Ancient Egyptians, as far as it can be known. Although there are no erotic carvings such as one finds, for example, on Hindu temples, and texts referring to sexual intercourse are usually discreetly worded, there was nothing sly or furtive about Egyptian sex. The reticence was due to religious, not moral reasons. In official inscriptions love-making is either described in a vein of high poetry, as in the already-quoted story of how the god Amun visited Queen Ahmose in the form of her husband, or in terms of vigorous animality as when the Vizier Imhotep, the great minister of King Djoser (2800 BC), consults the ancient writings to find out the source of the Nile. Having read them he returns to the King, who is concerned about 'the seven lean years' due to abnormally low flooding, and tells His Majesty:

> There is a city in the midst of the waters (from which the Nile rises) named Elephantine. It is the Beginning of the Beginning. . . . It is the joining of the land, the primeval hillock of earth, the throne of Re. . . . 'Pleasant of life' is the name of its dwelling. 'The Two Caverns' is the name of the water; they are the two breasts which pour forth all good things. It is the couch of the Nile, in which he becomes young (again). . . . He fecundates (the land) by mounting as the male, the bull, to the female; he renews (his) virility, assuaging his desire. He rushes twenty-eight cubits (high at Elephantine); he hastens at Diospolis seven cubits (high). Khnum is there as a god . . .[1]

In the more sophisticated love-poetry of the New Kingdom there is often a powerful but thinly-veiled eroticism, as in this example, in which a girl addresses her 'brother,' i.e. her beloved:

> *My brother, it is pleasant to go to the pool*
> *In order to bathe thee in thy presence*
> *That I may let thee see my beauty in my tunic*
> *of finest royal linen*
> *When it is wet.*
>
> *I go down with you into the water,*
> *And come forth again with a red fish*
> *Which lies beautiful on my fingers.*
> *Come and look at me . .*[2]

The ardour of the lover is expressed in another poem which might have been addressed to a young officer of chariots by his beloved:

Would that thou wouldst come (to the sister speedily)
Like a horse of the king,
Picked from a thousand of all steeds,
The foremost of the stables!
It is distinguished in its food,
And its master knows its paces.
If it hears the sound of the whip,
It knows no delay,
And there is no foremost of the chasseurs
Who can stay before it (to hold it).
How well the sister's heart knows
That he is not far from the sister![3]

In all these poems and songs the words 'brother' and 'sister' merely imply 'beloved'; they do not necessarily imply a consanguineous relationship, although these existed, particularly among royal and noble families. They are the poetry of a high civilisation, such as that which flourished at Thebes under Amenophis III, and were sung at feasts and festivals where the guests were invited—as the tomb-inscriptions testify—to 'spend a merry day!' In another song the little sycamore-tree in the garden sees the young lovers enjoying their 'merry day' but promises to be discreet.

It slippeth a letter into the hand of a little maid, the daughter of its chief gardener, and maketh her run to the beloved; 'Come, and pass the time in the midst of thy maiden. The garden is in its day. There are bowers and shelters there for thee. My gardeners are glad and rejoice when they see thee. Send thy slaves ahead of thee, supplied with their utensils. (Of a truth) one has already drunken when one hasteneth to thee, before thou hast drunken. But the servants come from thee with their vessels, and bring beer of every sort and all manner of mixed loaves . . . Come and spend the day in merriment, and tomorrow, and the day after, three whole days, and sit in my shadow. Her lover sitteth on her right hand. She maketh him drunken, and heedeth all that he saith. The feast is disordered with drunkenness, and she stayed on with her brother. Her . . .

[word missing] is spread out under me, when the sister walketh about. But I am discreet, and speak not of what I see. I will say no word . . .[4]

Some of the stories, and even myths about the gods, are considerably more basic, as when Re recovered his good humour when Hathor lifted her skirt. And in the Turin Museum today there is a pornographic papyrus—rarely shown—in which a bald-headed priest and a Theban tart are capering together accompanied by some very coarse hieroglyphic annotations. Homosexuality was not unknown; one story has it that the Pharaoh Pepi II was in love with one of his generals, and in another the god Seth tries to seduce Horus. It is true, as Professor Posener comments:

The Egyptians . . . did not confine eroticism purely to within the idea of cosmic fecundity. Indeed, in spite of an official creed, concerning sexual union among the gods, the Egyptians descended to attributing suggestiveness, even vice, where the great Min (god of fertility) intended none.[5]

At the same time Egyptian civilisation, even at the height of its sophistication, reveals fewer examples of perversion and pornography than those of, say, Greece and Rome.

The scope and variety of sexual diversion available to the Pharaohs, with their enormous harems, must have been considerable, and not surprisingly they occasionally became jaded. There is an amusing story, very popular in the New Kingdom, about Snofru, father of Khufu, who built the Great Pyramid. The bored monarch summons his chief magician, one Zazamonkh, and asks him to produce some new diversion. After pondering for a while Zazamonkh replies:

'If thy majesty would but betake thee to the lake of the Great House! Man thee a boat with all fair maidens from the inner apartments of thy palace. Then will thy heart be diverted, when thou shalt see how they row to and fro. Then, as thou viewest the pleasant nesting-places of thy lake, and viewest its fields and its pleasant banks, thine heart will be diverted thereby.' And His Majesty said 'I will do this; get thee to thine house, but I will go boating.'[6]

And he does, improving on the magician's original idea by dressing the maidens—'twenty women, those with the fairest limbs and with beauteous breasts'—in fishnets. 'And the heart of His Majesty was glad when he heheld how they rowed.'

Just as the diversion was at its height an accident occurred. The leading girl 'became entangled in her braided tresses and a fish-pendant' (hair-ornament) 'of new malachite fell into the water.' The King of Egypt offered the girl a new one, but being a woman this did not satisfy her. 'I want my pot down to its bottom,' she answered, i.e. 'I want my own thing back.' So the King has to summon Zazamonkh again, while the boat, presumably with Snofru as passenger, drifts across the lake, as the girls refuse to row. The magician, equal to the occasion, folds back the waters of the lake, retrieves the fish-pendant, and the entertainment proceeds.

Whether this was one of Amenophis's diversions one does not know, though it sounds very much in keeping with his character. Certainly he had a pleasure-lake near his palace, and I sometimes wonder if the incident took place in his reign, and was tactfully put back to the time of Snofru by the story-teller. The lake was created for Queen Tiye and Amenophis proudly commemorated this epochal event on one of his scarabs. It reads:

Year 11, third month of the first season, day 1, under the majesty of Amenophis III, given life; and the Great King's Wife, Tiye, who liveth.

His majesty commanded to make a lake for the Great King's Wife, Tiye, in her city of Zeruka. Its length is 3,700 cubits [about one mile] and its width 700 cubits [about 1,000 feet]. His majesty celebrated the feast of the opening of the lake, in the third month of the first season, day 16, when his majesty sailed thereon in the royal barge, 'Aten-Gleams.'[7]

This pleasure-lake, the outline of which can still be detected in places, was excavated—it is said in fifteen days—near the royal palace which Amenophis built on the west bank of the Nile near Medinet Habu. The sailing of the royal barge upon it was no doubt accompanied by a gorgeous festival, with many gilt and decorated vessels carrying musicians and singers, and much feasting and entertainment in the palace. Among the on-lookers there would be, no doubt, Kirgipa, daughter of the King of Naharin, who had arrived in Thebes in the previous year, accompanied by 317 more Asiatic ladies. This too was commemorated on an inscribed scarab which was duly dispatched to the governors of the provinces and the Pharaoh's foreign possessions.

> Year 10 under the majesty of . . . the son of Re, Amenophis III, Ruler of Thebes, who is granted life; (and) the Great King's Wife, Tiye, who liveth; the name of whose father was Yuya, the name of whose mother was Thuya. Marvels brought to his majesty—Life! Prosperity! Health!; Kirgipa, the daughter of the chief of Naharin, Satirna (and) the chief of her harem-ladies, 317 persons.[8]

The tomb of Tiye's parents, Yuya and Thuya, was discovered by Mr. Theodore Davis in 1906 in an isolated branch of the Valley of the Kings. It had been entered only once by ancient robbers, and most of the magnificent funerary furniture remained intact, together with the mummies. From the inscriptions archaeologists could now learn something about the parents of one of the most illustrious Queens of Egypt. The fact they were honoured by burial in the valley normally reserved for royalty is another indication of the esteem in which Tiye was held by her uxorious husband.

They came from a town called Ipu (modern Akhmim) in Upper Egypt where Yuya had been Prophet and Overseer of the local god, Min, not a very important post. His name occurs in several inscriptions; sometimes it is rendered as Aau, sometimes as Aay or Aai, at other times as Yaa or even Yau. These suggest that the pronunciation of the name was difficult to render into Egyptian, and that Yuya could have been a foreigner. He must have been about twenty when Tuthmosis III died, so that he could have been one of the foreign princes brought back as captives after one of the King's Asiatic campaigns; this again cannot be proved, but the face of his daughter Tiye does not look Egyptian. Her mother, however, was called Thuya or Tuau, which is a common Egyptian name.

Among Thuya's titles were 'Royal Handmaid' (lady-in-waiting); 'the favoured-one of Hathor' and 'Royal mother of the Great Wife of the King.' The more one turns over the scanty details of this family the more puzzling becomes their relationship with the King. For it was not only Amenophis III who married into it. Hayes points out that one of Yuya's titles is 'Father of the God' and that this:

> 'seems to have been the regular designation of the Pharaoh's father-in-law, which Yuya shared with his predecessor Yey, and his successor Ay' [who later became Pharaoh]. Like them too he was also honoured with the rank of Commander of the Cavalry. The similarities of the names Yey, Yuya and Ay and the fact that at least two of them appear to have had ties with the town of Akhmim suggest that they belonged to the same family and may have been father, son and grandson. *This would mean that for three generations the Kings of Egypt took as their wives girls of a single Upper Egypt family* who in the last two instances were their first cousins. [our italics][9]

But here one must halt before one is drawn into the bewildering vortex of the so-called 'Amarna Period' and its complex family relationships. We shall have to consider them later. Let us turn again to the face of Queen Tiye, with its delicate, slightly retrousse nose, its small firm chin, sensuous mouth and long slender neck. What kind of world did she inhabit? What did she see through those shrewd, Oriental-looking eyes?

It was a world of such splendour, luxury and magnificence as would have astonished her predecessors, Ahmose and even

Hashepsowe. They would also probably have envied her, because she and her husband had inherited the wealth and power won by the warlike Tuthmosids. During a reign of thirty-seven years Amenophis is recorded as having made only one military expedition and that was a short campaign in Nubia made not long after his accession. During the reign of his son and successor Amenophis IV, a period of seventeen years following his father's death, the Pharaoh never led his armies out of Egypt. Yet such was the prestige of the Theban kings, made tangible by garrisons scattered throughout what are now Syria, Israel and the Lebanon, and such was the wealth gained by trade and tribute, that not only vassal-chieftains but even kings of such mighty states as Mitanni and Babylon wrote to the Pharaoh in terms of almost servile respect.

'Send me a great deal of gold,' writes the King of Babylon. . . . 'If, during this harvest, you send the gold concerning which I wrote to you, then I will give you my daughter.'

'Send me much gold, more gold,' writes King Tushratta of Mitanni, brother of the Mitannian princess whom the Pharaoh had married, 'for in my brother's' (i.e. Amenophis's) 'land, gold is as common as dust . . .'

Only occasionally do these letters from distant outposts of the Empire sound a note of warning, and the faint sound of battle is heard.

'Teshub, my Lord, gave my enemy into my hand, and I routed him,' wrote Tushratta. 'There was none among them that returned to his own land.' And Aki-izzi, lord of Katna, an Egyptian province pleaded 'O my Lord, if the trouble in this land lies upon the heart of my Lord, let my Lord send troops, let them come!'[10]

Queen Tiye knew about these letters, which were found many years ago in the ruins of Akhenaten's city of El Amarna, of which we shall speak later. In several she is mentioned by the Asiatic kings and chieftains in terms which suggest that she was the confidant and adviser of the King. But evidently Amenophis believed that the garrisons, assisted by reinforcements sent under the command of his Army chiefs, would be sufficient to withstand any threat, without the tiresome necessity for his personal presence. There is in fact a record of a successful campaign in Syria led by one of his Army commanders.

Remaining in Egypt, the Pharaoh devoted himself to the glorification of his already-splendid capital. Tiye lived in a palace—the foundations of which still exist—in which suites of rooms, their plastered walls decorated with naturalistic coloured frescoes of plants, birds and other wild-life, opened on to pillared courtyards which gave shade from the omnipresent sun. Fish swam in cool basins where lotuses bloomed; plants and flowers brought from Asia were reflected in artificial pools; and when her chariot took her through the great gateway she would see, to the north, the enormous funerary temple of her husband rising against the superb backcloth of golden cliffs.

Within it stood a colossal sculptured group showing Tiye and her husband seated side by side, her arm around his waist and their daughters standing in front of the throne. Its height was that of a modern two-storey building and it now dominates the largest gallery in the Cairo Museum. Near the temple stood a stela in which Amenophis recorded his building enterprises, including his Mortuary Temple.

Now his majesty was pleased to build a very great monument, without equal since the beginning of time. He built it to be monument for his father Amun, Lord of the Thrones of the Two Lands, erecting for him an august temple on the starboard of Thebes, an everlasting fortress of sandstone, embellished with gold throughout, its floor shining with silver and all its doorways with electrum [gold and silver alloy]. It is very wide and long, adorned for eternity, and made festive with this exceptionally large stela. It is extended with royal statues of granite, of quartzite and of precious stones, fashioned to last forever. They are higher than the rising of the heavens; their rays are in men's faces like the rising sun . . . Its workshops are filled with male and female slaves, the children of chieftains of all the countries which his majesty conquered. Its magazines have stored up uncountable riches. It is surrounded by villages of Syrians, peopled with the children of chieftains; its cattle are like the sands of the shore . . .[11]

Today, all that remains of this great building 'adorned for eternity' are the twin colossi of Amenophis III which rise above the cultivated land, their huge battered faces staring endlessly across the river. One of them became famous in Greek and Roman times as the singing 'statue of Memnon,' because at dawn, when the heat of the sun caused the rock to expand, it gave out a melodious sound. It is said that the Emperor Hadrian camped beside the colossus to hear its voice at dawn.

Crossing the river, Tiye would see, where Luxor now stands, another temple rising, with lotiform and papyrus-bud capitals, and sculptured scenes—imitating those at Deir el Bahri—purporting to show how her husband's father was Amun-Re himself, who appeared to his mother Mutemwiya in the form of Tuthmosis IV.

Tiye might, perhaps, have accompanied Amenophis III on one of his famous lion-hunts, for he was an accomplished sportsman, and in one scarab—distributed as usual—he boasts of having slain '100 fierce lions, brought down with his own arrows.' As an archer he claimed to be the equal of his grandfather Amenophis II and an inscription exists which records how His Majesty, rapidly circling a target in his speeding chariot 'like the golden circlet of the sun,' fired his arrows into a three-inch copper plate 'so that they stuck out a hands-breadth on the other side.' Archery from a fast-moving chariot was one of the royal and noble pastimes, and this feat, naturally, took place 'before the people of the land.' There is no reason to doubt its truth; after all the Pharaoh had plenty of time to practise, and able tutors. Horses and chariots, which had been introduced into Egypt by the Hyksos, introduced a somewhat knightly element into Egyptian sport. They were expensive and highly prized, and the young blades of Thebes no doubt showed them off with the same delight as a modern youth with a new sports car. We know this is true because a disgruntled scribe mentions the fact in a warning to one of his pupils whose parents had just bought him a chariot 'costing 5 *deben.*'

> He [a young officer] hasteneth to get steeds from the stall of his majesty's stable. When he hath obtained goodly horses, he is glad and exulteth. He cometh with them into the town, and he trampleth it underfoot with zest. Happy is he when he thus trampleth . . . for he knoweth not yet what is in store for him [i.e. when he goes into action with his regiment].[12]

There must have been many such young men. Tiye herself had a son who was probably so equipped. Then there were the other occupants of the women's quarters of the palace, many other royal wives and hundreds of concubines. These, too, bore children, and even allowing for the high mortality rate there must have been hundreds of young men and women, princes and princesses, besides the sons and daughters of the noble families who attended the Pharaoh and his 'Great Royal Wife.' The now-deserted walls at Medinet Habu must once have throbbed with eager young life. Amid this Tiye moved, the undisputed ruler of them all, inferior only to the King in rank and power.

Nor was hers a closed world. She stood at the centre of the most powerful empire in the world, surrounded by the men who governed it. There was a constant coming and going of great ministers of state, officials from the provinces and ambassadors of foreign states. In the royal harem were the daughters of foreign kings, such as Princess Tadukhipa, whose father, King Tushratta of Mitanni, could claim Amenophis III as his son-in-law. And there was also, inevitably, the powerful hierarchy of the Amun priesthood, the priests in their flowing white robes, surrounded by their retinues, moving along the frescoed corridors or sitting in audience with the Pharaoh in the rooms of state. They were becoming a problem for several reasons.

First, because, thanks to the wealth which had poured into the temple of their god, and his glorification by Amenophis's predecessors, their power was beginning to rival that of the King himself. Second, because, like all long-established priesthoods, they were innately and strongly conservative, guardians of entrenched beliefs and customs which had served Egypt well in the past when Egypt was the earth and the earth was Egypt.

But now the Egyptians had become aware of a world beyond their own, of peoples who had never heard of Osiris and Isis, Hathor and Anubis, Horus and Ptah. The people of Canaan worshipped Baal and Astarte; those of Babylon worshipped the great mother-goddess Ishtar, 'clothed with pleasure and love . . . laden with vitality, charm and voluptuousness' and her consort Anum. Tuthmosis III had conquered the lands in which these deities were revered and forced them to accept the dominion of Egypt. But the ultimate battle is fought not with arms but in the minds of men. Amenophis III has been decried as an indolent, luxury-loving Pharaoh, inferior to his war-loving ancestors, the fighting Tuthmosids. But it could be that he was a highly intelligent man who preferred diplomacy to war. There is evidence of this in the Amarna letters exchanged between the Pharaoh and the kings of Asia, as we shall see.

To hold the empire it was not enough to deploy troops and garrison cities. If some way could be found by which the peoples of Egypt's dominions could, in their religious worship, build on common ground with their Egyptian rulers, there would be a basis for a stable, prosperous and enduring society. But this could not be achieved if the entrenched priesthood of Amun-Re who lived in a closed world, insisted on retaining and reinforcing the beliefs of their forefathers.

We cannot be certain, from the sparse evidence available, that Queen Tiye was a party to this movement towards integration. All we know is that during the reign of her husband and her son, Amenophis IV, such a movement was made, and that from some of the letters from foreign kings found at El Amarna, it is clear that her influence and advice were sought. There is also the undoubted fact, attested by all Egyptologists, that during this period the Queens of Egypt exercised an influence greater than any of their predecessors, or of any of their successors save Cleopatra.

There is another possibility. We know for a fact that in Asia from the earliest times the cult of female deities was predominant. The earliest known deity, worshipped in western Asia and later in the Aegean islands colonised by Asiatics, was a Mother-Goddess. This fact *might,* if Tiye *was* of Asiatic origin, be correlated with the feminine influence which is apparent both in the reigns of Amenophis III and his extraordinary son and successor Amenophis IV, later called Akhenaten.

> *She is their queen; they continually cause her commands*
> *to be executed.*
> *All of them bow down before her,*
> *They receive her light before her.*
> *Women and men indeed revere her.*[13]

—as the Babylonian 'Hymn to Ishtar' relates.

A study of Tiye's face emphatically does not suggest a philosopher-queen or a female intellectual. She is a woman, essentially feminine and intuitive, accustomed to form judgements through her emotions and instincts and find reasons afterwards. Being a mature woman she would also be essentially 'down-to-earth,' more interested in people than abstractions. She may have enjoyed her position at the fulcrum of power, but it is more likely that her main consideration was the welfare of her husband and son and she would judge men and events from this basis. Through them she would become aware of the tension resulting from the conflict between the narrow traditionalism of the priesthood and the need for a universal god who would be acceptable to Egyptian and Asiatic alike.

And the attempted solution of this problem may have been partly hers.

---

[1] Pritchard, J. B., *Ancient Near Eastern Texts,* Princeton University Press, 1958

[2] Erman and Blackman, *Literature of the Ancient Egyptians,* University Books, Inc., New Hyde Park, New York, 1964

[3] Erman and Blackman, op. cit.

[4] Erman and Blackman, op. cit.

[5] Posener, G. (ed.), *A Dictionary of Egyptian Civilisation*, Tudor Publishing Co., New York, 1961

[6] Erman and Blackman, op. cit.

[7] Breasted, J. H., *Ancient Records of Egypt,* Volume II, Chicago University Press, 1906-07; 1927

[8] Breasted, J. H., op. cit.

[9] Hayes, W. C., *The Scepter of Egypt,* New York Graphic Society for the Metropolitan Museum of Art, Greenwich, Conn., 1959

[10] Pritchard, J. B., op. cit.

[11] Breasted, J. H., op. cit.

[12] Erman and Blackman, op. cit.

[13] Pritchard, J. B., op. cit.

7

Party Scene

I AM WELL AWARE THAT THE SKETCH I HAVE TRIED TO DRAW OF Tiye and her world is a pageant rather than a play; the figures move stiffly but do not speak. This, unhappily, is inevitable in a work of fact, since the principal players have been given no lines. However, in order to give the picture a little more depth and colour, and before we move into the realm of religious and political controversy, let us look more closely at that world, as it would be seen by less exalted eyes than the Queen's.

In a long, low-ceilinged room near the palace a number of women sit cross-legged on the floor. Three of them have, in front of them, piles of flax fibres. Their lithe brown fingers move very quickly, picking up the dried strands and rolling them, on their left knees, into loosely twisted slivers or roves. Other girls then roll the thread into balls and put them into bucket-like pots; each pot has a lid with a small hole in the centre through which the thread is drawn by other women. These stand, with a spindle in each hand, rapidly spinning the fine linen thread which they then wind on to pegs on the walls.

The girls wear simple, one-piece, shift-like garments reaching only to the knee, and leaving one shoulder bare; and they are barefoot. There is a continuous hum of chatter, mingled with rhythmical singing, but the process is organised for rapid, systematic production. One group sorts out and rolls the fibres, and places them in the 'suspension-pots'; another group spins; a third group operates hand-looms, rectangular frames resting on the floor, interweaving the warp and the weft, and in some cases introducing coloured embroidered patterns. In scores of Theban workshops—including a large number manned by male weavers—this scene is repeated, except for a few workshops in which the spindles are suspended from the ceiling, an innovation introduced by the Hyksos invaders who also brought the horse and chariot to Egypt. These are the women whose labour produced the fine, semi-transparent linen from which the court dressmakers made the gowns worn by Tiye and her great ladies.

Not a line of this description owes anything to imagination. It is based on a model, dating from the Twelfth Dynasty (about 2000 BC), found among many others in the tomb of a Theban official named Meket-Re. It is illustrated in Plate 23.

Linen, in varying degrees of fineness, was the principal apparel worn by the upper and middle classes. Wool was also woven, and sometimes worn over the exiguous linen gown to protect its wearer against the cool night air. Silk, imported from China, and cotton from India were both unknown until Graeco-Roman times. By the time of Amenophis III and Tiye, fashion in dress, hair-style and wigs (worn over close-cut hair) had become more elaborate and sophisticated than in the early years of the New Kingdom. The climate of Egypt is never cold, except in winter during the night; usually the air is dry and warm and in summer extremely hot. Servant-girls at parties are shown almost naked, and their mistresses's gowns, though of elegant cut and with ankle-length skirts, revealed at least as much as they concealed.

It is sometimes stated that because the dress of Egyptian women appears to vary little from age to age, and is usually shown as a uniform white in the tomb-paintings, the contemporaries of Hashepsowe, Tiye and Nefertiti were not 'fashion-conscious.' This is simply not true, as a close examination of statues and paintings will show. It is true, of course, that as Egyptian civilisation was more static and conservative than ours, the variations were generally slower and more subtle; also the tomb-painters were governed by strict religious convention, and were not interested in the exact delineation of current fashion. But these variations occurred, in both female and male dress.

> . . . the simple linen kilt from the hips to the knees, which had once satisfied all, not excluding the king, had now given way to an elaborate costume, with long plaited skirt, a rich tunic with flowing sleeves; the unpretentious head-dress of the old time had been replaced by an elaborately curled wig hanging down to the shoulders; while the once bare feet were shod in elegant sandals . . . A noble of the landed class from the court of Sensuret, could he have walked the streets of Thebes in the days of Amenophis III, would have been almost at a loss to know in what country he had found himself; while his own antiquated costume, which had survived among the priests, would have awakened equal astonishment among the fashionable Thebans of the day.[1]

As this passage from Breasted indicates, both sexes, during this period, wore long robes of linen, which were pleated elaborately with the aid of starch, so that the laundresses must have been kept extremely busy, particularly as garments were frequently washed. The tunic worn above the robe was also pleated horizontally, and from the appearance of the sleeves, which often curve upwards like the roof of a pagoda, must have been stiffly starched, unless this also was merely an artistic convention.

The women's gowns were not invariably white, though this seems to have been the most popular colour. But sometimes we see guests at a banquet wearing coloured robes; the ladies shown on the wall-paintings in the tomb of Nakht, Astronomer of Amun under Tuthmosis III, wear attractive gowns the colour of ripe wheat, swathed tightly round their slim figures, rather like a sari. They sit easily, legs tucked under them on cushions, their long black wigs encircled by gay circlets of blue with a patterning of red, their bare shoulders adorned with collars of red and blue beads. Apart from the wigs, and the lotus flowers they are inhaling, they could be a group of young modern Egyptians at an informal party. (See Plate 21.)

A more formal and elegant style of dress is shown in the well-known tomb of Ramose, who lived under both Amenophis III and his son Amenophis IV. Here the great official and his family are entertaining their friends and their wives. These include May, King's Master of the Horse, and his wife, a priestess of Mūt. There is also Neby, Ramose's father, and his beautiful wife Ipuia. The wife of May, whose name is Werel, shows the fashion of the late Eighteenth Dynasty at its height. She sits beside her husband, each on a graceful chair, her arm placed affectionately round his shoulders. She wears a very long curled wig, reaching below her shoulders. A very broad collar made up of hundreds of tiny lapis and carnelian beads covers the upper part of her chest, but below that she is naked down to her very high waistline, the gown being fastened by a clasp just below the breasts. The skirt fits closely around her thighs, which are visible through the diaphanous linen, and spreads in elegant folds around her ankles (Plate 19). The other ladies of the party are similarly—but not quite similarly—gowned.

From this and hundreds of similar scenes it is clear that Egyptian women were not segregated, but encouraged to share in the social life of their menfolk. One wonders what they talked about, these lovely and obviously intelligent women, when they sat at table with their friends of both sexes. The inscriptions above the pictures give us no clues; they are almost invariably mere lists of names and ranks, together with a few scraps of usually frivolous dialogue. The servant-girls hand the ladies favours, with the greeting 'Spend a festive day!' A woman calls for more wine as she 'wants to drink to the point of drunk-en-ness.' The musicians play and the dancing-girls dance; some-times the words of a song are given, usually a love-song. Scholars treasure the pathetic fragments which remain, and they have become 'Egyptian literature.' But in fact they were merely the popular songs of the day.

Although the royal and noble palaces had separate quar-ters for men and women, the women moved about freely. Herodotus, visiting Egypt in the fifth century BC, was shocked to see women walking the streets, going to market, and enjoy-ing a social freedom which was unthinkable in Athens. Today it is the Muslims who veil their women; the Copts, descended from the Ancient Egyptians in many cases, go unveiled, readily receive Europeans, and enjoy alcohol, which the strict Muslim is forbidden to touch. So it was in Ancient Egypt.

That the Egyptian loved and honoured his womenfolk is clear from many inscriptions and literature which praise them, always for their feminine qualities. The Queen is 'the charming one, adorned with the two plumes, she whose voice delights her hearers, full of grace, of a pleasant disposition, affectionate and filling the palace with her waves of perfume.'

Again, in male-dominated societies such as those of Baby-lon and Assyria, sons were much longed for, daughters less highly regarded; the same is true in many Muslim lands today. How the Ancient Egyptian father felt about his daughters is indicated by the affectionate names he gave them. Here are a few, translated by Sir Alan Gardiner: 'Beauty comes,' 'Ruler of her father,' 'She is healthy,' 'My own.'

A touching example, evidently given to his baby girl by a father whose wife died in childbirth, is 'Replace her.'

Of course Egyptian men were not without the familiar male prejudices. 'As foolish as a woman's words' wrote one disgruntled scribe. But another wrote:

> She is profitable of speech, agreeable in her conversation,
> of good counsel in her writings; all that passes her lips is like

the work of the Goddess of Truth, a perfect woman, greatly
praised in her city, giving the hand to all saying that which is
good, repeating what one loves, giving pleasure to all. . . .[2]

Again, one wonders if it was the feminine influence in
Egyptian society which made the Ancient Egyptians, to all appearances, considerably more humane than their contemporaries, even in warfare. They were certainly not effeminate;
their record as warriors and conquerors proves their masculine
qualities. But one could quote numerous examples of their humanity. The custom of killing the slaves and servants of the
dead to accompany them in the After-Life, a custom which continued in Asia and elsewhere down to the fifth century BC, was
abandoned by the Egyptians nearly 3,000 years earlier. In war
they fought savagely in defence of their country, as when the
'Sea-Peoples' invaded Egypt and were defeated in a great sea-
battle by Ramesses III. Yet in the sculptured scene depicting this
battle, amid the carnage, we see the crew of an Egyptian warship rescuing their drowning enemies from a sinking vessel.
Formal Egyptian religion, which was largely a matter of ritual,
has little moral content, but in the popular myth of Isis and
Osiris there is feminine tenderness, and in the Wisdom Literature we find such passages as:

> Do not use violence against any man either in the country
> or the town, for they are born of the Eyes (of the sun) and come
> from him and his heart is troubled by wrong-doing.

And this one:

> Do not laugh at a blind man or tease a dwarf
> Nor injure the affairs of the lame
> Do not tease a man who is in the hand of god*
>
> Nor be fierce of face against him if he errs.
> For man is clay and straw
> And god is his builder . . .[3]

So though we do not know what the Queens of Egypt

* i.e. the insane.

said to their divine lords, or the great ladies such as Ipuia and Werel to their husbands, their influence can be felt, perhaps, in what their menfolk thought and wrote.

When the lady Werel and her husband left the party she would draw round her shoulders the elegant cloak which, in the picture, she has let slip over her arms. She might also have a woollen cloak. Outside the great gate, guarded by porters, carrying chairs would be waiting, and, led and escorted by servants bearing torches, and by guards, they would be carried through the moonlit streets of Thebes to their own villa. Entering their own spacious walled garden, perhaps pausing to admire the reflections of the lotus flowers in the ornamental pool, they would see before them a pillared portico, also lit by servants holding lamps, and above it a two-storied building gleaming white, dappled by shadows thrown by the palm and sycamore trees.

Passing the state rooms, now silent and dark, on the ground floor, they would climb a flight of stairs to the private apartments. There were in fact two suites of rooms, one for the women of the house, including female servants, maids, serving-women, and the children's nurses; the other was for the male members of the household. Each suite had its own separate entrance.

Werel's bedroom would be simply but elegantly furnished. A bed of cedar-wood embellished with gold stood near the window, through which she could see the silver-glittering Nile and the dark shape of the Theban hills beyond the far bank. Inlaid boxes and cupboards stood against the pale walls, on which there were no pictures but instead delicate painted frescoes of natural scenes—the reed-fringed Nile, perhaps, with wildfowl rising above them. There would be flowers set in bronze bowls, like that illustrated (Plate 22), and perhaps a small statuette of Hathor or Isis.

While one servant folded back the fine linen sheets on the bed, another helped Werel undress. The big wig was removed and placed on a stand. Werel combed back her short hair with an ivory comb, while the servant stood with a polished silver mirror mounted on a gold-plated handle with a little figure of Hathor near the top. Spread out on her dressing table were her cosmetic jars of alabaster rimmed with gold, her perfumed unguents, her tubes of kohl, eyebrow tweezers, small razors and other implements. She unclasps her jewellery, unfastens the clasp below her breasts and slips out of her dress, which one maid takes away while another holds out a sleeping-robe. Next Werel removes her make-up, probably using cleansing-cream (such as was found in the equipment of the three Syrian wives of Tuthmosis III), while the maid stands by with a bowl in which she washes her hands.

Werel is weary. Shall she take a bath before retiring to bed? There are a shower-room and other conveniences near by, and the maid is ready with warm water. While Werel is standing by the window making up her mind the other servant is folding the elaborate court dress and preparing it for the laundrywomen. Another girl trims the lamps, which are of translucent alabaster so made that the flame illuminates a coloured picture painted on the side of the bowl. Then she puts away her mistress's jewellery in ebony caskets inlaid with ivory.

Her husband also was tired. Probably he will not come to her tonight. From the high window she looks across the garden, across the moonlit river to the royal palace on the far bank. There has been an important function there, and she can see the lights of torches moving down to the river as the guests leave. Perhaps Queen Tiye, whom Werel once met, is also at this moment wondering whether to take a bath or succumb to her weariness and go to sleep.

---

[1] Breasted, J. H., *A History of Egypt*, Charles Scribner's Sons, 1921

[2] Breasted, J. H., *Ancient Records of Egypt,* Volume II, Chicago University Press, 1906

[3] Pritchard, J. B., *Ancient Near Eastern Texts,* Princeton University Press, 1958

8

The Beautiful Woman Has Come

TIYE HAD A SON, ALSO NAMED AMENOPHIS, WHICH MEANS 'Amun-is-satisfied.' He grew up in the huge palace at Medinet Habu among the sons and daughters of his father by other wives. When he was still in his 'teens he married a girl of overwhelming beauty. So overwhelming, in fact, that even today, 3,000 years later, millions who know nothing else about Ancient Egypt pay homage to her portrait and her name, which was Nefertiti, meaning 'The Beautiful Woman Has Come.'

This portrait-bust, taken to Berlin by German excavators who discovered it at El Amarna, has been reproduced in millions. Everyone knows that slender neck, firm but feminine chin, delicately modelled nose, languorous, heavy-lidded eyes, and mouth whose curves are neither too sensual nor too self-controlled, neither too profligate nor too grudging of their love. It is a miracle of balance. Even the Greeks at the peak of their

genius never portrayed a face like this. Their goddesses are goddesses, their women, women. Nefertiti is both.

Any attempt to penetrate the secret of its allure must fail.
There are some faces which, like certain music, poetry and
painting, enrapture for a time and then gradually lose their
power. One breaks the chains, and is free to seek new experiences: a different kind of music, poetry and painting. But just
as the genius of Shakespeare, Mozart, and Michelangelo perpet-
ually regenerates its power, so the sculptured face of Nefertiti
holds Man in eternal subjugation.

Among all the attempts by Egyptian, Babylonian, Greek
and Roman sculptors to deify Woman, only the artist who created this bust has succeeded. And his triumph is due, not to
technique only, nor even the loveliness of his model. He has
walked the perilous knife-edge between the real and the ideal,
and arrived safely on the other side. The face he has immor-
talised is the perfect equipoise between what we long for and
what we know to be possible. His Nefertiti combines the sensual and the spiritual, and to my mind is perhaps one of the
few convincing arguments for the existence of God. We are,
as some Victorian rationalist observed, 'apes imperfectly depiled.'
We may have struggled painfully out of the primeval slime, and
the mud still clings to our feet, but our eyes are on the stars.
The ideal of beauty lies beyond the grasp of most of us.

But the portrait of Nefertiti, one mere mortal creature out
of billions, born over 3,000 years ago, seems to bridge the canyon
between Man and God. The stone has been made flesh. She is
divine but she is also human, not least because she does not
scorn to use the artificial aids by which women, then and now,
enhance their beauty. She uses green eye-paint of malachite
powder to emphasize the liquid depth of her eyes; her lips are
painted, her cheeks rouged, and her eyebrows darkened and
made more symmetrical. The deep collar of interlinked beads of
carnelian and lapis sets off the slender neck, just as, in another
full-length statue, the vertical pleating of her diaphanous linen
gown moulds and reveals the feminine contours of her body.

If I have described the Queen's physical appearance at some length it is because the sculptor who saw her tells us far more than the scholar, grubbing about among worn inscriptions and fragmented papyri. The arguments concerning her birth and parentage, the reign-length of her illustrious husband, the husbands of her daughters, her influence upon the beliefs of Amenophis IV—later renamed Akhenaten—have occupied the minds of many scholars for seventy years and produced acres of learned prose from Moscow to Chicago. All this is, no doubt, of immense value to scholarship. In 3000 AD, if records have been destroyed, scholars will achieve a high reputation if they know what kind of hat was worn by Lord Avon, and what brand of pipe-tobacco was favoured by Mr. Harold Wilson. The same is true today of the so-called 'Amarna Period.' For instance, Professor Fairman says that after Amenophis III was too old and senile to rule, his son Amenophis IV shared the throne as 'co-regent.' This view is supported by Mr. Cyril Aldred and other Egyptologists. But Sir Alan Gardiner writes:

> In the letters (from King Tushratta of Mitanni) to Queen Tiye it is clearly implied that the new king ascended the throne only after his father's death, and the same is asserted even more clearly in a letter to the young ruler from the great Hittite monarch Suppiluliumas. Hence the much-canvassed co-regency must be an illusion.[1]

My own theory, however, is based on the existence of a co-regency, since this seems to fit the known facts. The issue of 'co-regency or no co-regency' is of more than academic importance, as we shall discover. So is the issue of Nefertiti's parents. At one time it was suggested that she was none other than the Mitannian princess Tadukhipa, who is recorded as having been sent to the Theban court by the Mitannian king as bride to Amenophis III; this would fit nicely into the theory that the religious revolution which took place during the latter's reign was inspired by his Asiatic wife. Unhappily for this theory inscriptions found at El Amarna say that Nefertiti's sister was an

Egyptian, and that her nurse was also Egyptian, the wife of an elderly officer named Ay who ultimately became Pharaoh. Professor W. C. Hayes states in his *Scepter of Egypt* that Nefertiti was the niece of Queen Tiye; that Nefertiti's father was Queen Tiye's brother, the Cavalry Commander Ay. This official, who later became Pharaoh, could have been the son of Yuya, whose body, with that of his wife Thuya, was discovered by Mr. Theodore Davis in the Valley of the Kings (see page 80), and this lends weight to Hayes's argument that 'for three generations the kings of Egypt took as their wives girls of a single Upper Egyptian family, who in the last two instances were their first cousins.'

The family relationships of Amenophis III and IV, Tiye and their successors are tiresomely complicated but need to be grasped if one is to understand the parts played by Tiye, Nefertiti and the two short-lived queens who followed them. Having read all the relevant documents and weighed the arguments and counter-arguments I have drawn up a 'family tree' (see page 227), with the warning that not all authorities will accept it, and, even if they do, it will almost certainly become out of date if new inscriptions are discovered.

First, however, it is important to remember that the Kings of Egypt not infrequently married their full sisters and even their daughters, and had children by them. This is one of the most extraordinary aspects of Egyptian civilisation, because whereas nearly all cultures throughout the world have rigid laws forbidding consanguineous relationships, the Ancient Egyptians did not. However repellent this seems to our minds, it is a biological fact that such marriages do not necessarily or invariably produce mentally-infirm or physically feeble offspring; in fact, as with the breeding of dogs and horses, it may actually refine and improve the stock, for a time. Some of the greatest of the Pharaohs, men of high intelligence and fine physique, were the products of such marriages.

The danger is that if either party to the marriage inherits a physical or mental defect which can be transmitted (or is

'recessive') the chances of this appearing in subsequent generations are much greater than they would be in children of parents
not closely related. But the consanguineous marriages do not
make this inevitable; they merely shorten the odds.

Looking at such marriages from an emotional and sexual
standpoint one must bear in mind the conditions under which
royal children were brought up. As the male and female members of the household lived in separate suites of apartments, the
infants would not be brought up in close proximity, as they
usually are today. When, after puberty, they were thrown together, their close relationship would only be in the blood; it
was not something consciously felt. Therefore such children
would be unfamiliar with each other, and just as likely to fall
in love as, say, first cousins sometimes do today. Moreover many
of these royal unions were 'dynastic' marriages, arranged for
reasons of state.

But not all of them by any means, whatever the 'realists'
may say. Egyptian literature contains numerous examples of
passionate love-poetry; and you do not have love-poems without
that extraordinary phenomenon known as falling in love. One
such poem contains the following lines which will be immediately recognised by any woman who has been in love:

> My heart only thinks of your love ... I run quickly towards
> you with my hair disarranged ... but I will set my curls and be
> ready in a moment.[2]

I am convinced that the marriage of Tiye and Amenophis
III was a love-match, especially as the Queen was not of the blood
royal; the fact that the couple married when both were mere
children (by our standards) need not deter us. In Ancient Egypt
people grew up more quickly than they do today. A boy of six-
teen was a man and could already have fathered several children. As for Tiye's son Amenophis IV there can be no doubt
that he was passionately devoted to Nefertiti. Inscriptions which
he caused to be carved praise her as:

*The heiress, great in favour, lady of grace, sweet of love,
Mistress of the South and North, fair of face, gay with the two
plumes, beloved of the living Aten, the Chief Wife of the King,
whom he loves, Lady of the Two Lands, great of love, Nefertiti,
living for ever and ever.*[3]

Such homage is exceptional, even for a Queen of Egypt,
and there is ample evidence to prove that it was no mere ritual
formality. What we have now to consider is why Nefertiti was
given such honour, why she figures in her husband's monuments
with even greater prominence than that afforded to Tiye by
Amenophis III. There can be little doubt that the answer to this
question must be found in the religious revolution carried out
by her husband, though its seeds were sown in the reign of his
father.

Amenophis III, a luxury-loving hedonist, was not the stuff
of which revolutionaries are made, though Tiye may have been.
But there is no evidence that he had any intention of departing
from the traditional religious beliefs of his ancestors. Like the
Tuthmosid Pharaohs, he enlarged and beautified the temple of
Amun-Re at Karnak, and at Luxor he built another temple,
much of which still stands as he left it, dedicated to the 'Theban
Triad,' Amun, Mūt and Khonsu. He also built a temple for the
goddess Mūt, consort of Amun, near the Sacred Lake at Karnak,
adorning it with 600 colossal diorite statues of this goddess in
the guise of the lioness-headed Sekhmet—another example of
how Egyptian deities changed their forms, much to the confusion of the amateur student of Egyptian religion. For, originally,
Sekhmet was the mother-goddess of the earlier triad of deities
worshipped at Memphis during the Old Kingdom. Now she
had become identified with the Theban goddess Mūt.

On the walls of his labyrinthine tomb near the Valley of
the Kings, Amenophis III is shown in association with many of
the long-familiar deities, Isis, Osiris, Anubis and the rest; and,
of course, like all his predecessors of the Eighteenth Dynasty,
he accompanied the sun-god Amun-Re in his daily journey

across the sky and his nightly voyage through the twelve caverns of the Underworld.

But the sun-god had a number of other forms. Sometimes he was shown as an enormous beetle; sometimes he was the falcon-headed Re-Harakhte, 'Re-in-his-horizon,' and in yet another form he is the 'Aten,' which means 'the sun's disk.' 'It is often difficult to tell,' writes Gardiner, 'when this term has or has not a religious implication' and he points out that in the famous 'Story of Sinuhe' which dates from the Twelfth Dynasty, the death of King Ammenemes I is described in these words:

> He went aloft to heaven and became united with the disk [*itn*], the limb of the god being merged in him who made him.

It is futile, Gardiner continues, to dispute whether the word *itn* refers to the deity or not. Less ambiguous is the phrase 'lord of all that the disk surrounds' . . . here the word translated 'disk' obviously refers to the visible celestial body.

This is the epithet usually applied to 'the living Aten' which appears so frequently on the monuments of Amenophis IV and Nefertiti; but it also appears on those of his predecessor Amenophis III, and this is very interesting. That there was already a cult of the Aten in Thebes under Amenophis III is clear, since there is a tomb of the period, a description of which is so far unpublished, whose owner describes himself as 'Steward in the Mansion of the Aten,' and it will be remembered that the royal barge in which Tiye sailed on her great lake bore the name 'Aten-gleams.' There are other inscriptions, e.g. at Soleb in the Sudan. But at this period, towards the latter part of the old King's reign, and before his son enjoyed supreme power, it was merely a minor cult.

Amenophis IV, who was probably Nefertiti's cousin, appears to have been crowned in Thebes in about 1370 BC and ruled from there for six years, presumably from the great palace built by his father; it was certainly large enough for both of them. He was in his early twenties, an unprepossessing youth with a lean, scrawny neck, pendulous, narrow jaw, thick lips, cadaverous cheeks and high but narrow forehead. His body, too, was misshapen, with unusually wide, almost feminine hips, and a distended belly. In appearance he resembles no Pharaoh of whom we have any record.

He has all the signs of extreme abnormality; whether or not he was diseased has been the subject of endless discussion which is unlikely to cease. Here I shall stick to the known facts and then try to summarise the theories and speculations, of which there are many. The facts are obtained (a) from inscriptions, (b) from archaeological research carried out at El Amarna and elsewhere and (c) from an extraordinary series of letters in the cuneiform script of western Asia, sent to Amenophis III, Tiye, Amenophis IV and their officials by the rulers of foreign powers such as Mitanni, Babylon and the Hittite Empire and also from the governors of Egypt's foreign provinces.

The existence of these documents has made it possible to know more about the reigns of Amenophis III and IV than we can learn purely from their own monuments and inscriptions; through them for the first and only time prior to the ninth century BC we can catch a faint glimpse of Egypt through the eyes of her neighbours. As we have referred and shall refer to them frequently an account of their discovery may be of interest.

El Amarna is a deserted Ancient Egyptian site roughly midway between Cairo and Luxor. As we shall see, it became for a short time the capital of Egypt, and the foundations of its buildings remain, half buried in the sand. The Egyptian *fellah* has found from experience that ancient mud-brick makes a good fertiliser which is called *sebakh*. In 1885 a peasant woman was digging for *sebakh* when she came upon a large number of baked-clay tablets with inscriptions which we now know to be in the cuneiform writing used throughout western Asia at the time when the Pharaohs of the New Kingdom ruled. The woman hawked the tablets round from dealer to dealer, but at first they were not regarded as genuine, and in the process of transport (in a sack carried on a donkey) many were destroyed. By the time they were recognised only about 300 survived, but these turned out to be the files of the Pharaohs' Foreign Office. Some, dating from the reign of Amenophis III, must have been transferred from Thebes when the court moved to the new capital, but the majority date from the reign of Amenophis IV.

From them we sometimes get dramatic glimpses of conditions within the Egyptian Empire which had been won by the Tuthmosid kings. Since they deal with affairs of which Tiye and her husband and son must have been aware, and which they must often have discussed, it is worth quoting from a few of them.

Although Amenophis III never seems to have appeared in person at the head of his armies (and this is one of the most frequently-expressed complaints of his governors and vassal-chiefs) he was evidently kept aware of conditions in the provinces and sometimes sent military help when it was needed. Here is a letter from one of the vassal-chiefs, Biridiya.

> At the two feet of the king, my lord, my Sun-god, seven and seven times I fall. Let the king know that ever since the archers returned (to Egypt) Lab'ayu has carried out hostilities against me, and we are not able to pluck the wool, and we are not able to go outside the gate in the presence of Lab'ayu, since he learned that thou has not given archers; and now his face is set to take Megiddo, but let the king protect the city, lest Lab'ayu seize it. Verily the city is destroyed by death from pestilence and disease. Let the king give one hundred garrison troops to guard the city lest Lab'ayu seize it. Verily there is no other purpose in Lab'ayu. He seeks to destroy Megiddo.

In another letter Lab'ayu, the man accused of seeking to destroy Megiddo, writes protesting his loyalty to the Pharaoh.

> I have heard the words which the king wrote to me, and who am I that the king should lose his land because of me? Behold I am a faithful servant of the king, and I have not rebelled and I have not sinned, and I do not withhold my tribute,

and I do not refuse the requests of my Commissioner. Now they wickedly slander me, but let the king, my lord, not impute rebellion to me!

Another letter, this time from Amenophis III to the prince of Gezer, is typical of many, and reveals that the Pharaoh took a lively and personal interest in Egypt's foreign imports.

To Milkiu, prince of Gezer. Thus the king. Now I have sent thee this tablet to say to thee; Behold, I am sending to thee Hanya, the commissioner of the archers, together with goods, in order to procure fine concubines, weaving-women, silver, gold, (linen) garments, turquoise, all (sorts of) precious stones, chairs of ebony, as well as every good thing, totally 160 deben. Total: 40 concubines; the price of each concubine is 40 (shekels) of silver. So send very fine concubines in whom there is no blemish . . . And mayst thou know that the king is well, like the Sun-god. His troops, his chariots, his horses are very well. Behold the god Amun has placed the upper land, the lower land, the rising of the sun and the setting of the sun under the two feet of the king.[4]

Other letters are from great kings, including Tushratta of Mitanni, the powerful kingdom on the upper Euphrates which acted as a buffer-state between Egypt and the rising power of the Hittites of Asia Minor. Both Tushratta and the Hittite King Suppiluliumas sent congratulatory messages on the accession of Amenophis IV. That of Tushratta was addressed to his mother, Tiye, and that from Suppiluliumas, though addressed to the young Pharaoh, also refers to Tiye, a clear indication that the Queen-Mother must have had considerable influence on foreign affairs.

If Amenophis III was still alive at this time, as most specialists on the 'Amarna period' believe, he was probably a sick and prematurely-ageing man. That he was ill is proved from at least two sources. His mummy indicates that in later life he suffered severe pain from dental abscesses, and in a letter from the King of Mitanni the latter says he is sending a magical statue of the goddess Ishtar in the hope that she may help cure the Pharaoh of his illness. The statue was sent under suitable escort and later returned to Mitanni. This incident in itself proves that foreign gods were respected, even by the 'son of Re.'

These significant details, seen in association with what we know of Amenophis IV during the first six years of his co-regency, help us to fill in the picture. The ageing Amenophis III, now become fat and flabby, as we can see from a statue of him made late in his reign (Plate 26), has little control over affairs. His wife, aided by her great officials, does what she can to guide the young Pharaoh, who, from his face and what we know of his subsequent actions, must have been an obstinate and headstrong young man. It would appear that from his early youth he had formed an intense dislike for the god Amun and his priesthood. At first this hatred was kept in check—perhaps through the influence of his mother. Even so, though he permitted himself to be represented, at Gebel Silsila, worshipping Amun-Re, the accompanying inscription is curiously worded, in that the King describes himself as:

> *first prophet of Re-Harakhte-Rejoicing-in-the-Horizon in his name the sunlight which is Aten.*

This was the first step. But before more than a few years had passed Amenophis IV was no longer content to represent the sun-god in human shape; the well-known figure of Re-Harakhte—a human figure with a falcon's head crowned with the sun-disk—gave way to an entirely new conception of the deity. In the tomb of Ramose already described there exists the earliest known representation of the 'sole god' whom the young king intended should replace Amun-Re; and not only Amun-Re but, apparently, every one of the thousands of human- or animal-headed deities which the Egyptians had worshipped since the dim beginnings of their history. The 'new' god was in fact the 'Aten' whose cult had already appeared during the reign of Amenophis III. The god was depicted simply as the sun's disk with descending rays, each terminating in a human hand. But the regal nature of the deity was indicated by the royal uraeus that hung from the top of the disk, just as it adorned the brow of the Pharaoh. And the Pharaoh's intimate association with the god was shown equally clearly. In Ramose's tomb we see for the first time a scene which was to be reproduced again and again. It is a balcony, on which stand Amenophis and Nefertiti. Below them, in adoring attitudes, stand or kneel the chief magistrate, officers of the royal harem and various servants, receiving golden necklets as gifts from the royal couple. And above them shines the Aten, each descending ray holding the hieroglyphic symbols for 'life,' 'dominion' or 'power.'

> An exaggerated liveliness and a visible emotional content are conspicuous; a bolder sweep of line and backs bowed lower stress the deference owed to the king; and one can hardly be deceived in the impression that the peculiarities of Amenophis's own body have been consciously imitated in the shapes given to his subjects.[5]

At round about the same time there appeared at Karnak colossal statues of the young Pharaoh in which his gross physical deformities were blatantly emphasized, almost to the point of caricature. In one he is shown completely nude and without genitalia. In the other the hips and thighs are ostentatiously feminine. And the thin face above the meagre neck is that of a fanatic. Before long whatever moderating forces had tried to influence the king were powerless. He changed his name from Amenophis ('Amun-is-satisfied') to Akhenaten ('Serviceable-to-Aten').

---

[1] Gardiner, Sir Alan, *Egypt of the Pharaohs,* Oxford University Press, New York, 1961

[2] Posener, G. (Ed.), *A Dictionary of Egyptian Civilisation,* Tudor Publishing Co., New York, 1961

[3] Weigall, Arthur, *The Life and Times of Akhenaten*, G. P. Putnam's Sons, New York, 1923

[4] Pritchard, J. B., *Ancient Near Eastern Texts*, Princeton University Press, 1958

[5] Gardiner, Sir Alan, op. cit.

9

'*Lady-of-the-Two-Lands*'

Six years after his coronation, Akhenaten moved from Thebes with his wife, two daughters, and followers. Nor did he move to an already existing city such as Memphis, which had been the capital during the Old Kingdom when Re was the supreme god. Instead he had created an entirely new capital on a virgin site where no town had existed before or would ever exist again. This site, about half-way between Luxor and modern Cairo, is a crescent-shaped plain on the east bank of the river, backed by a semi-circle of cliff-like hills. Nowadays it is called Tell el Amarna or simply El Amarna, which is more correct. To Akhenaten it was Akhetaten, which means 'The Horizon of the Disk.'

Practically all that we know about Nefertiti and her extraordinary husband has been obtained from this deserted site, which has an awesome desolation and melancholy unparalleled anywhere else in Egypt. Though a trickle of tourists is now beginning to visit it—usually of the more dedicated variety—it can never achieve the popularity of Luxor, Karnak or Giza, because there is nothing to see save the half-buried mud-brick foundations of Akhenaten's huge, rambling city and palaces, and carved but badly mutilated tombs hewn out of the cliffs. When I revisited it recently the site looked exactly as when I first saw it nearly twenty years ago. And its fascination was as powerful as ever.

Standing on the cliff-top, or wandering along the bridle path which, 3,330 years ago, was patrolled by Akhenaten's city police, one looks down over the brown, sandy plain where a complex, rectilinear pattern of darker lines reveals faint lineaments of streets, palaces, temples, houses, workshops and storerooms. Some distance away clusters the village of El Till; a woman swathed in black moves slowly across the plain on a donkey, and sometimes the sun catches the glint of the rifle carried by one of the turbanned *ghaffirs* who guard the tomb. Occasionally, to relieve his boredom, one of these guardians fires a round; the echo slams back from the cliffs, then reverberates into silence again. A wind gently stirs the sand, so that a yellowish haze dims the fecund green of the cultivated land bordering the river. That is Akhetaten. This, for more than twenty years, was the home of the loveliest woman who ruled Egypt.

In certain places on both the east and west of the river the cliffs have been cut and chiselled into large flat surfaces, and then carved with lengthy inscriptions. There are fourteen of these 'boundary stelae' set up in the sixth year of Akhenaten's reign, and in niches below them are battered but still-recognisable statues of the King, Nefertiti, and their two daughters. The hieroglyphic inscriptions describe how the royal pair, on the thirteenth day of the eighth month in year 6, set out in their golden chariot from the tent in which they had spent the night, in order to demarcate the frontiers of their 'holy city' which was to be dedicated to the worship of 'the living Aten.' First Akhenaten drove southward until he came to a place where the sun's rays shining upon him indicated that this was to be the southern boundary.

The inscription goes on to state that Akhenaten swore an oath by the god, and by his hope that, he, Nefertiti, and their daughters would live to a ripe old age, that he would never pass beyond this boundary, and beyond two others on the east bank and three on the west. In another, longer inscription he goes into much more detail, summoning his courtiers and explaining to them that all land within these boundaries belonged to the Aten and how Akhetaten was to be planned and built. Again he swears never to pass its boundaries, nor, in a curious phrase, allow Nefertiti to persuade him to do so. He ends by giving instructions for the building of certain sanctuaries for the god, and a family tomb to be made in the eastern mountain in which, he says, he and his family must be buried 'even if they should die in another town.'

In 1891, Sir Flinders Petrie began to excavate the buried city, and his work continued over many years, first by German and then by British archaeologists. It was the German archaeologists who discovered the world-famous portrait bust of the Queen, and a number of other superb works by the King's master-sculptor, whose workshop was identified. These excavations disclosed the foundations of an enormous complex of buildings within an area eight miles long and three miles broad. There were great palaces, several temples, a royal estate, mansions of the nobles and officials, a workmen's village, military and police barracks, and administrative buildings in one of which, called 'the place of the Pharaoh's Dispatches,' were found more cuneiform letters and documents similar to those discovered by the *sebakh*-digger in 1885.

Most of these structures had been of mud-brick and timber, but the principal royal palace, according to the late J. D. S. Pendlebury, was 'the largest secular building in the ancient world, and the only one in Egypt to be constructed of stone.' The western frontage facing the river was nearly half a mile long and within its enclosure-wall were huge state apartments, a Coronation Hall 120 yards along each side, a northern and southern harem with hundreds of rooms and with colonnades

opening on to sunken gardens and ornamental pools, and domestic quarters which must have housed thousands of servants.
Nefertiti had lived in a palace which could have accommodated
Versailles and Fontainebleau within its walls and left room
to spare.

But as even she could only occupy one room at a time it is
better to forget, for the time being, the bewildering prolifera-
tion of rooms, corridors, courtyards and gardens and concentrate
on more intimate details. Thanks to Akhenaten's habit of pub-
licising his domestic life in pictures, sculpture and inscriptions
we are better able to do this than at any site in Egypt. We know
what the palace and temples looked like, not only from the plans
drawn by archaeologists who excavated them, but because in
the tombs of the nobles hewn out of the eastern cliffs we are
permitted glimpses of these buildings through the eyes of artists
who knew them and had seen their occupants.

This in itself was a revolutionary change. Whereas in the
royal tombs at Thebes we see only pictures of the great deities,
and the spirits who haunted the Egyptian Underworld, at El
Amarna it is different. Only one god is represented, the Aten
disk with its descending rays. But we see the King and Queen
again and again, with their daughters, sometimes driving
through the city in their chariot, at other times showering gifts
on the great official whose tomb they have honoured with their
presence. These officials, Ay the 'Divine Father,' Panhesy the
Chief Steward, Mahu the Chief of Police and others, were also
permitted, in carved reliefs, to illustrate their own lives and
functions.

But the most extraordinary manifestation is the art itself.
For more than 2,000 years, ever since the beginnings of Egyptian
civilisation, there were only certain rigidly-prescribed ways in
which members of the royal family could be represented. In the
monumental sculpture of the Old Kingdom the pyramid-build-
ing kings such as Chephren, Menkaure, etc., are figures of aloof,
regal dignity, more like gods than men. The Pharaohs of the
Middle Kingdom are more realistically represented, and their

faces sometimes bear the marks of age and suffering; but they are still superhuman, and their stance never varies: standing, one foot forward, their hands clenched at their sides, or seated stiffly, one hand on knee, the other clutched to the breast and holding some hieratic symbol. On carved reliefs we see them striding forward with one upraised arm holding a club in the traditional attitude of the king smiting his enemies which goes back to 3200 BC.

As for their Queens, they are also shown in stiff, stylised poses, and very rarely with their husbands. It was only with the arrival of Amenophis III that the Queen was given equal prominence on her husband's monuments and in the colossal seated group which once stood outside the funerary temple of that King (now in the Cairo Museum). Tiye is seated beside the Pharaoh, smiling contentedly, with her arm affectionately round his waist—an attitude which had been permitted non-royal personages as far back as the Old Kingdom but seldom to Pharaohs and their consorts. (See Plate 31.)

This feminine encroachment was carried to the ultimate extreme in the reign of Akhenaten. In one of the Amarna tomb-reliefs she is shown riding in Akhenaten's chariot as he drives through the streets of his capital, and not only has she her arm round his waist; she appears to be kissing him. In another chariot-scene the royal couple are accompanied by their infant daughter who is mischievously poking the rump of one of the horses with a stick. The affection which Akhenaten and Nefertiti felt for their children—all daughters—is touchingly conspicuous. There is a small statuette of the king kissing his daughter, who sits on his knee, and, most moving of all, a scene on the wall of the Royal Tomb showing the King and Queen mourning the death of their daughter Meketaten, who died while still in her teens. In the death-chamber, while the royal parents lament over the body lying on a bed, a woman leaves the room holding a baby to her breast. Evidently Meketaten died in childbirth. (See Plate 30.)

It is difficult to associate these scenes of almost cosy domesticity and family affection with a monarch who, like his father, also maintained a huge harem, but in one of the tomb-reliefs we get an intimate glimpse of this: the bored guards lounging in the corridors, and, within the rooms, girls practising dances or playing musical instruments, while others are having their hair dressed. The foundations of this building were found. It was of great size, contained hundreds of rooms for the harem-ladies and their attendants. The key to this puzzle probably lies in the Pharaoh's identification with the sun-god, the creator and maintainer of life. He was much more than a temporal ruler; like his primitive ancestors he was linked in the minds of his subjects with the creative principle, with fertility in man, animal and plant. All the pharaohs claimed to be sons of Re, but Akhenaten carried this conception much further. To him there was only one god, the Aten, and it would almost seem, from a study of the pictures, that only he, and Nefertiti, could directly worship the god. They, and the fertility expressed in their fecund union, embodied the life-giving power of the Aten, and their subjects worshipped him through them.

Or so it would seem; but there are many varying views on this subject and it is doubtful if the true answer will ever be known. It seems certain, however, that the influence of Nefertiti was paramount, and she may have been an even more fervent Atenist than her husband. The fact that, on his boundary stelae, he states that he will not stray beyond his city's boundaries *even if the Queen should try to persuade him,* may be highly signifi-cant.

They had at least six daughters, all of whom are shown on the monuments, and two, Meritaten and Ankh-es-en-pa-aten, eventually became Queens. Two other royal children, both ap-parently sons of Amenophis III in his latter years, were brought up at El Amarna. These were Smenkhkare and Tutankhaten, later called Tutankhamun. But authorities differ basically on the precise relationships between these and other royal person-ages of the Amarna period, and it is only fair to the reader to summarise some of these conflicting views.

Of Tutankhaten, later Tutankhamun, Sir Alan Gardiner writes:

> When the wrappings of the mummy revealed his face, the discoverers were so much struck by its semblance to that of Akhenaten that they conjectured him to be the latter's son by an unofficial marriage; other scholars believed that they had found evidence of his being the son of Amenophis III; it is better to admit that nothing is definitely known about his parentage.[1]

Madame Desroches-Noblecourt, however, points out that an inscription at Soleb and at Gebel Barka in the Sudan, both set up by Tutankhamun after he became king, state that his father was Amenophis III. Unlike some scholars, who think that these inscriptions are a general reference to a royal ancestor, she is prepared to accept them literally, but she scouts the idea advanced by some authorities that Amenophis III married his own daughter, Sitamun, and so fathered Tutankhamun and also Smenkhkare. She believes that Tiye herself was the mother, and that the Queen bore Tutankhamun when she was about forty-eight. In this case he would have been Akhenaten's full brother.

Madame Desroches-Noblecourt is also quite unconvinced that Nefertiti was the daughter of the nobleman Ay, in which case she would have been Tiye's niece. She leaves Nefertiti's parentage an open question, but throws in an intriguing observation.

> Was she even Egyptian? There is no evidence to the contrary and her beauty was of the noble Theban type . . . but the coloured bust now in Berlin shows the rosy tint of her complexion, which suggests that she was careful to avoid sunlight, or, alternatively, *that she was of northern stock*.[2] [our italics]

Any man would be rash to question a lady of such academic eminence but I would dare to ask what Madame Noblecourt means by northern? Not northern Egypt or Syria surely, where one is just as likely to become sunburned as in Thebes. The rains begin at Cyprus. Dare one suggest that the paragon of Egyptian Queens could have come from somewhere in the Aegean, e.g. Cyprus or Crete, with which the Ancient Egyptians had close and friendly relations? I admit that the possibility is unlikely, since the Pharaoh would feel bound to announce his marriage to a Cypriot or Minoan princess in his inscriptions.

The belief, held by several authorities, e.g. Professors Fairman and Hayes, that Akhenaten also married his own daughter Ankh-es-en-pa-aten (later renamed Akhesnamun) will be examined later. Meanwhile we must look more closely at the Aten-cult and the reasons why it was promoted with such fanatical energy by Akhenaten and Nefertiti. The bare facts of the story lend themselves to a variety of interpretations, ranging from the sentimental to the cynical. To some the 'heretic king' was the world's first monotheist, or, as Breasted wrote, 'the first individual in human history,' and he quotes the following lines from the famous 'Hymn to the Aten' which Akhenaten caused to be inscribed in the tombs of his nobles:

How manifold are all thy works!
They are hidden from before us,
O thou sole god, whose powers no other possesseth.

Breasted interprets the King's apparent scorn for tradition as:

an acceptance of the daily facts of living in a simple and unconventional manner. For him what was right and its propriety was evident by its very existence. Thus his family life was open and unconcealed before the people. He took the greatest delight in his children and appeared with them and the Queen, their mother, on all possible occasions . . . whenever he appeared in the temple to offer sacrifice the Queen and the daughters she had borne him participated in the service.[3]

Arthur Weigall goes even further when he writes that the King

did his utmost to elevate the position of women and the

sanctity of the family by displaying to the world the ideal conditions of married life. He made a point of caressing his wife
in public, putting his arm around her neck in the sight of all
men; and in a little ornament . . . he is shown kissing the
Queen, their lips being pressed together. . . . He spoke of his
wife always as 'Mistress of his happiness . . . at hearing whose
voice the King rejoices.' . . . Even on the most ceremonious
occasions the Queen sat beside her husband and held his hand,
while their children frolicked around them; for such things
pleased that gentle Father more than the savour of burnt-
offerings.[4]

Why public caresses should 'elevate the position of women
and the sanctity of family life' and what it had to do with 'the
gentle Father' is not clear. It was, no doubt, the saccharine sentimentality of this and other accounts which produced a brutally
sceptical reaction. Thus J. D. S. Pendlebury, the distinguished
archaeologist who, with Professor Fairman, conducted a long,
scientific excavation of Akhenaten's city, commented:

So much has been written about Akhenaten in the character of Christ before his time that it must be pointed out that
Atenism was in no sense a way of life but merely an exercise in
theology. . . . Today the impression that the art and civilisation
of Amarna gives us is that of an ephemeral butterfly age with
that total lack of moral standards usually associated with happy
morons.[5]

Though archaeology strives for objectivity, archaeologists
are bound to be subjective in their approach to personalities. I
imagine that Pendlebury, who died gallantly in Crete fighting
alongside the Resistance, must have found Akhenaten's flabby
pacifism more than a little irritating. But he goes too far. Akhenaten's achievements were too great to be dismissed in this way,
and the very fact that, at a distance of more than three thousand
years, he can still arouse such heated controversy attests to the
power of his personality, and that of his Queen.

The main pitfall to be avoided—and this applies to the

study of all ancient civilisations—is in looking at the people of the 'Amarna Age' from the wrong end of the time-scale—our end. Instead of seeing them always in relation to our own civilisation it is safer to consider them against the primitive background from which their ancestors had emerged. In this I agree with a comment by Mr. Cyril Aldred, who writes that 'the Egyptians must be regarded as a primitive people more akin to some modern Africans than ancient Greeks, and their habits of thought are more likely to be understood by anthropologists than grammarians.' Though I would add the rider that we ourselves are much nearer the primitive than most of us care to accept.

It is obvious that only a major religio-political rupture could have caused the King of Egypt to desert his ancestral capital and found a new one. It is also certain that this momentous decision was prompted by a rift between the priesthood of Amun and the young Pharaoh and his adherents. This is proved on three çounts: (a) that before he left Thebes, Akhenaten had encouraged the Aten-cult which had already appeared in the reign of his father; he built a temple to the Aten in Thebes itself; (b) that not long after he had settled in his new city, and when his father was either dead or too senile to intervene, Akhenaten set about a systematic campaign of destruction; workmen were sent to most of the major temples, monuments and tombs with orders not only to obliterate the name Amun (even on the monuments of Akhenaten's father) but also, as far as possible, to mutilate those of the other gods. They could not, of course, be completely successful, but sufficient traces of their handiwork remain, e.g. in the funerary temple of Hashepsowe, to show that they did their best; (c) after Akhenaten's death the Amun priesthood took their revenge by erasing the name of the hated 'heretic king' whom they called 'that criminal' wherever they found it.

If either Akhenaten or his Queen had left any written record of their beliefs we would be in a better position to understand why these events took place. But the only written evidence we possess which throws light on the Aten-cult is the so-called

1. PRECEDING PAGE: *A capital in the Hathor shrine, Hashepsowe's Funerary Temple at Deir el Bahri; the features resemble those of the Queen.* © *Paul Elek Productions, Ltd.*

2. ABOVE FAR LEFT: *Life-size limestone statue of Queen Hashepsowe from her temple at Deir el Bahri.* © *Metropolitan Museum of Art.*

3. ABOVE LEFT: *Head of seated statue of Hashepsowe in red granite, Deir el Bahri.* © *Metropolitan Museum of Art.*

4. BELOW LEFT: *Cosmetic jars and kohl-tube inscribed with the cartouche of Hashepsowe.* © *Metropolitan Museum of Art.*

5. ABOVE: *The Funerary Temple of Hashepsowe at Deir el Bahri; the Valley of the Kings lies beyond the cliffs.* © *Paul Elek Productions, Ltd.*

6. ABOVE: *Sen-en-mut with Hashepsowe's infant daughter Nefru-Re; he was her guardian and tutor.* © *Cairo Museum.*

7. ABOVE RIGHT: *Studies for a portrait of Sen-en-mut on a fragment of limestone found near his tomb at Deir el Bahri.* © *Metropolitan Museum of Art.*

8. BELOW RIGHT: *Sketch of a rat on reverse side of same fragment.* © *Metropolitan Museum of Art.*

31.4.2

9. ABOVE LEFT: *Limestone figurine showing lady having her hair dressed while nursing her child (18th Dynasty).* © Metropolitan Museum of Art.

10. BELOW LEFT: *Egyptian woman of the 18th Dynasty showing characteristic wig and necklace.* © Metropolitan Museum of Art.

11. ABOVE: *Girdles of gold and semi-precious stones worn by one of Tuthmosis III's Asiatic wives.* © Metropolitan Museum of Art.

12. NEXT PAGE, ABOVE: *Covered spoon in the form of a young girl swimming after a gazelle (18th Dynasty).* © Metropolitan Museum of Art.

13. NEXT PAGE, BELOW: *Part of the jewellery of Princess Sith-Hathor-Unet (12th Dynasty); a leopard-head girdle surrounds necklace, both of gold and amethyst.* © Metropolitan Museum of Art.

14.   TOP: *Tableware of three Asiatic wives of Tuthmosis III (18th Dynasty), of gold, silver and gold-mounted glass and alabaster.* © *Metropolitan Museum of Art.*

15.   BELOW LEFT: *Vanity case, mirror, and cosmetic jars from the tomb of Princess Sith-Hathor-Unet (12th Dynasty).* © *Metropolitan Museum of Art.*

16.   BELOW RIGHT: *Close-up of another mirror from same tomb showing Hathor-head handle.* © *Metropolitan Museum of Art.*

17.   ABOVE: *Portrait head of Queen Tiye in later life.* © *F. L. Kenett.*

18.   RIGHT: *The lady Depet, one of the guests at a banquet given by the Vizier Ramose; from his tomb (18th Dynasty).* © *F. L. Kenett.*

19.   LEFT: *The lady Werel with her husband, May, Master of the Horse, both guests at the banquet depicted in the tomb of the Vizier Ramose (18th Dynasty).* © *Paul Elek Productions, Ltd.*

20.   ABOVE: *The "Berlin bust" of Queen Nefertiti.* © *F. L. Kenett.*

21.　ABOVE LEFT: *Young girls, guests at a banquet, wearing corn-yellow gowns, jewellery in red, yellow and green, with vari-coloured headbands; from an 18th Dynasty tomb.* © *Paul Elek Productions, Ltd.*

22.　BELOW LEFT: *Flower bowl of bronze with tiny figure of the cow-goddess, Hathor, standing in the water.* © *Metropolitan Museum of Art.*

23.　ABOVE: *12th Dynasty model showing women spinning and weaving linen fibres; from the tomb of Meket-Re, Thebes.* © *Metropolitan Museum of Art.*

24.　NEXT PAGE, TOP LEFT: *One of the "Amarna tablets" from Akhenaten's Foreign Office files.* © *The British Museum.*

25.　NEXT PAGE, TOP RIGHT: *Head of one of Akhenaten's daughters by Nefertiti, probably Meritaten.* © *F. L. Kenett.*

26.　NEXT PAGE, BELOW: *Amenophis III in old age.* © *The British Museum.*

'Hymn to the Aten,' parts of which are inscribed on the walls of the Amarna tombs, and which may have been composed or inspired by the King, though there is no proof of this. Ancillary evidence is confined mainly to the naturalistic art which distinguishes the period, and which has no precedent in Egyptian civilisation.

The 'Hymn to the Aten' praises the life-giving power of the sun-god in all its aspects. The extracts quoted are from Sir Alan Gardiner's translation.[6] It begins:

Thou arisest beauteous in the horizon of heaven, O living Aten, beginner of life when thou didst shine forth in the eastern horizon, and didst fill every land with thy beauty.

Thou art comely, great, sparkling, and high above every land, and thy rays enfold the lands to the limit of all that thou hast made, thou being the sun and thou reachest their limits and subjectest them to thy beloved son [i.e. Akhenaten].

The hymn goes on to describe the rising of the sun, when

the Two Lands are in festival, awakened they stand on their feet, thou hast lifted them up,

and poetically evokes the reawakening of life after its nightly death.

All animals frisk on their feet. All that flyeth or alighteth live when thou arisest for them. Ships fare north and likewise fare south ... The fish in the river leap before thy face, etc.

The sun is compared with a mother

bringing to life the son in the body of his mother; soothing him by the cessation of tears.

Even the 'chick in the egg' is not beneath the attention of the omniscient god.

... Thou has made for him his completion so as to break it, even the egg, and he cometh forth from the egg ... and he walketh upon his two feet when he comes forth from it.

the hymn continues, breaking now into philosophic contemplation.

> How manifold are thy works,
> They are mysterious in men's sight. Thou sole god, like to whom there is none other. Thou didst create the earth after thy heart, being alone, even all men, herds and flocks, whatever is upon earth . . .

The Aten is now seen as the Creator-God who fashioned all countries and all mankind, not only Egypt.

> Thou settest every man in his place, and makest their sustenance, each one possessing his food, and his term of life counted; tongues made diverse in speech and their characters likewise; their complexions distinguished, for thou has distinguished country and country.

It is this and certain other passages which have suggested that Atenism may have had a political motive, that it was an endeavour to find a deity which would be acceptable to both the Egyptian and the foreigner.

> All distant lands, thou hast made their life. Thou hast set a Nile-flood in the sky, and it descendeth for them and maketh waves upon the mountains like the Great-Green [sea] to drench their fields in their villages. How efficacious are thy plans, thou lord of eternity. A Nile-flood in heaven, it is thy gift to the foreign countries. . . . But the Nile-flood comes forth from the netherworld for the land of Egypt.

Towards the end of the hymn the unique function of the King as interpreter and representative of the god is emphasised.

> *There is none other that knowest thee except thy son NeferKheprure-wa-enre* [Akhenaten]. *Thou hast caused him to be skilled in thy ways and in thy strength.*

And after repeating the statement that life ceases with the setting of the sun and begins again when it rises, the royal poet continues:

Thou raises them up for thy son who came forth from thy body, the King of Upper and Lower Egypt, living on Truth, the lord of the Two Lands NeferKheprure-wa-enre, the son of Re, living on Truth, lord of glorious appearings, Akhenaten great in his duration; with the king's great wife, whom he loves, the lady of the Two Lands, Nefernefruaten—Nefertiti, may she live and flourish for ever and ever.

Many writers, impressed by the beauty of this poem and its obvious resemblance to Psalm *civ,* have represented it as something unique, a new universal, philosophical conception born in the mind of a deeply religious thinker. In fact most of it can be paralleled in much earlier Egyptian religious poetry originating in Heliopolis, the cult-centre of the earlier sun-god Re. This fact, however, hardly lessens Akhenaten's achievement, because whereas the earlier poet-philosophers were apparently content with the co-existence of Re with thousands of anthropomorphic deities, the 'heretic-Pharaoh' saw the illogicality of this and tried to sweep away what Gardiner rightly calls 'the vast accumulations of mythological rubbish inherited from the past.' Atenism, Gardiner continues, 'was no mere physical theory but a genuine monotheism.'

In this Akhenaten can lay claims to greatness, even if it was a negative greatness. For the poem contains no trace of moral teaching, no single indication of how men should behave towards their fellow-men. The much older Wisdom Literature from which we have quoted, though it has no religious context, abounds in moral precepts not unlike those of Christianity and other world religions. There is none of this in Atenism, which lends weight to Pendlebury's criticism that it was merely 'an exercise in theology.'

So much for the literary content of the new faith, so far as it is known. When we come to its expression in sculpture and painting we are on difficult and disturbing ground. For there is something in the so-called 'naturalistic' art of the Amarna period which baffles minds which can easily accept its theology. For, side by side with his religious revolution, Akhenaten instituted an entirely new kind of artistic expression which appears to have been bound up inextricably with his own grotesque physical appearance. Unlike all preceding and succeeding Pharaohs he seems to have insisted on his artists reproducing the royal face and body as they really were, even to the extent of caricaturing their physical defects.

During the early years at El Amarna this tendency increased, and there can be little doubt that the King himself was responsible for it since his master-sculptor specifically states in an inscription that 'His Majesty taught me.' Not only Akhenaten but the Queen, her daughters, and the courtiers were all depicted in the same way. All have Akhenaten's long skull, pendulous chin, swollen belly and broad, feminine hips. To the modern mind it is incredible that Nefertiti, who from later, more realistic sculpture is revealed as an extremely lovely woman, should permit herself to be represented as she appears on the stela reproduced in Plate 33. Neither she nor her daughters were deformed, yet even in the later, more truly naturalistic works of art the emphasis always is on a soft, over-feminine voluptuousness, highly acceptable in a woman but bizarre when transferred to the male body.

There are numerous other instances of this feminising tendency. In most Pharaonic statues the Queens are shown with their feet together, the King's with one foot striding forwards. There are examples of Amarna art where this is reversed. Again, it was customary in the time of the Tuthmosids and the earlier part of Amenophis III's reign for women to wear long wigs, with curls descending to their shoulders, while men usually wore a short cap-like wig. During the latter part of the reign of Amenophis III, and during the Amarna period, women are often depicted wearing the short male wig.

All these facts, coupled with the increasing prominence given to Queens Tiye and Nefertiti, strongly suggest an overwhelming feminine influence, and as this reached its peak during the reign of Akhenaten, and subsided afterwards, the implication seems to be that it was associated with the religious revolution which Akhenaten appears to have initiated. Unless, and there are some grounds for believing this, the original impetus came not from the 'heretic king' but his Queen, the 'Lady of the Two Lands.'

---

[1] Gardiner, Sir Alan, *Egypt of the Pharaohs,* Oxford University Press, New York, 1961

[2] Desroches-Noblecourt, C., *Tutankhamen*, New York Graphic Society, Greenwich, Conn., 1963

[3] Breasted, J. H., *A History of Egypt*, Charles Scribner's Sons, New York, 1921

[4] Weigall, Arthur, *The Life and Times of Akhenaten,* G. P. Putnam's Sons, New York, 1923

[5] Pendlebury, J. D. S., *Tell el Amarna*, Lovat Dickson and Thompson, 1935

[6] Gardiner, Sir Alan, op. cit.

10

The Enigma of Nefertiti

IT IS DIFFICULT TO ASSESS THE IMPACT OF AKHENATEN'S AT-tempted religious revolution on Egypt as a whole, but we have a few clues. If it had been slight the priests of Amun would have disregarded it, whereas it is clear that they felt it was suffi-cient of a menace to cause them to induce the young Pharaoh to take himself from Thebes and agree not to stray beyond the frontiers of his new capital. Again, when the heretic was dead and his successor installed at Thebes, they felt it necessary to undo, as far as possible, the harm he had done by erasing his memory and that of his god.

Against this we must set the following facts. It is often stated that 'the court followed Akhenaten to El Amarna.' In fact, as Gardiner interestingly points out, of all the officials to whom Akhenaten donated tombs near his new capital, only one is definitely known to have come from Thebes. 'The rest were *novi homines*, many of them probably hangers-on whose ostensible devotion to the Aten masked a determination to gain as much material reward as possible.' When the golden collars and other rich gifts were being distributed from the 'Balcony of Appearances' so often shown in the Amarna tombs, these men were there to receive them, in attitudes of grovelling obeisance.

As for the common people who flocked to Akhetaten in the wake of the court, the field-workers, craftsmen, jewellers, carpenters, quarrymen, plasterers, smiths, grooms, etc., they and their families probably knew little of the new cult and cared less. They would see Akhenaten and Nefertiti driving along the Sikkit es-Sultan (the Arab name for the Royal Way which still exists) and mass at the entrances to the great temples of the Aten to which only the priests and the Royal Family were admitted. But they themselves continued to honour the older gods. When Pendlebury excavated the workmen's quarters at El Amarna he found many small statuettes of Bes and other minor deities.

Within Egypt as a whole there were a few Aten temples here and there, including one at Heliopolis. There may have been other Aten-sanctuaries in Nubia, where certain rock inscriptions testify to the presence of some of the King's favoured officials. There is absolutely no evidence of Akhenaten's universal god in Syria-Palestine, whose inhabitants continued to revere their native deities.

Thebes would be a depressed city. For ten or twelve years after his son's accession Amenophis III lingered on in his great, rambling palace on the west bank of the Nile, accompanied by Queen Tiye, though she occasionally paid state visits to Akhetaten, as we know from certain tomb-inscriptions. Though ageing and increasingly decrepit, as we can observe from his sculpture portraits (see Plate 26), Amenophis III's interest in foreign concubines continued, and the 'Amarna letters' contain many requests for fresh supplies from Syria-Palestine. Occasionally he appears to have short-changed his suppliers, as when Tushratta of Mitanni sent him this pained reply to a request that the Mitannian king should send the Pharaoh one of his daughters.

Gillia, my messenger, has brought to me my brother's [Amenophis's] message; when I heard it, it seemed to me very good, and I was very glad indeed and said 'So far as I am concerned, even if all the friendly relations which we have had with one another ceased, nevertheless, on account of this message, we would forever continue friendly.' . . . Let my brother make our friendship ten times greater than with my father, and I ask of my brother a great deal of gold, saying 'More than to my father let my brother give me and send me. Thou sentest my father a great deal of gold . . . but thou sentest me (only) a tablet of gold that is as if it were alloyed with copper. . . . So let my brother send gold in very great quantity, without measure, and let him send more gold to me than to my father. . .

As for the girl whom Amenophis III wished to purchase the wily Tushratta comments:

> Inasmuch as my brother sent his messenger, Mani, saying 'My brother, send me thy daughter for my wife, to be Queen of Egypt,' I did not grieve the heart of my brother . . . And as my brother wished I presented her to Mani. And he beheld her and when he saw her he rejoiced greatly; and when he brings her safely to my brother's land, then may Ishtar and Amun make her correspond to my brother's wish.[1]

But apparently Amenophis had to send quite a number of messengers, and more gold of better quality, before the goods were delivered. 'In this vein,' Breasted comments, 'the men who were now shaping the destinies of all hither Asia wrote to one another.'

Some time between the tenth and twelfth year of Akhenaten's co-regency, his royal father died and was buried in a magnificent tomb in a side valley leading off the Valley of the Kings. His mummy has survived, and shows him to have died in his fifties. If the co-regency theory is correct the two young male children brought up partly at El Amarna could have been his, either by Tiye or by Sitamun, but more likely the latter. Of these two boys one, Tutankhaten, incorporated in his name that of the 'new' god, and the other, Smenkhkare, incorporated that of the earlier Sun-god Re.

We cannot be sure if Tiye remained at Thebes or moved permanently to El Amarna, but there is a well-known sculptured relief in the Tomb of Huya, Superintendent of the Royal Harem and Chamberlain to Tiye, which shows a royal banquet given by Akhenaten to the Queen-Mother. While Nefertiti nibbles at a small roast duck which she holds in her hand, Akhenaten attacks a large bone wrapped round with strips of meat. A pleasing domestic touch is provided by the royal children; Tiye is passing some titbit to her daughter Meketaten who sits beside her on a small chair, while next to Nefertiti sit her daughters Meritaten and Ankh-es-en-pa-aten, seated together on cushioned chairs, each with her footstool.

Much can be learned about Ancient Egyptian dining habits from this and similar scenes at Amarna. The host, hostess and their guests sat at small separate tables while the servants moved swiftly and expertly between them, refilling the wine-cups (Akhenaten is shown with a huge one) and replenishing the tables with food. We see joints of meat, poultry, dishes of confectionery, bread, cakes, vegetables and fruit of various varieties. The tables are massed with lotus-flowers in bowls, and even the wine-jars are festooned.

In these scenes the diners eat with their hands, but knives and spoons were in use, though not at this time forks. Meat such as beef, mutton, and pork was eaten by the rich, though, as Egypt is a hot country, it had to be eaten fresh, as there were no means of freezing it. It might be roasted, boiled, or fried, presumably in animal-fat, though the olive-tree was known in Pharaonic Egypt. Fish was popular with all except royal or priestly personages, to whom it was forbidden by a religious taboo. Bread was the staple diet, and many varieties of cakes made from flour. The tomb of Meket-Re mentioned in a previous chapter contained a model bakery. Among fruit and vegetables were figs, dates, grapes, pomegranates, cucumbers, onions, water-melons and sweet melons; but citrus-fruits did not come into use until Graeco-Roman times, and neither did sugar. Honey was probably used for sweetening, and salt was also known.

In the same tomb-relief of Huya, Queen Tiye is shown holding to her lips a fine goblet of wine, and this, one may be sure, would be of rare vintage. Akhenaten, like other Pharaohs, took a pride in his 'cellar,' as we know from the numerous wine-jar sealings found on the site of his city, some bearing such inscriptions as 'Year so-and-so, fine wine of the king, from the vineyard so-and-so.' Wine had been enjoyed in Ancient Egypt from as far back as 3200 BC, and throughout the Old, Middle and New Kingdoms the vine was lovingly cultivated. In many tomb-paintings of the New Kingdom we see vine-trellises, and in one famous sepulchre, that of Sennufer, the ceiling of the tomb had been left rough and then painted to represent clusters of grapes hanging from such a trellis.

Other paintings show the whole process of wine-making, from the gathering and pressing of the grapes, the fermentation of the juice in vats and, after ageing, its storage in tall *amphorae,* each sealed with a stopper of plaster bearing the name of the grower. In each case of rare wines the name of the vineyard and the vintage year were also given, thus:

> Year 10 of the King. . . . high quality wine, three times good, Syrian stock, from the great vineyard (called) *The Food of Egypt* on the western arm of the Nile . . . made under the supervision of the Chief Overseer of the Vineyard, Nakht.

Beer was also brewed by a simple and effective method. After kneading barley into a dough it was lightly baked and then left to soak in water, with the addition of other substances, such as dates. After the liquid had fermented it was strained through a cloth into pots. Good beer was highly regarded throughout the Two Lands, and, taken in sufficient quantity, could be potent. An old scribe admonishes his pupil:

> I am told that thou forsakest writing, thou givest thyself up to pleasures; that thou goest from street to street where it smelleth of beer, to destruction. Beer, it scareth men (from thee), it sendeth thy soul to perdition.

The association of excessive drinking with other forms of debauchery is clear from the rest of the scribe's admonition. In Ancient Egypt as in modern times Wine and Women often went together.

> Would that thou knewest that wine is an abomination that thou wouldst take an oath in respect of *shedeh* that thou shouldest not set thine heart on the bottle. . . . Thou art taught to sing to the flute . . . and to pipe. . . . Thou sittest in the brothel and the girls encircle thee . . . Thou sittest in front of the wench and art besprinkled with oil; thy garland of *ishet-penu* hangeth about thy neck and thou drummest on thy paunch . . .[2]

Though such scenes are unlikely to have occurred in Akhenaten's halls of state, one imagines that, when the Great Ones were holding high festival in the Palace, as on the occasion of Tiye's visit, the drinking-houses of the city would have witnessed somewhat less elegant celebrations. And probably some of the dancing-girls whom one glimpses practising their steps in the royal harem had graduated from a less luxurious environment.

To the over-censorious, such scenes might well justify Pendlebury's criticism of the Amarna Period as 'an ephemeral butterfly age with that total lack of moral standards associated with happy morons.' Yet in essence they are no different from those which had decorated Egyptian tombs from the Pyramid Period onwards. Feasting, dancing, hunting, and the pleasures of the harem were the normal pastimes of the great. The only difference in the Amarna tombs is that some (not all) of these activities are depicted in greater detail, and that the royal family are shown, not only worshipping their god, but also enjoying the same temporal pleasures as their noble subjects.

But there is something else, a delicacy, a softness, a listless atmosphere of decadence. The King lolls on his throne, his rounded paunch almost resting on his plump thighs, while the Queen offers him flowers, or gently massages his body with oil. Flowers, trees, birds are delineated with extreme naturalism which seems to reflect that delight in nature expressed in the Aten-hymn. In art the revolution was as profound as that in religion, and if we are to believe the statements in the tomb of the master-sculptor Dhutmose it was the King who inspired and encouraged these freer forms of expression.

During the twenty years during which he reigned from Akhetaten, the Pharaoh and his Queen seem to have devoted themselves almost entirely to the worship of the Aten. In the huge temples, in which the altars were open to the sun—unlike earlier and later Egyptian temples—we see the King, always accompanied by Nefertiti and her daughters, making offerings to the deity. Every nobleman and high official, in his tomb-reliefs, is either sharing in this adoration or receiving from the King and Queen the rewards of his loyalty and service.

We know from excavation that there was a flourishing trading and commercial quarter. Great ships arrived at and departed from the wharves, and near the northern limits of the city was a Customs House where dues were levied. But there is no evidence that the King ever left his city, and the administration of the kingdom and Egypt's foreign dominions was left to the great officers of state. In Akhenaten's Foreign Office scribes read and translated the letters which flowed in from the rulers of Mitanni, from Babylon, from the king of the Hittites and from the governors of Egypt's vassal states in Syria-Palestine.

Those from the Great Powers were usually requests for gold; those from the petty kinglets of such fortress-towns as Gebal and Simyra were usually urgent pleas for military help, which never came. For something sinister was happening in those lands which had been won for Egypt by the strong arm of Tuthmosis III. By 'won for Egypt' it is not implied that these cities and lands were Egyptian colonies in the modern sense. Recent research has thrown doubt on whether Tuthmosis's 'Egyptian Empire' ever really existed. As Gardiner comments:

> The defeat of Mitanni by Tuthmosis I may have brought
> about an attempt in that direction, but there is no evidence that

his success was followed up in the next two reigns. It would be perverse to minimise the splendid achievement of Tuthmosis III, but this started with the uprising of a vast coalition of petty Palestinian and Syrian chieftains, and, even after Mitanni had again been vanquished, thirteen more separate campaigns were needed in order to maintain Egyptian suzerainty. We may guess, though it is little more than guesswork, that while the seaports were strongly held, military governors were stationed at key-points. At all events the many small city-states . . . will have considered themselves at most as vassals of Pharaoh, to whose protection they looked as the least of several evils.[3]

It was these governors whose letters were found at El Amarna in 'The House of the Pharaoh's Dispatches.' One of them, King Abdu-Heba of Jerusalem, a Canaanite monarch, wrote numerous letters to Akhenaten pleading for military aid against the '*Apiru*,' once identified with 'Hebrew' but now known to be merely a generic term for 'outcasts' or 'bandits.' Here is an extract from one of these letters:

> To the king, my lord, my sun-god, say; Thus Abdu-Heba, thy servant. At the two feet of the king, my lord, seven times and seven times I fall [etc., etc.]. . . . It is vile what they have done against me. Behold, I am not a governor nor even a petty officer of the king, my lord; Behold, I am a shepherd of the king, and a bearer of the royal tribute am I. It was not my father and not my mother, but the arm of the mighty king which placed me in the house of my father. . . . Let the king take thought for his land! The land of the king is lost; in its entirety it is taken from me; there is war against me, as far as the lands of Seir and as far as Gath-carmel! All the governors are at peace, but there is war against me. . . . The army of the mighty king conquers the land of Nahariam and the land of Cush, but now the 'Apiru capture the cities of the king. There is not a single governor remaining of the king—all have perished! Behold Turbazu has been slain the very gates of Sile, yet the king holds his peace. Behold Zimreda, the townsmen of Lachish have smitten him,

slaves who had become 'Apiru. Yaptih-Hadad has been slain
in the very gate of Sile, yet the king holds his peace. Wherefore
dost not the king call them to account? So let the king take
care of his land; let the king decide, and let the king send
archers to his land! But if there are no archers here this year all
the lands of the king, my lord, will be lost![4]

Another letter from Abdu-Heba contains the lines:

Behold the deed which Milkiu and Shuwardata did to
the land of the king, my lord! They rushed troops to Gezer,
troops of Gath and troops of Keilah; they took the land of
Rubutu; the land of the king went over to the 'Apiru people.
But now even a town of the land of Jerusalem, Bit-Lahmi by
name, a town belonging to the king, has gone over to the side
of the people of Keilah. Let my king hearken to 'Abdu-Heba,
thy servant, and let him send archers to recover the royal land for
the king. But if no archers are sent, the land of the king will
pass over to the 'Apiru people.[5]

Responsibility for dealing with these letters lay with Tutu,
equivalent to Foreign Secretary (or Minister for Colonial Affairs) of Akhenaten. How much the Pharaoh was kept in touch
with affairs in his Empire is unknown, but there are hardly any
records of replies to the vassal-kings, let alone reinforcements.
Presumably the Egyptian commissioners on the spot would send
reports, or they should have done; if they did not, then the Minister, lacking accurate intelligence, would be hard put to weigh
the conflicting claims of the governors.

Faced with such a situation a Pharaoh such as Tuthmosis
III would have led an army to Palestine himself to find out the
truth. Akhenaten did not, but relied entirely on correspondence
and the reports of his commissioners. Sometimes these officials,
no doubt confused by contrary reports, sent troops to attack the
wrong objectives, as when the Nubian mercenary troops of the
Pharaoh, stationed in Jerusalem, had sacked the residence of
Abdu-Heba himself, much to the latter's chagrin. However, one

must keep a sense of proportion. The squabbles and treacheries of these petty kings, fighting among themselves, but each protesting his loyalty, were annoying but could hardly be considered dangerous. The real threat came when Suppiluliumas, King of the Hittites, whose power was to rival that of the Pharaoh himself, began exploiting these quarrels in order to aggrandise his territory. Again, Tuthmosis III, a statesman as well as a warrior, would probably have recognised this threat, but apparently Akhenaten or his advisers did not.

To what extent was this inaction prompted by Akhenaten's religious views? Attempts have been made to present him as a pacifist, an early believer in non-resistance. This I believe is doubtful. It is more likely that Akhenaten, brought up at the court of the indolent Amenophis III, when the despatch of a few troops and ships was sufficient to pacify the squabbling chieftains, never took the threat seriously, and if, as often happened, the intriguing kinglets were able to grease the palm of the Foreign Minister, the latter would use his influence to restrain the Pharaoh from intervening. In any case it seems highly probable that Akhenaten, whose mother wielded strong influence over his father, and who was married to a woman of equally strong personality, would be more likely to listen to their pacific advice than take that of his Army commanders such as Horemhab.

Indifference and a fanatical absorption in his religion are more likely causes of the Pharaoh's neglect of military affairs than a consciously-implemented policy of pacifism. Non-resistance is too modern a concept.

Here again we are straying into the dangerous field of speculation, but there are certain pointers to this theory, especially in the case of Nefertiti. One glance at that strong-boned face, that intelligent brow and firm lips is sufficient to suggest that she was no cypher. Considering the honour in which she was held, and the adoration lavished on her by her husband, she must have exerted power over him and been at least superficially cognisant of foreign affairs. His face too exhibits a strong personality, but whereas hers is calm, resolute and self-controlled, his is neurotic. He looks like a man of strong passions which could be manipulated and used; also his physical abnormalities may have been paralleled by nervous and mental instability, perhaps at times approaching madness.

The possibility of Akhenaten having been mentally abnormal has exercised the minds of two generations of scholars. Weigall, writing in 1921, suggested that he was an epileptic, basing this theory on the bones of a young man found in a tomb at Thebes and then believed to be that of Akhenaten. Elliot Smith, the anatomist who conducted the autopsy, said that the skull was misshapen and was that of a man who suffered from epileptic fits and who was probably subject to hallucinations. But since Smith made his report inscriptions have been found which prove that the King lived to be at least forty, whereas the bones appear to be those of a young man of not more than twenty-five. Unless the King suffered from a disease which inhibited the normal development of the bones—a theory which has been strongly promoted and equally strongly contested—the skeleton could not have been his. Nor is its alleged abnormality now universally accepted.

In fact this matter, as we shall see later, has been the subject of a fierce academic controversy for at least twenty years, and the fascinated amateur, watching the ebb and flow of battle from a safe distance, may anticipate another vigorous offensive at any time. Sir Alan Gardiner, who brought his vast philological knowledge to bear on the coffin inscriptions, died a few years ago, but the main contestants, Professor H. W. Fairman and Mr. Cyril Aldred, are in excellent shape.

Until this matter is settled we are left with numerous statues and sculptured reliefs of Akhenaten which certainly make him appear abnormal, and as he himself inspired the naturalistic art of which they are examples they may be considered accurate. Also he came near the end of a long dynasty, the earlier rulers of which were in some cases the products of consanguineous marriages. Tuthmosis II and Tuthmosis III both married their half-sisters, and it is possible that Tuthmosis IV, Akhenaten's grandfather, was the product of a similar relationship. The genetic hazards of continued inbreeding are well-known; the progressive weakening of the stock would make it increasingly vulnerable to disease, and we know that Amenophis III, Akhenaten's father, was a sick man in his later years. It seems to me highly likely that the heretic Pharaoh suffered from a disease which would affect both his mind and body, though this may not have been apparent in his early youth, when he married Nefertiti.

Madness and genius are often closely allied, and—a most important point—incipient madness, or what we might call an obsessional neurosis, would not necessarily jeopardise the right of a 'divine King' to rule, since the Ancient Egyptians, like some modern primitives, believed that lunatics were possessed by a god. The Wisdom Literature quoted earlier contains the significant line:

> *Do not tease a man who is in the hands of god.*

The ravings, visions, hallucinations of an unbalanced mind might, by their very incomprehensibility, seem divinely inspired. So it may have been with Akhenaten, who had the good fortune to come to the throne in a time of peace when the Egyptians did not need a military genius to lead them.

It has been suggested that the Aten-cult was little more than a political manoeuvre designed to offset the growing power of the Amun priesthood, and also to establish a common focus of worship for both the Egyptians and the peoples of the lands which they wholly or partially controlled. It is an attractive theory which may contain a germ of truth. We know that the cult was encouraged in the time of Amenophis III, who was certainly no religious fanatic, and Tiye may also have supported it. But political strategy masquerading as religious revolution is surely too sophisticated a concept for the Ancient Egyptians, who took their religion seriously. It seems more likely that Akhenaten was less of a politician than a schismatic; a thinker and a mystic who found in what had been a minor cult a burning focus for his ideals and aspirations. If he had been of common birth he would have been powerless to effect a change, since the Egyptians were not given to following minor prophets. But he was the divine Pharaoh, the son of Re, with the power to put his ideas into action.

But even he could not have done this alone; he would need support and encouragement, and this, I believe, he obtained from Nefertiti. Once again we must look at her face for an answer. There is no fanaticism there, but there is determination, self-control, wisdom and not a little ruthlessness. She, too, had grown up at a court where her mother-in-law, Queen Tiye, enjoyed a power and influence which had not been accorded to any of her predecessors, save Hashepsowe. She may or may not have shared Akhenaten's devotion to his god, but I suggest it would be Nefertiti, and not her husband, who would know how to realise his aims and ambitions in terms of practical politics.

The initial split with Thebes and the Amun-cult may even have been amicable. A diplomatic Queen, perhaps in alliance with her mother-in-law, might have persuaded the Theban priesthood to agree to the Pharaoh worshipping his god unhindered, provided that he remove his presence from Thebes and, with his fellow-schismatics, found a new city and not stray beyond its boundaries, *nor permit the Queen to persuade him to do so,* as referred to previously. This strongly suggests that the King was a malleable man under the influence of a stronger personality, which is borne out in the portraits. The priests of Amun may have feared Nefertiti as much as they feared her husband.

From what we know of Akhenaten's subsequent actions it may be surprising that he did not use his power at the outset to promote the Aten-cult boldly in Thebes itself; after all he was the Pharaoh in command of the armed forces. He had no compunction, later, in defacing Amun's monuments and prescribing the worship of the Theban deity and all the other gods. The answer probably lies in the personalities of Tiye, Nefertiti, and possibly Amenophis III himself, if he was still alive, i.e. if the co-regency existed. They might have counselled a more diplomatic approach. In any case, once the idea had been put to him Akhenaten may have welcomed the prospect of a clean break with a city he obviously hated.

It is only possible to speculate on Nefertiti's motives. Obviously her husband worshipped her; he never tires of praising her beauty and charm on all his monuments. Most probably she loved him, but was her devotion to the Aten-cult prompted by a shared religious enthusiasm or a desire for unrestricted personal power? History does not lack examples of ambitious and beautiful women, who, without being actual rulers, enjoyed exercising power through their husbands or lovers. If this is true it would explain why, when eventually Akhenaten appeared to be seeking a compromise with Thebes, the Queen's steel-tempered will never faltered.

There are a number of reasons for thinking that this happened. The scanty clues have been obtained from the Amarna letters and from archaeological discoveries made by Pendlebury and Fairman at Akhetaten, but these have to be understood in relation to events which took place in and outside Egypt during and after Akhenaten's reign. Hindsight necessarily comes into play.

As the years pass, the pleas from the governors of Egypt's vassal-states become more and more urgent. The reason, our hindsight tells us, is the increasing power of the Hittite Empire, but it is highly unlikely that Akhenaten and his advisers realised this at first. Suppiluliumas, the Hittite King, was a cunning strategist. His armies, rolling down from their homeland in the high tableland of central Asia Minor, had defeated and engulfed the state of Mitanni which, ever since Tuthmosis III had defeated the Mitannian King, had acted as a buffer between Egypt's Syrian dependencies and any hostile threat from the north. Tushratta had been murdered and the Hittites controlled his vast territory on the Great Bend of the upper Euphrates.

Then, as in later times, the petty kings of what are now

Syria, Jordan, Israel and the Lebanon were forced to accept the protection of whichever Great Power appeared the strongest. Under Tuthmosis III, Amenophis II and Tuthmosis IV, there had been no doubt that Egypt was that power. They regularly paid tribute to Egypt, and Egyptian commissioners and garrisons helped the vassal-kings or governors to control their lands. But with the steady encroachment of the Hittites the situation was deteriorating rapidly. Far too wily to confront Egypt with an open attack Suppiluliumas had adopted a policy of subversion and infiltration, playing one petty kinglet off against another. And at the end of these local wars, whichever Canaanite or Syrian chieftain had won or lost territory, one may be sure that Suppiluliumas had gained in strength and influence.

But among the hundreds of letters which the Pharaoh's messengers brought to El Amarna, some breathe a passionate and steadfast loyalty, even when their writers are hardest-pressed and at the point of despair. Such are the letters from Ribbadi, governor of Gebal, on the coast of the Lebanon. Remains of this strategically-important city and port, later renamed Byblos, still exist. One imagines the governor as a man advanced in years, a tough old soldier who remembered better days, when 'the King's voice was for all' as he says. His enemy was one Aziru.

> Behold Aziru has fought my chiefs, and the chiefs whom I despatched to the city of Simyra he has caused to be seized in the city. Both the city Beruta (Beirut) and the city of Ziouna (Sidon) are sending ships to the city. All who are in the land of the Amorites have gathered themselves . . . I need men to save the rebellion of this land . . . Give me soldiers!

But no help was sent and Simyra fell. Ribbadi writes in sorrow and indignation to the Pharaoh:

> Grievous it is to say what he has done, the dog Aziru. Behold what has befallen the lands of the King on account of him; and he cried peace unto the land, and now behold what has befallen the city of Simyra—a station of my Lord, a fortress

... and they spoil our fortress ... ah, the cries of the place ... a violent man and a dog. ...[6]

One wonders if General Horemhab, who commanded Akhenaten's idle army, knew of this appeal and many like it. If he did know, his frustration may be imagined, for he was a capable soldier as was proved in later years. But no troops were sent, though the sea-journey to Gebal was not far. But now another rebel, Abdesherah, was threatening the Pharaoh's territory.

> March against him and smite him

Ribbadi appeals in another letter

> ... the land is the King's land, and since I have talked and you have not moved the city of Simyra has been lost. There is no money to buy horses, all is finished, we have been spoiled ... give me thirty companies of horse with chariots ... men, men ... there is none of this for me ... not a horse ...[7]

However carefully the King's ministers tried to conceal this unwelcome news, it would be bound to spread, not only in Akhetaten, but in Thebes where the humiliated priests of Amun walked in the dishonoured temple of their god. And there would be not a few voices raised in protest, voices which pointed out that in the days when Amun-Re reigned as supreme deity he had given the Pharaoh victory after victory, making his enemies see him 'as Lord of Radiance' and causing him to 'smite the Asiatics.'

We can assume this with some certainty because of what the Amun priesthood felt about Akhenaten after his death. We cannot be certain what happened to him, and to Nefertiti, during the closing years of his reign, when the shadows of defeat, disillusion and failure had begun to darken the courts of the Sun-King. Certain archaeological clues may be significant. When Pendlebury and Fairman excavated at Akhetaten they discovered that some time after year 12, in a particular building called Maruaten, Nefertiti's name had been constantly erased. In its place had been inscribed that of her eldest daughter Meritaten. We also know that this daughter was married to the boy Smenkhkare, who later became a short-lived Pharaoh.

In the ruins of the Northern Palace the archaeologists found the name of Nefertiti, associated not with that of her husband but with Smenkhkare's brother Tutankhaten. This may seem slight evidence on which to base a theory, but it is practically all we have, and it has been suggested, I think with reason, that at this period Akhenaten and Nefertiti were estranged, each living in a separate palace. The cause of the rift is unknown, but only a cataclysmic clash of wills could have parted two individuals so obviously devoted to each other. We do know, however, that near the end of Akhenaten's reign the boy Smenkhkare returned to Thebes and became Pharaoh; possibly he reigned for a time as co-regent, just as Akhenaten may have been co-regent with Amenophis III. There are several indications that Smenkhkare had replaced Nefertiti in Akhenaten's affections. One is the fact that the boy's name is shown on inscriptions of this period with the *nomen* 'Nefernefruaten—beloved of Wa'enre.' 'Nefernefruaten' had always been borne by Nefertiti when she was in favour. 'Wa'enre' is a standing epithet of Akhenaten. Even more remarkable is a stela which shows two kings seated together under the sun-disk. Although the cartouches contain no hieroglyphs they cannot be other than Akhenaten and Smenkhkare, says Gardiner; but the pose in which they are depicted is so intimately affectionate that some Egyptologists think it indicates a homosexual relationship.

Here again one must be on one's guard. Looked at in modern, secular terms the inference would be obvious. Akhenaten had fallen in love with his young half-brother and had been rejected by Nefertiti. But as Madame Desroches-Noblecourt points out, the ideal of the royal couple, always shown together, touched by the Aten's rays, was an essential part of the Amarna theology. 'The two principles (male and female) were inextricably bound to each other and neither could alone ensure the eternal cycle of Egypt's life.'

Therefore, this scholar argues, in substituting Smenkhkare for Nefertiti, even though the former was male,

> Akhenaten was simply carrying to the extreme his pursuit of a dream-ideal, and insisting upon perpetuating this symbol of life passing from the Aten to the double-principle of the couple.[8]

There is another faint clue in support of this theory. The body of a young man found in a Theban tomb and believed to be that of Smenkhkare was arranged in its coffin in a way normally reserved for women, with one arm at the side and the other across the breast.

> It would not be too daring to suggest that the young co-regent's limbs were so arranged in death to eternalize the symbolic role that Akhenaten, in his mystic folly, had wished him to play.[9]

We may never know whether this strange attachment, amorous, spiritual, or both, was the cause or the result of the King's estrangement from Nefertiti. My own opinion is that the cause was less personal than political, or politico-religious. Either, as some believe, Nefertiti had decided that Egypt must return to the old faith whereas Akhenaten would not, or Akhenaten was weakening while the Queen remained firmly attached to Atenism. On balance I think the latter is more likely to be true. We know that, after a period of living in close association with Akhenaten, Smenkhkare returned to Thebes and reigned for a short time as Pharaoh. Gardiner suggests that he did this after Akhenaten's death, others that he reigned for a time as co-regent in Thebes while the older king remained at Akhetaten. His right to the throne would be based on his marriage to the King's eldest daughter, Meritaten.

Tutankhaten, on the other hand, was evidently Nefertiti's protégé, living with her at the Northern Palace, and married to her third daughter Ankh-es-en-pa-aten. (Meketaten, the second daughter, it will be remembered, had died young.) From objects found in his tomb it is evident that Tutankhaten, later called Tutankhamun, had been brought up as an Atenist. Whoever the renegade was, Akhenaten or Nefertiti, the overall picture is dramatic. For this was not merely the end of a short-lived 'exercise in theology' (vide Pendlebury) nor even, as some idealists have suggested, the end of a noble attempt to introduce a purer religion to a people who were not ready for it. What we are watching at El Amarna are the death-throes of the Eighteenth Dynasty.

Far to the south the Tuthmosid warrior-Pharaohs sleep in their still unrifled tombs, surrounded by their glittering funerary equipment. Tuthmosis III, the scourge of the Asiatics, is there, not far from the tomb of his father Tuthmosis II. Amenophis II, who could shoot an arrow through seven copper plates, lies in his silent tomb, his great bow beside him in his sarcophagus. And on the western side of the cliffs which guard the Royal Valley, in hope of eternal life, lie the mummified bodies of the soldiers, sailors, and great officers of state who served these Pharaohs: Rekhmire, the great Vizier of Tuthmosis III, receiving, on the painted walls of his funerary chapel

the tribute of the foreign lands;

Ahmose of El Kab who

sailed the King . . . triumphant, when he ascended the river . . . in order to cast out violence in the highlands . . . I showed bravery in his presence in the bad water, in the passage of the ship by the bend;

and the old warrior Amenemhab, comrade-in-arms of Tuthmosis III at the siege of Kadesh

. . . His majesty sent forth every valiant man of his army, in order to breach the wall for the first time . . . I was the one that pierced it, being the first of all the valiant. I went forth . . . I brought back lords as living prisoners.[10]

But the mighty men who made Egypt great now lie in eternal silence beneath the hills of western Thebes. The proud capital they knew is a city of memories; the great gods they worshipped receive no sacrifice, and even their sacred names have been defaced. If the ghosts of the Tuthmosids and their followers ever left their tombs and crossed the river 'at the time of the cool north wind' they would find the splendour of Thebes dimmed. Few men walked its streets, or crossed the sunlit courtyards of its royal palace; they would listen in vain for the rattle of war-chariots and the tramp of soldiers. Here and there, in the neglected temples, they might perhaps overhear murmurs of discontent, rumours and plotting. The very stillness vibrated with a sense of dread and omen.

In Akhetaten, as the sun-god kissed the eastern cliffs, the chanting of priests floated across the eight-mile length of the city, across the villas of Panhesy, of Huya, of Ay and the other courtiers who were now the custodians of Egypt's greatness. In his many-pillared palace, surrounded by gardens bright with flowers, the fifty-year-old Pharaoh, sick in mind and body, talked listlessly to the youth who would soon become Pharaoh. Miles to the north, in her own splendid palace, Nefertiti, no longer young but still beautiful, watched and waited, guarding the next heir to the throne, the child Tutankhaten.

And hundreds of miles away, where the hills of the Lebanon loomed dark against the sunset, Ribbadi, now a hunted refugee, dictated his last letter to the Pharaoh, his lord.

Ribbadi to the king, my Lord, at thy feet seven times I bow . . . Lo, it is not granted to my sons to take root of me, as the prophets have perceived of old. Behold my brother has commanded, he went out as my deputy. It is of no use, the soldiers of the garrison failed with him, and so the evil is done, and they made me flee from the city. It is not defended from the enemy. . . .

Behold the city of Gebal was a city truly like our eye; there was plenty of all that was royal in her midst. The servants of the chief city were at peace, the chiefs were our well-wishers when the King's voice was for all . . . It is the chief city of the

land they have wasted for me. But the King my Lord will protect me, and restore me to the chief city, and to my house as
of old.

O King my Lord, O King my Lord, save the city from
shame. . . .[11]

---

[1] Breasted, J. H., *A History of Egypt,* Charles Scribner's Sons, New York,
1921

[2] Erman and Blackman, *Literature of the Ancient Egyptians,* University Books, Inc., New Hyde Park, New York, 1964

[3] Gardiner, Sir Alan, *Egypt of the Pharaohs,* Oxford University Press,
New York, 1961

[4] Pritchard, J. B. (ed.), *Ancient Near Eastern Texts,* Princeton University Press, 1958

[5] Pritchard, J. B., op. cit.

[6] Weigall, Arthur, *The Life and Times of Akhenaten,* G. P. Putnam's
Sons, New York, 1923

[7] Weigall, Arthur, op. cit.

[8] Desroches-Noblecourt, C., *Tutankhamen,* New York Graphic Society,
Greenwich, Conn., 1963

[9] Desroches-Noblecourt, C., op. cit.

[10] Breasted, J. H., *Ancient Records of Egypt,* Volume II, Chicago University Press, 1906-07; 1927

[11] Weigall, Arthur, op. cit.

11

The So-Called Tomb of Tiye

THE END OF THE 'AMARNA PERIOD' IS, IF ANYTHING, EVEN MORE obscure than its beginning. It is undoubtedly one of the most absorbing periods of Egyptian history which has aroused, and continues to arouse, deep controversy.

The detailed and exhaustive excavations carried out at El Amarna by J. D. S. Pendlebury and his assistants between 1926–7 and 1931–6 were not published until 1951. Even allowing for the interruption caused by the Second World War, and Pendlebury's tragic death, this is a good example of how long it takes to produce the detailed, comprehensive, scientific publication of a site. The amateur, wandering in amazed admiration through the three big volumes of *The City of Akhenaten* and frequently lost in a mass of necessary technical detail, occasionally finds precious nuggets of information which have an instant human appeal. For instance, in his description of what he calls 'The Royal Estate,' Pendlebury makes this comment on a suite of rooms unearthed in the King's House:

The south side of this court is occupied by a small block of buildings along the south and west side of which run corridors. At the west end of the block are two sets of three bedrooms, the niche at the back in which the bed itself was set being remarkably shallow, only 1 metre. To the east the building is divided into two, the northern half consisting of a room with two closets opening off it, the southern half of a room within the main room. The mud floor and what was left of the mud-plastered walls of this small room were covered with streaks of paint, yellow, red, blue, green, black, where people had wiped their brushes. Indeed the very brushes and other paraphernalia of painting were found here. It is hard to resist the conclusion that these were the quarters of the six princesses with their night-nurseries and their playroom.[1]

Any parent who finds it difficult to envisage Nefertiti's domestic way of life may at least find a point of contact here.

In the same block Pendlebury located 'a little suite of rooms which formed the bedroom, bathroom and latrine of the King himself.' He writes:

It consisted of two main rooms, there being two L-shaped screen walls within the door of each. . . . The western of the two main rooms is divided into two small closets at the south end, in both of which are screen walls. A bath slab of stone with a stone basin to catch the water survives in one. Probably a latrine seat was in the other. In the eastern room there is an inner chamber at the south end. It was in the antechamber to this inner room that the famous fresco of the princesses was found by Petrie. Many fragments belonging to this or to a similar scene were found by us among the debris. Most important were a fragment showing the front of the Queen's face. . . .[2]

I cannot resist quoting two more brief extracts from Pendlebury's description, if only to demonstrate the enthusiasm and imagination—as well as scholarly observation—which were typical of his work. Writing of the Police Barracks he describes the parade ground, with mangers and tethering-stones on each side, the trough for watering the horses, and the stables with cobbled floors, and then comments:

> Thus a 'flying squad' could be kept in perpetual readiness for an emergency . . . (the barracks) lie at the extreme edge of the city commanding an admirable view of the whole plain so that any criminal making a break for the High Desert would quickly be spotted. Furthermore, as we can say from personal experience, the surface of the desert hereabouts offers an admirable ground for galloping, so that if a disturbance should break out in any part of the city it would be possible to reach the point nearest to it very quickly before turning in to traverse the narrow winding lanes.[3]

And of the main highway through the city along which Akhenaten and Nefertiti drove in their chariot with their daughters, the archaeologist has this to say:

> The main thoroughfare was the *Sikket es-Sultan* as it is called today. This highway—its name is translated 'Royal Road' . . . . is still in use, particularly for droves of camels brought down from the Sudan to Cairo, legitimately brought that is, for stolen camels still use the *Darb el-Harami* or Robbers' Gorge some fifteen or twenty miles up in the high desert which comes out opposite Minia.

The unique fascination of Egyptology is the continuity of past and present, which Pendlebury obviously felt. After his description of the Police Barracks with their mangers and tethering-stones he writes:

> The season after the excavation of this building a member of the staff taking a walk towards the High Desert suddenly noticed, about half a mile to the east, a neat row of mangers similar to those described . . . complete with tethering stones. This had clearly not been the scene of a casual excavation by the villagers. It was too tidy and there was no dump of sand. Eventually it appeared that a troop of the Frontier Camel

Patrol had stopped here for some days during the previous summer and had unwittingly made an encampment of a nature precisely similar to, though simpler than, that of their predecessors over 3,000 years before.[4]

Alas, the remains of the Northern Palace provided very scanty information about the Queen who is believed to have spent her latter years here. There were, however, objects bearing the cartouches of Nefertiti and Tutankhaten, just as others found in the later part of Akhenaten's palace bore his cartouche with that of Smenkhkare. Another interesting clue was the fact that in a number of cases the doors of public and private buildings had been bricked up. We know that after Akhenaten's death in year 17 of his reign his followers left the city and returned to Thebes, though probably not immediately, nor all at once. If they had intended to leave permanently they would obviously have taken their furniture and other possessions with them, in which case it would have been pointless to seal the doors. The fact that they did this suggests that, at the time of their departure, they were still uncertain about the future of Akhetaten.

This, then, demolishes the theory that following the death of the Pharaoh there was an immediate reaction against Atenism, and a hurried evacuation of the capital. The process must have been much more gradual. Yet the great city which Akhenaten had built with such high hopes less than twenty years before must have been gradually deserted over a comparatively short period. There is no evidence that any of the noble tombs were ever occupied; indeed a number were never finished, and to this day one can see half-excavated columns and walls on which the designs have been merely drawn in ink on plaster, but never sculpted in relief.

The great family tomb which Akhenaten built high up in a lonely wadi to the east may or may not have received his body and that of his Queen; there is insufficient evidence to support either belief. Nor is it known when or how Nefertiti died. We hear nothing more of her after Akhenaten's death, nor has her body ever been found. Pendlebury comments:

No objects which must have come from her burial were found in the Royal Tomb. The only clue we have is that in the 'eighties of the last century a body of men was seen marching down from the high desert with a golden coffin, and shortly afterwards appeared golden objects bearing her name, whether genuine or faked it is hard to say. That is a well-known story and is told of almost every site in Egypt; but, true or false, the possibility remains that someone one day will gaze into the sepulchre of that great and unhappy lady.[5]

In the Cairo Museum are the shattered remains of four granite sarcophagi which once stood in Akhenaten's tomb; and Pendlebury, when he excavated there, came upon a few parts of the King's magnificent alabaster canopic chest in which the viscera of the mummy were normally kept. But these fragments did not contain the tell-tale stains of black resinous material which would have marked them indelibly if the chest had ever been used. The smashed sarcophagi would be the work of the traditionalists when they arrived, years later, to wreak posthumous revenge on the heretic King. But when the agents of the Amun priesthood entered the tomb to wreck its contents the body was almost certainly not there, though that of Princess Meketaten probably was.

One wonders if Akhenaten and his theologians had formulated any ideas concerning the After-Life. They must have believed in one, or they would not have encouraged the building of elaborate tombs; but Osiris, god of the dead and of resurrection, naturally never appears on the inscriptions, and even the shawabtis, wooden figures buried as 'servant-substitutes,' though of Osirid shape, are not inscribed with the familiar spell ordering the figure to work for its master or mistress in the After-Life. Nor was an image of Osiris or Isis ever found among the ruins of Akhetaten, a clear indication of the division between the Aten-cult and the most popular of all Egyptian religious myths.

But when Tutankhamun died in Thebes, he was buried with the full Osirian ritual, in an anthropoid coffin of Osirid shape, and on the wall of his burial chamber he is shown as the mummified Osiris. Yet it must have been Smenkhkare, his short-lived predecessor, who undertook the reconciliation with the older faith, since we know that he returned to Thebes, while his brother Tutankhaten remained for a time at El Amarna, probably until the death of Nefertiti.

The reconstruction of the last dying years of the Eighteenth Dynasty rests mainly on a series of discoveries made at Thebes in the early years of the present century. Following Petrie's initial excavations at El Amarna in the eighteen-nineties, there was a great wave of interest in the personalities of the Amarna period. The tomb of Amenophis III was known and his mummy had been identified, along with those of his Tuthmosid ancestors. But what had happened to Akhenaten, Nefertiti, Tiye, and the Amarna princesses? And where were the bodies of Smenkhkare and Tutankhamun?

The first decade of the twentieth century was marked by a surge of archaeological activity in the Theban Necropolis, especially in the Valley of the Kings. Wealthy amateurs such as Lord Carnarvon and the American millionaire Mr. Theodore Davis worked in collaboration with professionals such as Mr. Howard Carter and Mr. Arthur Weigall. Davis, as we have seen, was rewarded by the discovery of the tomb of Tiye's parents Yuya and Thuya, and in 1907 he and Weigall came upon an uninscribed sepulchre near the entrance to the Royal Valley which was at first acclaimed as that of Queen Tiye herself. This much-ravaged tomb, one of the smallest in the Valley, has probably aroused more scholarly conflict than all the others put together; and as this still continues in the pages of learned journals it is worthwhile summarising the successive stages of the battle, which has raged intermittently for sixty years.

First it should be realised that most of the great Pharaonic tombs of the New Kingdom had been plundered thousands of years ago. Even in Graeco-Roman times the majority of the royal tombs which tourists visit today were already show-places. Ptolemaic soldiers, Roman officials and their wives scribbled or

27. ABOVE: *Queen Tiye, wife of Amenophis III and mother of Akhenaten.* © *Lehnert and Landrock.*

28. ABOVE: *Young girls, wearing transparent gowns of fine linen, perform a ritual at the jubilee festival of Amenophis III. Kheruef, owner of the tomb, was High Steward of Queen Tiye.* © *Leonard Cottrell.*

29. ABOVE RIGHT: *Nefertiti and Akhenaten driving through the "Holy City" of Akhetaten with one of their daughters; the Aten disk with descending rays protects the royal couple. From one of the Amarna tombs.* © *Egypt Exploration Society.*

30. BELOW RIGHT: *Scene in the Royal Tomb at Amarna showing grief of the royal family over the death of Princess Meketaten. In the upper section a nurse carries a newborn child; the grieving mourners suggest the Princess died in childbirth.* © *New York Graphic Society.*

31.   ABOVE: *Queen Tiye with her husband, Amenophis III.* ©
Cairo Museum.

32. ABOVE: *Portrait head of Akhenaten.* © *F. L. Kenett.*

33. ABOVE: *Example of early "Amarna art" showing Nefertiti, Akhenaten and their daughters in grossly deformed style. Compare with Plates 20 and 32. © Staatlichen Museen zu Berlin.*

34. ABOVE: *Tomb-relief from Amarna. Nefertiti and Akhenaten (left) entertain Queen Tiye (right) at a state banquet. Two of Nefertiti's daughters are seated beside her, while Tiye passes a titbit to her own small daughter.* © *Egypt Exploration Society.*

35. BELOW: *Palette with paints and reed brushes bearing Princess Meketaten's cartouche.* © *Metropolitan Museum of Art.*

36. NEXT PAGE: *Queen Nefertiti in later life, probably in her forties.* © *Staatlichen Museen zu Berlin.*

37. ABOVE: *Portrait of a King of the Amarna Period, probably Smenkhkare.* © *F. L. Kenett.*

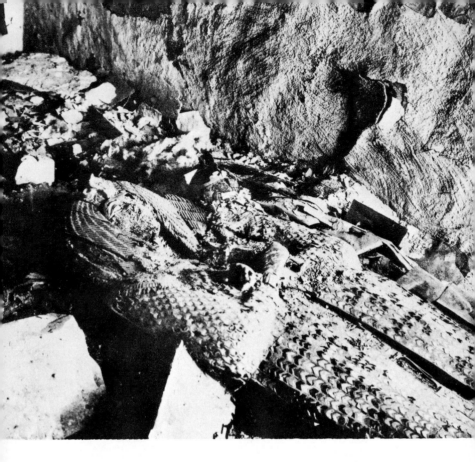

38. ABOVE: *Coffin of a royal personage as found in the so-called Tomb of Tiye. Originally made for a female member of the royal family, its inscriptions were altered to denote a man; it contained a male body, generally believed to be Smenkhkare.* © *Egypt Exploration Society.*

39. ABOVE RIGHT: *Portrait head, believed to be Princess Ankh-es-en-pa-aten (later to become Queen Ankhesnamun).* © *Metropolitan Museum of Art.*

40. ABOVE FAR RIGHT: *Lid of canopic jar representing Princess Meritaten, found in so-called Tomb of Tiye.* © *Metropolitan Museum of Art.*

41. BELOW RIGHT: *Head of Tutankhamun with royal head-dress bearing the uraeus.* © *Metropolitan Museum of Art.*

42. ABOVE: *One of the four protecting goddesses in gold-covered wood placed around the canopic chest of Tutankhamun. Although representing Isis, the features appear to be those of Queen Ankhesnamun.* © *Ashmolean Museum.*

43. RIGHT: *Queen Ankhesnamun with her husband, Tutankhamun, in the garden of their Palace. Painted ivory plaque from a coffer found in the tomb.* © *Ashmolean Museum.*

44. ABOVE LEFT: *Ay, chief minister to Akhenaten and later to Tut-ankhamun, with his wife; from their Amarna tomb.* © *Cairo Museum.*

45. BELOW LEFT: *Portrait head of Ay.* © *Metropolitan Museum of Art.*

46. ABOVE: *Ay's rival, General Horemhab, from his tomb near Memphis.* © *F. L. Kenett.*

47. NEXT PAGE: *Queen Nefertari, from her tomb in the Valley of the Queens.* © *Paul Elek Productions, Ltd.*

carved their names on the walls, sometimes accompanied by fatuous messages, such as 'I, Philaistrios, having seen these tombs of astounding horror, have spent a delightful day.'

But by a miraculous chance over thirty royal and priestly mummies, including those of some of the mightiest Pharaohs, had survived. They were found, not in the original tombs but in two secret caches where they had been reburied by the priests responsible for guarding the Necropolis, probably round about 1000 BC. One batch of royal mummies was found in a deep shaft in the cliffs just behind Hashepsowe's funerary temple; the other lay in the tomb of Amenophis II. He still lay in his original sarcophagus, but around him slept a number of royal guests, some of whom were his predecessors and others his successors on the throne of Egypt.

However, a consultation of the 'King-lists' showed that a number of Pharaohs and their Queens were missing, including —not surprisingly—Akhenaten, Queen Tiye, Smenkhkare and his wife Meritaten, and Tutankhamun and his wife Ankhesnamun. Since these had evidently not been buried at El Amarna it seemed possible that if their bodies had survived, they might yet be found in the Theban Necropolis. The excitement of Egyptologists may be imagined when Davis and Weigall, burrowing into the sand and rubble which choked the entrance to the Valley, came upon a rock-cut chamber containing the battered remains of a gilded wooden shrine bearing the name Tiye. And near it, resting on a wooden bier which had collapsed under its weight, lay a wooden coffin encased in gold and inlaid with carnelian and lapis, within which lay a mummy.

Davis confidently expected this to be that of the great Queen herself, but was disappointed when Elliot Smith, the anatomist, pronounced that the bones were those of a young man.

Then the philologists got to work, carefully copying and studying the inscriptions on the wood-and-gilt shrine, the coffin, the gold bands on the mummy, and other funerary objects found in the tomb. These proved to be extremely confusing. The shrine,

a sort of tabernacle which had been made to enclose the sarcophagus, bore inscriptions in which the name Akhenaten fig-
ured prominently. In these the King states that the shrine was
made for his mother, Queen Tiye. But this ponderous wooden
structure, from which the gold casing was peeling, was dismantled, nor was there any sarcophagus. In fact from the position
of one section, lying aslant in the entrance-passage, it appeared
that an attempt had been made to remove the shrine to some
other place, and that this attempt had had to be abandoned.

In this process it had been badly battered, but sufficient remained of the inscriptions to show Akhenaten and his mother
worshipping the Aten-disk. But close examination showed that
the cartouches had been altered, apparently twice. First the
name of Akhenaten's father, Amenophis III, had been erased,
and over it, in red ink, was that King's second name Nebmare.
This was evidently Akhenaten's work, of which many other
examples have been found. Since his father's name incorporated
that of Amun it had to be altered. But there had been further
alterations; the name of Akhenaten had been hammered out,
though it was still faintly visible. The assumption is that the
shrine was made for Queen Tiye during the early part of the
Amarna period—it was usual for royal personages to have their
funerary equipment made during their lifetimes—but that, later,
the hated name of Amun had been erased. Still later, when
Akhenaten was dead and discredited, other hands had tried to
obliterate *his* name.

But if this was Tiye's shrine and Tiye's tomb, who was the
young man lying in the coffin? A close study of the coffin, and
the golden bands on the mummy, showed that the former had
once borne the cartouches of the heretic King himself, but these
had been partially erased and the gold bands encircling
the corpse had also been mutilated. The cartouches had been
cut out. Thus a new theory began to form in the minds of the
archaeologists. Could this, perhaps, be the body of Akhenaten
himself? The facts as then understood seemed to point in this
direction. Weigall, who excavated the tomb with Davis, pro-

duced a highly plausible reconstruction of the events leading to the burial in his book *The Life and Times of Akhenaten* in 1910.

On entering the tomb, Weigall had found the remains of three separate walls sealing the approach corridor. On top of this heap of stones lay one side of the dismantled shrine. The other three sides were within the burial chamber, also dismantled, as if an attempt had been made to remove them at some time. At one side lay the coffin, which was of the *rishi* type, i.e. covered with 'feathered' ornament in gold, carnelian and lapis-lazuli, and on the foot was an inscription which Gardiner translated as follows:

> I breathe the sweet breath which comes forth from Thy mouth. I behold Thy beauty every day. It is my desire that I may hear Thy sweet voice, even the north wind, that my limbs may be rejuvenated with life through love of Thee. Give me Thy hands, holding Thy spirit, that I may receive it and may live by it. Call Thou upon my name unto eternity, and it shall never fail.[6]

This, by the way, is Gardiner's original translation published by Weigall in his book, which first appeared in 1910. Later the translation had to be modified, as we shall see.

On the brow of the coffin-lid, which was of anthropoid shape, was a bronze uraeus, but it was apparent on close examination that this did not form part of the coffin as it was originally made, but had been added. There were other puzzling features, not made easier to understand by the damage the coffin had sustained. Part of the gold mask on the coffin-lid had been ripped off and the lid itself had come loose. At some remote period flood-water had trickled into the tomb through a fissure in the rock, and the resultant dampness had rotted the legs of the wooden bier on which the coffin had rested. When these eventually collapsed—but not all at once—the coffin had tilted forward, so that the lid jerked off, and at the same time the magnificent golden pectoral (chest-ornament) had slid from its original position and was found with one claw of the sacred vulture resting in the left eye-socket of the skull. The dampness had so rotted the mummy-wrappings that the shock of the fall pulverised them, so that all that remained of the body were the skull and bones.

In a wall recess above the coffin stood the canopic jars containing the viscera, and elsewhere in the tomb the discoverers came upon certain toilet articles bearing the name Tiye. But the 'magic bricks,' which were found in the places which they normally occupied in such tombs, bore the name Akhenaten. Once Elliot Smith had established that the bones were male, Davis and Weigall concluded that the body must be that of Akhenaten; at this time it was not known that the King had lived to the age of forty-one and was about twenty-five when he came to the throne. Weigall's interpretation of the evidence may be summarised as follows:

(a) The shrine had been made for Queen Tiye, and was intended to enclose her sarcophagus and coffins. (At this period there were usually three coffins, one inside the other, as in the case of Tutankhamun.)

(b) During his lifetime Akhenaten had altered the name of his father Amenophis III to 'Nebmare' in order to erase the name of the hated god.

(c) This was Tiye's tomb; Akhenaten had first been buried at Akhetaten.

(d) Some time after the court had returned to Thebes and the old religion was re-established, certain faithful followers of the dead king had removed his body from the original tomb and placed it beside that of his mother.

(e) Still later, probably during the reign of Horemhab, when he and the Amun priesthood were determined to vilify the memory of the hated heretic, their agents entered the tomb and removed Tiye's body, probably re-interring it in the sepulchre of her husband, Amenophis III. They tried to remove the great wooden shrine but found the effort too great, so they left it in a dismantled condition. At the same time they seized the opportunity to erase Akhenaten's cartouche wherever they found it, e.g. on the shrine, on the coffin, and even on the gold bands encircling the mummy, front and back. They did not dare molest the body itself since, heretic though he had been, Akhenaten was royal and therefore sacred. But someone tore off the gold mask as loot, and hid it under his robes. Then the tomb was re-sealed, stones piled against the entrance, and the body was left in peace for 3,000 years.

On the face of it this was a highly convincing interpretation of the known facts and was widely accepted when published by Davis and Weigall. The coffin and mummy were removed to the Cairo Museum where the coffin, after some restoration, was put on display. Then, in 1916, the philologist Daressy, after carefully studying the much-damaged inscriptions, produced evidence which proved that the coffin had originally been made for a queen or princess, but later had been adapted for a man. One clue was the uraeus which, though it bore Akhenaten's name, had been fixed to a coffin not originally intended to have it, but other evidence was much more convincing. One example must suffice. In two instances where the inscription on the coffin-lid had contained the suffix pronouns for the first person singular, these had been changed from the feminine to the masculine form; from a squatting woman to a bearded god. It was as if, in modern English, the word 'her' had been altered to 'him.'

From this and other evidence Daressy concluded that the coffin had been intended for Tiye but had been 'usurped' by a king. For various reasons he could not accept Akhenaten, Davis and Weigall's candidate, but proposed Tutankhamun. At this time the latter's tomb still awaited discovery, but it was known that Tutankhamun had reigned for a very short time and had died young. In fact that is all that *was* known about him.

Six years later Tutankhamun's tomb was discovered, with the King's body lying within it, so another name had to be assigned to the lonely occupant of the 'Tomb of Tiye.' This time it was that of Tutankhamun's brother, the young Pharaoh Smenkhkare, who was also known to have died young. But there were still those who remained unconvinced. Since the name Akhenaten appeared on the coffin, and on the 'magic bricks,' it seemed certain that whoever put the body there believed it to be that of the great religious revolutionary. Could Elliot Smith have been wrong? Could the bones be those of an older man? So in 1931 Dr. Douglas Derry re-examined the bones, and was able to piece together the pieces of the damaged skull with more success than Elliot Smith had achieved. But the hopes of the 'Akhenaten' camp were dashed when Derry announced that the bones were definitely those of a young man, at most twenty-five years of age. He also stated that he could detect no signs of abnormality in the skull, nor in the pelvis which, it had been suggested, was unusually broad for a man.

Mr. Rex Engelbach, then Curator of the Cairo Museum, regarded this as conclusive justification for his own strongly-held belief that the body was that of Smenkhkare. Among the rising generation of Egyptologists Professor H. W. Fairman took the same view, on both archaeological and inscriptional grounds. The tomb was that of a ruler of the Amarna period. It was male, so it could not have been Tiye; it was too young to be that of Akhenaten; Tuthankhamun's body had been found, so the only other possible candidate was Smenkhkare. One would have thought that there the matter would be allowed to rest. And so it was; but only for twenty-six years.

In 1957 Sir Alan Gardiner, who fifty years earlier had translated the inscriptions, opened the counter-attack. In an article in the *Journal of Egyptian Archaeology* for that year, intriguingly titled 'The so-called Tomb of Tiye,' he criticised Davis's careless and inadequate publication of the find, threw serious doubts on Weigall's interpretation of the evidence, and started a number of hares. On the subject of the tomb's owner he was noncommittal, saying of Elliot Smith and Derry, 'it is

not for a mere philologist to arbitrate between two such distinguished physiologists.'

> None the less [he continues] the absence of the name of
> Smenkhkare from any of the furniture in the tomb would be
> extremely strange. There is only one exception, a fragment of
> gold bearing the words 'beloved of Wa-en-re,' i.e. of Akhenaten,
> these words being an integral part of the nomen of Smenkh-
> kare as found in a box in the tomb of Tutankhamun.[7]

Anyone familiar with Sir Alan's method of approach
would know immediately that this was merely gentle sparring.
The heavy blows, one senses, will follow later. And they do,
one after the other. By the time one has read the article, Weigall's
plausible reconstruction of the tomb's history is in the same state
of disintegration as the monument itself. Not only that, but one
begins to wonder if, after all, the question of the coffin's occupant
is still not settled.

As a philologist, Gardiner's main concern is with the inscriptions, particularly those on the foot end of the coffin. These,
he points out, occupy the place which, on earlier and later
coffins, was always used for a recitation by the goddess Isis in
which she welcomes the dead man and assures him of her protection. But in this case, as the coffin was intended to be occupied by Akhenaten, obviously the goddess could have no place
on it.

Gardiner then asks,

> Who was the royal lady that in the time of Akhenaten
> (for it is clearly he who is addressed) stood to him in the same
> relation as Isis to her brother and husband Osiris? The answer
> must of course be: his spouse Nefertiti.

Although the cartouche had been cut out Gardiner states
that

> I am personally convinced that it was she who is here pre-
> sented as voicing her hope to enjoy her husband's company in

the hereafter. An additional reason for holding this view is that —unless I am mistaken—Nefertiti was the sole female relative of Akhenaten who ever fell into such disfavour that her name was erased.[8]

Bearing this in mind, the prayer which Weigall thought was that of the Pharaoh to his god now becomes that of Nefertiti to her husband, and is all the more moving, especially in the new translation which Gardiner prints in his article:

> Recitation by (Queen Nefertiti) I shall breathe the sweet breath that comes forth from thy mouth, and shall behold thy beauty daily. (My) prayer is that (I) may hear thy sweet voices of the north wind, that my flesh may grow young with life through thy love, that thou mayst give me thy hands bearing thy spirit, and I receive it and live by it, and that thou mayst call upon my name eternally, and it shall not fail from thy mouth (my beloved) brother, thou being with me to all eternity, living like the (living) Aten . . .[9]

'Clearly,' Gardiner continued, 'we have here no empty formula, but the expression of a wish the fulfilment of which Akhenaten had indeed himself planned,' and goes on to mention the king's intention, expressed on his boundary stela, to be buried, with his wife and family, in his tomb near Akhetaten.

But, as Daressy had observed, the feminine first person suffixes in this inscription had been changed to masculines, and the only male who might hope to dwell beside Akhenaten for eternity was Smenkhkare, after the latter replaced Nefertiti in the King's affections. So here again, on this damaged, mutilated coffin, the inscriptions appear to confirm the tragic estrangement of Akhenaten from his Queen.

Gardiner had no doubt that, whichever body it contained, the coffin had been *intended* for Akhenaten, and whoever placed the body in the tomb believed it to be his; he cites as proof of this the 'magic bricks' bearing his name, intended as a protection against evil spirits. But he rejects Weigall's theory that the tomb was originally that of Tiye. His theory, briefly summarised, is that certain devoted followers of the Pharaoh had preserved his body from the destructive fury of those who wrecked his family tomb at El Amarna; that later, perhaps during the reign of Tutankhamun, it was decided to bring it back to Thebes and bury it in a small sepulchre, probably already excavated for someone else. Searching around among the stores of funerary equipment they found the shrine which Akhenaten had made for his mother's burial, and a coffin, perhaps the middle one of a nest of three, which had been made for one of the princesses, perhaps Meritaten, but adapted for the King.

But, in the haste and confusion (and perhaps the need for secrecy) the job was mishandled. First, they got hold of the wrong mummy. Then, when they came to erect the shrine there was insufficient room to assemble it in the short time available. All they could do was to place the royal coffin on its bier, hurriedly put a few ritual objects in position, including the magic bricks, place the canopic jars in the niche (and even these had ill-fitting stoppers carved with a head which may be that of Meritaten), seal the tomb and leave.

Later, Gardiner suggests, the tomb was re-entered by the agents of Horemhab, who cut out the cartouches of the King wherever they appeared on the coffin, and hammered out those on the shrine. But whoever these intruders were they were not robbers, who would have stripped the gold from the shrine and the mummy and taken the gold pectoral which was found lying on it. If the tomb had been intended for Tiye it would surely have contained her sarcophagus and other funerary furniture. But nothing was found belonging to the Queen save a few toilet articles.

> It must be remembered [adds Gardiner] that Queen Tiye never suffered from the hatred incurred by her son. If the tomb had belonged to her, it is incredible that it should ever have been depleted in so ruthless a manner.[10]

As for the still-unknown original occupant of the coffin, it may be, as Gardiner suggests, that the agents of Horemhab found and destroyed the mummy, substituting that of Smenkh-kare, though this seems unlikely. Gardiner admits that his theory is a makeshift one, and much of the mystery remains. But once having reopened the controversy, Sir Alan was quickly followed by other scholars, notably Professor Fairman and Mr. Cyril Aldred, who hastened to put forth their own views.

[1] Pendlebury, J. D. S., *The City of Akhetaten,* Part III, Egypt Exploration Society, 1951

[2] Pendlebury, J. D. S., op. cit.

[3] Pendlebury, J. D. S., op. cit.

[4] Pendlebury, J. D. S., op. cit.

[5] Pendlebury, J. D. S., *Tell el Amarna,* Lovat Dickson and Thompson, 1935

[6] Weigall, A., *The Life and Times of Akhenaten,* G. P. Putnam's Sons, New York, 1923

[7] Gardiner, Sir Alan, *Journal of Egyptian Archaeology,* Volume 43, December 1957

[8] Gardiner, Sir Alan, op. cit.

[9] Gardiner, Sir Alan, op. cit.

[10] Gardiner, Sir Alan, op. cit.

12

Whose Body?

THE SEARCH FOR FACTS CONCERNING EGYPT'S QUEENS LEADS one along some difficult and tortuous tracks. At times these can become so narrow and stony, so empty of life, that one almost forgets that one is dealing, not merely with bones and coffin-inscriptions, but with human beings. But this is the only way we can hope to get at the truth, so far as it can ever be known. Of all the great personalities of the Amarna period, the bodies of only two—Amenophis III and Tutankhamun—have been positively identified. Those of Queens Tiye, Nefertiti and Ankhesnamun have never been found. Therefore, the slightest clue which can throw light on them, even if it is only a clay jar-stopper with a reign-date, is important.

Not long after the appearance of Gardiner's article in the *Journal of Egyptian Archaeology*, two more bearing on the same subject were published in Volume 47 of that justly-esteemed journal. The first was headed *'Once again the so-called coffin of Akhenaten,'* and was by H. W. Fairman, Professor of Egyptology of Liverpool University. This was followed immediately by another titled '*The Tomb of Akhenaten at Thebes,*' by Mr. Cyril Aldred, Keeper of the Egyptian Department of the Royal Scottish National Museum and well known for his studies of the Amarna period, especially its art. Fairman concerned himself mainly with Gardiner's opinion that the inscription on the coffin-end was a prayer addressed by Nefertiti to her husband, and that when the body was placed in the coffin it was believed to be that of Akhenaten himself, on the evidence of the 'magic bricks' which Gardiner regarded as 'incontrovertible.'

Fairman, who in the period between the publication of Gardiner's article and his own had been to Cairo again and carefully re-examined both the mummy and the bricks, opposed these assumptions on philological grounds. Only a specialist in hieroglyphs could evaluate the arguments and counter-arguments expressed with such skill and learning by Gardiner and Fairman; these rest partly on conjectural restorations of the missing parts of the damaged and mutilated inscriptions. But even for the non-specialist there is excitement in watching two such agile contestants making play with the adverbs, pronouns and inflections of a long-dead language, and to feel, rippling through the smooth flow of learned prose, the sharp thrust and parry of scholarly debate.

Fairman strongly denies Gardiner's assumption that:

> because 'at the foot end of the sarcophagi of the Eighteenth Dynasty Pharaohs it is regularly Isis who speaks' it therefore follows that the speaker in line 1 of our text must have been Nefertiti, who impersonated Isis and was addressing Akhenaten as Osiris. It is also evident that this same idea is still basic to Gardiner's latest, modified approach to the interpretation of the coffin and its texts. A moment's reflection will demonstrate that this is pure assumption for which no adequate proof has been adduced. It is no proof to argue that, because the foot-end of Tutankhamun's gold coffin shows that he followed the old beliefs and practices, it automatically follows that Akhenaten,

or for that matter any other Aten-worshipper in the high Aten
Period, still adhered to the old funerary ways. It must first be
proved that for Akhenaten and his followers the old attitude to
death, to funerary practices, and to the After-Life was substan-
tially unaltered. There is in fact no evidence that this was so.
During the Amarna Period, Osiris and Isis and their cycle share
the same fate as all the other gods of Egypt, and their names,
and any references to the beliefs associated with them, either
disappear or are simply not mentioned. It seems extraordinary
in the actual circumstances that either Akhenaten or Nefertiti
should ever either overtly or implicitly impersonate Osiris, Isis
or any of the old gods.[1]

Fairman then goes on to suggest that the coffin was made
for Akhenaten's daughter, Meritaten, and that the prayer was
addressed by her to the Aten.

It will be realised [he writes] that the trend of the preceding argument is to demonstrate that the internal philological
evidence of the inscriptions on the coffin, combined with our
present knowledge of Amarna beliefs and practices, proves that
at no stage in its history could the coffin have been used for
Akhenaten.[2]

He then attacks Gardiner's opinion that the 'magic bricks'
provide 'incontrovertible evidence' that this was the heretic Pharaoh's tomb, on the grounds (a) that although one brick bore
Akhenaten's name, in its early form, there is no proof that the
others were so inscribed, as the hieroglyphs were too badly worn
or damaged to be recognisable; (b) that there is no proof that
magical bricks were used at the end of the Amarna Period, and
(c) that each brick, immediately before the name of the King,
bears the word Osiris, which Akhenaten would not have coun-
tenanced.

The conclusion is inescapable that the bricks cannot have
been part of the actual burial equipment of Akhenaten. I suggest that they formed part of the equipment being prepared at

Thebes at the beginning of the reign, and left behind and discarded when Akhenaten moved to El Amarna because they were no longer in accord with the new ideas.[3]

Summing up, Fairman concludes that the coffin was made for Meritaten, who was probably buried in it. Later, when Tutankhamun died after a short reign, his successor Ay appropriated some of the funerary furniture of Smenkhkare for Tutankhamun's tomb.

As a consequence [he continues] it was necessary to make a semblance of a decent burial for Smenkhkare, who, it may be suggested, was removed to a convenient but small tomb, put in a coffin made for Meritaten his wife, after the necessary inscriptional changes had been made, in parts hastily and clumsily, and without much care or attention to logic, and equipped with a small and makeshift collection of miscellaneous objects of various royal persons that happened to lie more or less conveniently to hand.[4]

One of the flaws in this argument appears to be this. If, as Fairman suggests, Smenkhkare's body had to be accommodated in his wife's coffin in order to provide funerary furniture for Tutankhamun (and it is known that some of his equipment was originally Smenkhkare's from the altered cartouches), then one of Tutankhamun's coffins must also have been Smenkhkare's; otherwise why the necessity for burying the latter in a coffin not his own? But there is no evidence which suggests that any of Tutankhamun's coffins had been usurped, though the 'coffinettes' containing the royal viscera certainly were.

The article ends with a strong suggestion that the only way to settle the argument concerning the identity of the body in the 'so-called tomb of Tiye' was to submit the bones to 'a new and exhaustive anatomical and pathological examination, using anthropometric and radiographic techniques.' Fairman concludes with the words:

... neither Elliot Smith nor Derry has ever reported hav-

ing observed a single one of the peculiarities that would undoubtedly be present if the remains were those of Akhenaten
and if he had really suffered from one or other of the endocrine,
pituitary, or other disorders which modern speculation has
inflicted on him. After fifty-four years of speculation and worse
can we not for the time being be prepared to accept the simple
facts? Philological evidence, the evidence of age, and the absence of any reported strange disorder, suggest that, as far as our
present knowledge goes, the body cannot be that of Akhenaten.[5]

It may well be asked what have these speculations to do
with Nefertiti? The answer is a great deal. For if it could be
proved that her husband had suffered from the endocrine abnormalities which his statues suggest, and which might be
proved if his body were found, it is highly unlikely that all her
six children, so ostensibly displayed on the monuments, were
his.

Mr. Cyril Aldred, who enters the ring on the page following
the end of Professor Fairman's article, throws doubt on the
belief that the body is that of Smenkhkare, and, with the support
of medical opinion, argues that it could, after all, be that of the
heretic Pharaoh. Had Davis and Weigall been right after all?
And was Gardiner, though he did not commit himself, also
coming round to the same opinion? In order to avoid too long
an exposition it is as well to state that Mr. Aldred, like all Egyptologists, had formed a theory and was then trying to see if the
known facts fitted it. His theory, briefly stated, is that the body
was that of Akhenaten, as Davis and Weigall had believed; that
the discrepancy between the minimum age of the king (as indicated by the inscriptions) and the apparent age of the skeleton
might be resolved if it could be proved that Akhenaten had
suffered from a disease which would have inhibited the normal
development of the bones. If the Pharaoh had suffered from
such a disease, his bones, though appearing to be those of a man
of twenty-three or twenty-five, could have been those of an older
man.

Much of his article is taken up with philological and archaeological discussion which, though interesting to specialists, cannot be adequately summarised. Drawing on his vast knowledge of Amarna art and customs, he points out that the coffin could not, in its original form, have been intended for a man, since its decoration, especially the presence of an 'imbricated shawl' around the chest, is typical of coffins made for royal female personages of the period, but not kings. He points out, also, that the wig worn by the head carved on the stoppers of the canopic jars exhibits the 'Nubian cut' favoured by ladies of the Amarna period; he noticed that the space for the royal uraeus had been cut into the striations of the wig after the jar had been made, and that the original inscriptions on each jar had been erased.

Yet great care had been taken to alter the style and inscriptions to make the coffin suitable for a king; there was the bronze uraeus fixed to the brow, the vulture-pectoral worn only by kings of this period, and though the texts on the coffin-ends and on the lid had been hastily and inaccurately changed, by cutting out certain hieroglyphs and inserting others on fragments of gold leaf the intention clearly had been to make them apply to a male member of the royal family. But was this King Akhenaten or Smenkhkare?

Aldred believed it was Akhenaten. The principal archaeological evidence he produces is that already mentioned by Gardiner, the presence of the four 'magic bricks,' two of which bore the name of the heretic king.

Despite the two different sizes and qualities of bricks, and their lack of amulets, they do form a complete set, each one having a different orientation. This and the way they had been distributed around the chamber shows that when first installed they had been regarded as fully effective for their function of protecting the deceased from intruders. In view of their cheap nature and ready manufacture it is exceedingly improbable that one king's bricks would have been utilised for the burial of another, or would have been regarded as effective for that purpose without changing the name.[6]

But Aldred's main argument, developed at considerable length, concerned the skeleton itself. He had not seen it, of course; it is doubtful if anyone had paid much attention to the bones since Dr. Derry had examined them a quarter of a century earlier, after which they had been locked away in the storerooms of the Cairo Museum. But as an artist and art historian with special knowledge of the Amarna period, Aldred had become intrigued, as so many have, by the peculiar physique and physiognomy of Akhenaten, as revealed in his many statues. If it could be proved that the King had suffered from some abnormality, as Elliot Smith and other anatomists had suggested, this would explain a number of puzzling features, e.g. the pronounced feminine characteristics, wide hips, protuberant belly, heavy thighs and prominent breasts. If these abnormalities were the result of a disease which also produced a progressive mental aberration, this would go far to explain why, at the end, Akhenaten failed and his followers abandoned him. Perhaps this was why 'the god had failed.'

Aldred enlisted the aid of a distinguished physician, Dr. A. T. Sandison, Senior Lecturer in the University of Glasgow and Honorary Consultant Pathologist to the Western Infirmary, Glasgow, who was asked:

(a) if the monuments, especially the Karnak colossi, show that Akhenaten was abnormal, and if so, what was the probable nature of the disease; (b) if the skeletal remains, as examined and described by Elliot Smith and Derry, show that the subject was likely to be abnormal, and if so, what was the probable nature of the disease; and (c) if the answers to the questions (a) and (b) could be reconciled.[7]

Dr. Sandison published his report in an Appendix to Aldred's article, and the gist of it was that 'Akhenaten suffered from an endocrine abnormality, and pending fuller publication,

the evidence of the skeletal remains found in Tomb 55 tend to
be compatible with this diagnosis.' Aldred adds the significant
note:

> In the past, one of the difficulties in the way of a more
> precise identification of Akhenaten's pathology, both from the
> bones believed to be his and from the extravagant representa-
> tions at Karnak and El Amarna, has been the impossibility of
> his being an endocrinopath and also the father of at least six
> daughters. This is, however, a contradiction which will have to
> be faced unflinchingly, and should it ever be proved that he
> suffered from a chronic endocrine disorder, some other candidate
> will have to be sought as the father of Nefertiti's children.[8]

At this point I must emphasise that, at the time of writing,
this point has most definitely *not* been proved, and, pending a
full report on the re-examination of the bones (which has recently taken place), there is no anatomical evidence to prove
that the skeleton found in Tomb 55 (formerly known as the
'Tomb of Tiye') is that of Akhenaten. Fairman, as we have seen,
strongly denies it, and the late Sir Alan Gardiner in his *Egypt
of the Pharaohs* states that 'this aspect of the problem must remain undecided.'

Meanwhile it is worth while to consider Dr. Sandison's
comments. Writing of the Karnak colossi he remarks on the:

> elongated face . . . prominent prognathous jaw (pro-
> geniac), large full lips, coarse nose, large ears, and rather oblique
> eyes [which, he states] strongly suggest that Akhenaten was the
> subject of endocrine disease, [especially when seen in association
> with the trunk and limbs]. The most striking feature is the
> width of the pelvis and prominence of buttocks and thighs. The
> abdomen is somewhat protuberant with a transverse umbilicus.
> The breast regions are full, although the clavicles are well de-
> fined. . . . The changes in the trunk and limbs must be regarded
> as *feminization* and might result from a feminizing adrenal
> tumour or some form of hypogonadal eunuchoidism.[9]

A most significant part of Dr. Sandison's report concerns the 'delayed union of the *epiphyses*' (our italics). The epiphyses are the expanded ends of the bones, and unlike the shafts, which are of compact bone, usually include a vaulted structure of spongy or cancellous bone with a thin cortex or outer layer of compact bone. In normal human beings the epiphyses have become united by the middle twenties at latest, in exceptional cases in the thirties, and this is one way by which an anatomist can estimate a skeleton's age at death. But, says Dr. Sandison, 'in true eunuchoidism . . . delayed union of the epiphyses is invariable; open epiphyses have been noted in an 80-year-old eunuch.'

Later in his report Dr. Sandison adds this comment:

> There is a syndrome characterized by failure of normal maturation of the gonads and by adiposity; this is due to a primary hypothalamic, hypothalamic-pituitary, or pituitary lesion. . . . The Syndrome is variously named the Frölich syndrome, the Babinski-Frölich syndrome, or the adiposogenital dystrophy of Bartels. The changes in the trunk and limbs noted in the Akhenaten monuments fit well with those occurring in this syndrome.

Recalling the Karnak colossus which shows the King apparently without genitalia the Doctor observes that

> in this syndrome the penis and testes remain of childish size . . . The penis may be embedded in accumulations of fat of such an extent that the genital appearance approximates to that of the female . . . Sterility is inevitable . . . patients have periods of introspection and depression alternating with euphoria and good spirits; patients are popular and companionable, may be musical and imaginative, while intellectual ability may often be above average.

His comments on Elliot Smith's report are naturally guarded, but he remarks that:

> the evidence of epiphyseal union led Elliot Smith to place

the age of the individual at above 25-26 years, possibly with some little variation in either direction. It seems unlikely that this will be significantly revised using the criteria given in recent texts. If, however, the individual suffered from hypogonadism, secondary to dyspituitarism, the age so derived would be quite fallacious; the remains might well be those of a man in the fourth decade of life. Such an individual would necessarily be sterile.

But he adds:

One consequence must receive consideration, however, and that is the virtual certainty that Akhenaten was incapable of procreation at the time of death and for many years previously. It is not inconceivable, however, that during an earlier period of hyperpituitarism, e.g. shortly after puberty, his potency and fertility might not have been grossly impaired.[10]

It will be seen how important these speculations are in any attempted reconstruction of the Amarna period, and especially in understanding the relationship between Akhenaten, Nefertiti and the royal children. Since Aldred's article was published, Professor Fairman was able to have the skeleton examined by a team of British and Egyptian anatomists and radiologists. They concluded that the skeleton was a male of nineteen or twenty, with no abnormalities of the cranium, with a normal mandible, and with no feminine characteristics of the pelvis, which, Fairman commented in a letter to the present author, was 'almost aggressively male.'

So the mystery remains unsolved. But even if it transpires that the body in Tomb 55 is not that of Akhenaten, this will prove only that those who placed the mummy in its coffin, and those who subsequently altered or mutilated the inscriptions on it, were mistaken in believing it to be his body. Then, it seems to me, the question of how the tomb arrived at the state in which Davis and Weigall found it, whether or not Tiye was ever buried in it, will be only of minor interest.

The question will remain: did the Pharaoh suffer from a

disease which, from a study of the statues, Dr. Sandison suggests may have produced feminine characteristics and prevented him from fathering children, at least in later years? Who, then, was the father of the children born to Nefertiti in his later life? One looks again, reflectively, at the portrait of Amenophis III in his declining years, a wreck of a man, admittedly, but apparently still capable of fathering Smenkhkare and Tutankhamun. Whatever his deficiencies, one suspects that impotence was not one of them.

Even more important is the question of whether Akhenaten's mental state, in the latter years of his reign, was the reason why the revolutionary religious cult which he inspired failed in the end to hold even the sophisticated few who appear at first to have supported it. When it became apparent their king was not truly god-inspired, but a mental cripple, there need not necessarily have been an immediate, violent revolution. Perhaps, at first, as Aldred suggests, there was a relatively peaceful accommodation with the Amun priesthood, effected by Ay, Horemhab and other former adherents to the great heretic, since Smenkhkare, a short-lived youth, could have had little influence, and his successor Tutankhamun was probably about nine years old when he came to the throne.

Then, when the court finally abandoned Akhetaten, a few devoted Atenists may have brought the bodies of Tiye, Meketaten and others back to the ancestral capital, and, hastily providing them with funerary furniture collected from the Necropolis workshops and store-rooms, quietly and privately interred them in several places, one of which was the much-debated 'Tomb of Tiye.' Then, years later, when Horemhab was Pharaoh, the full reaction set in. Akhenaten became 'that criminal' (according to the inscriptions). The agents of Horemhab and his successor Ramesses I ruthlessly destroyed what was left of the 'holy city,' sealing the accursed temple of the Aten under a layer of cement, wrecking the royal tomb, and defacing the name and figure of Akhenaten wherever they found it. Then, breaking into Tiye's tomb at Thebes (if it was hers) they removed her body, perhaps to lay it in her husband's sepulchre in the Royal Valley and, after mutilating the inscription on the coffin which they believed to be that of Akhenaten, left it in silence and darkness for 3,000 years.

---

[1] Fairman, H. W., *Journal of Egyptian Archaeology,* Volume 47, 1961
[2] Fairman, H. W., op. cit.
[3] Fairman, H. W., op. cit.
[4] Fairman, H. W., op. cit.
[5] Fairman, H. W., op. cit.
[6] Aldred, C., *Journal of Egyptian Archaeology,* Volume 47, 1961
[7] Aldred, C., op. cit.
[8] Aldred, C., op. cit.
[9] Sandison, A. T., *Journal of Egyptian Archaeology,* Volume 47, 1961
[10] Sandison, A. T., op. cit.

13

Tutankhamun's Queen

Smenkhkare's reign was so short that it is not even certain that he survived Akhenaten, with whom he reigned as co-regent. They may both have died in the same year. Nefertiti's end remains a mystery. She probably died at Amarna, before she could see Tutankhaten (as he was first named) grow to maturity. But he had already been formally married to her daughter Ankh-es-an-pa-aten, so that, on the death of Smenkhkare, he was next in line for the throne. Those who are familiar with the famous Berlin bust of Akhenaten's Queen may like to study the torso illustrated (Plate 36). Here is Nefertiti in her late thirties or early forties; still lovely, but the face is saddened by suffering, and the body has borne six children.

At Thebes Smenkhkare had already made certain moves towards a reconciliation with the Amun priesthood before he died, probably at the age of about twenty-three. A hieratic graffito of the third year of his reign attests that a certain Pwah, a 'scribe of the offerings of Amun in the Mansion of Ankh-heprure' (Smenkhkare), offers a hymn of praise to Amun. But the major effort was made during the reign of his successor Tutankhaten, who left Amarna, presumably after the death of his sponsor Nefertiti, and took up residence at Thebes. As a mere child, not more than ten or eleven years of age at most, obviously he could have taken no part in framing policy, which would be in the hands of the elderly courtier Ay, 'Master of the Horse,' who had been one of Akhenaten's most faithful adherents (judging from his tomb at El Amarna) and was almost certainly Nefertiti's father. It must have been Ay who arranged that Tutankhaten should change his name to the more acceptable Tutankh*amun,* and perhaps under Ay's direction and guidance the young monarch gave orders for the repair and reconstruction of the neglected temples of the old gods. On a large stela erected near the Third Pylon of the Karnak temple we see him offering to Amun and his consort Mūt, above a long inscription, part of which reads:

> When His Majesty arose as king, the temple of the gods and goddesses, beginning from Elephantine down to the marshes of the Delta had fallen into decay, their shrines had fallen into desolation and become ruins overgrown with weeds, their chapels as though they had never been and their halls serving as footpaths. If messengers were sent to Djahi (Syria) to extend the boundaries of Egypt, they had no success. If one humbled oneself to a god to ask a thing from him, he did not come, and if prayer was made to a goddess, likewise she never came . . . But after many days My Majesty arose upon the seat of his father and ruled over the territories of Horus, the Black Land and the Red Land being under his supervision.[1]

The child who had grown up under Nefertiti's tutelage, and who must have been taught to accept the Aten as sole god, now appears, with his young wife, in statues adorning the temples of the god whom his father-in-law had hated and persecuted. At Luxor, according to another inscription, he fashioned richly-bejewelled statues of the older gods, and depicted on the walls of the peristyle hall one of the great festivals of Amun-Re.

We need not merely conjecture that Ay was behind all this; a small fragment of gold leaf discovered by Theodore Davis in a mud-filled chamber in the Royal Valley depicts Tutankhamun, followed by his wife, in the conventional attitude of a Pharaoh smiting his enemies with a club. It is doubtful if the young king ever took part in a military campaign; the significant feature, however, is that on his left-hand side, in an attitude of adoration, is Akhenaten's former adviser, the 'Father of the God' Ay. The supposition that this supple official and experienced politician was now the power behind the throne is not too far-fetched.

Ankh-es-en-pa-aten's name was now changed to Ankhesn-amum. In the Karnak statues she appears beside her husband— who was probably a year or two younger than she was—as a slim, petite girl with high cheek-bones, firm, rounded chin and full lips. She strongly resembles the portrait-head on the canopic jars found in the 'Tomb of Tiye' which probably represents her elder sister Meritaten. Both, like their mother, were beautiful women. (See Plates 39 and 40.)

The young Queen, wife of a short-lived, minor monarch— almost the last of a dying dynasty—cannot rank in importance beside the figures of Hashepsowe, Tiye and Nefertiti. She owes her relatively slight fame to two main causes: (a) her husband's treasure-filled tomb, in which she is represented, was the only intact sepulchre of a Pharaoh ever found in modern times, and (b) she is to my knowledge the only Egyptian Queen who speaks to us directly, through certain letters of hers, copies of which were found at the Hittite capital in Asia Minor. There is also the fact that she was one of Nefertiti's daughters, one of that unhappy, ill-fated family who lived in the city of the Sun King, and who was intimately associated with her father Ak-henaten.

Just how intimately is a matter for speculation. It is said that, before her marriage to Tutankhamun, she had been her father's wife. The evidence for this, if it can be accepted as evidence, is a fragmentary block found at Hermopolis, in which the name of a princess *Ankh-es-en-pa-aten—ta-sheri* (Ankh-es-

en-pa-aten junior) appears with the name of her mother
Ankh-es-en-pa-aten, but the name of the father is missing.
Some authorities have argued that the father was Smenkhkare,
who may have married Ankh-es-en-pa-aten, as the next heiress,
after the death of his wife Meritaten. Some argue, on the strength
of another inscription, in which the name of the Queen and her
infant daughter appear on the same slab as the cartouche of
Akhenaten, that he was the father.

One eminent Egyptologist, in a letter to the author, suggests an even more complex marital pattern, basing his theory
partly on unpublished texts from Hermopolis. According to
this theory:

(a) After his estrangement from Nefertiti, Akhenaten married
Meritaten and had a daughter by her;
(b) When Smenkhkare was co-opted as regent Akhenaten gave
him Meritaten as his wife, while he himself married his third
daughter Ankh-es-en-pa-aten and had a daughter by her;
(c) On the death of Akhenaten, Ankh-es-en-pa-aten married
Smenkhkare;
(d) On the death of Smenkhkare she married Tutankhaten.

If this theory is correct then Ankh-es-en-pa-aten (later
Ankhesnamun) became Tutankhamun's wife only after she
had been married first to her father and then to her uncle, and
had a child by each.

This theory is, of course, based entirely on fragmentary inscriptions which merely give names and sometimes dates, but
they are, unfortunately, all we have. Sir Alan Gardiner, with
touching Victorian gallantry, comes to the rescue of Ankesn-
amun:

> . . . a slab of stone found at Ashmunen mentions a small
> daughter bearing the same name as hers but adding to it the
> distinguishing epithet 'the child.' On the strength of the presence
> on the same slab of the cartouche of her father Akhenaten, an
> incestuous marriage of the two . . . has been suggested, but quite
> unjustifiably. Even more tenuous are the grounds on which a

union with the aged official Ay has been deduced. It is the conviction of the present writer that the virtue of this beautiful young queen has been unjustly impugned.[2]

C'est magnifique ... but is it Egyptology? The use of such loaded words as 'incestuous' and 'virtue,' in this context, seems completely irrelevant to a civilisation whose standards and moral conventions were not necessarily ours. Some of the customs and usages which we take for granted would probably have shocked the Ancient Egyptians as much as some of theirs astonish us.

Whatever her history was, Ankhesnamun was undeniably lovely, and, if we are to judge from the paintings and reliefs from her husband's tomb, devoted to him. The representations of the couple on the many objects found in the tomb evoke a delicate, sensuous, richly luxurious life, exactly as one would have expected at the Amarna court where they were brought up. In fact it is mainly from these tomb-treasures that we can form an idea of that luxury, because some of the furniture, e.g. the famous golden throne, bears the Aten-symbol and must have come from Amarna. It was certainly not all funerary equipment made specially for the burial, but actual palace furniture which had been used. And since the child Tutankhaten was brought up in Nefertiti's Palace we are almost certainly looking at objects which she had known. Not only that, but among the hundreds of objects there were a number which had evidently belonged to Tutankhaten when he was a small boy, and these provide us with the most intimate human links with the royal children who played in the great palace of the Sun-King more than thirty centuries ago.

Although the story has been told many times, it is worth recalling the events which led to this, the most astonishing, miraculous and awe-inspiring discovery ever made in Egypt— quite unprecedented, and one which is most unlikely ever to be repeated. After Theodore Davis's concession had expired, the right to dig in the Royal Valley passed to Lord Carnarvon and Mr. Howard Carter. Davis had cleared a number of royal tombs, including those of Ay and Horemhab, Tutankhamun's successors, and had found that of Tiye's parents, Yuya and Thuya. It would seem impossible that the royal Necropolis, which, before Davis's arrival, had been indiscriminately plundered for more than 2,000 years, would yield any new discovery; in fact Davis himself said that, in his view, nothing more would be discovered in the Valley of the Kings.

But Carnarvon and Carter were undeterred. Carter, in particular, who had had long experience of excavation in the Theban Necropolis, was convinced that at least one more royal burial remained to be found, that of Tutankhamun. His reasons were sound. It was customary, when a funeral took place, for the relatives of the dead man or woman to hold a funeral feast in or near the tomb. Afterwards the objects used at this ceremony, including the surplus wrappings and bandages used at the embalming, were usually buried near the sepulchre. This was a common custom in ancient times; the Mycenaeans of prehistoric Greece also held such feasts and may even have copied the idea from Egypt.

Carter's hunch that the tomb of Tutankhamun existed rested on the fact (a) that Tutankhamun was known to have reigned, but his interment had not been found, and (b) that Theodore Davis had come upon a cache of baked-clay jars and stoppers impressed with the royal name. This significant discovery has tended to be overshadowed by the finding by Carter of the tomb itself, but it is worth repeating. The objects which Davis found in 1908—fourteen years before Carter and Carnarvon discovered the King's tomb—were distributed between the Cairo Museum and the Metropolitan Museum of Art, New York. The late Professor W. C. Hayes, former Curator of the Egyptian Department of the latter, describes them in his book *The Scepter of Egypt*. They included:

> One of the huge whitewashed jars in which the cache was stowed and fourteen pottery dishes, bowls and vases from the table service used at the funerary banquet, including an

elegant long-necked wine-bottle . . . Two big mud sealings are painted blue and stamped in several places with the official seal of the royal Necropolis—the canine animal of Anubis crouching above nine bound enemies. Smaller mud sealings from boxes, baskets or jars bear the names of Tutankhamun. . . . Three of the floral broad collars worn by guests at the banquet are made up of real leaves and flowers—one collar, for example, being composed of olive leaves, cornflowers and berries of the woody nightshade. . . .[3]

This floral collar could have been worn by Queen Ankhesna-mun, who would have been the principal guest at her husband's funerary banquet.

It is extraordinary that Davis—an indefatigable excavator who did not lack financial resources—failed to follow up this clue. Perhaps he was exhausted after many years of painful digging; as it was, his successors gained the glory of the discovery, mainly through the determination of Howard Carter, that patient genius who, having carefully mapped every inch of the Royal Valley, was left only with a small triangular patch of land immediately below the well-known tomb of Ramesses vi, an area normally closed to excavators since work in that area would have blocked entrance to this extremely popular tomb. In fact Carter's patron, Lord Carnarvon, was on the point of giving up the work after several unrewarding years, from 1916 to 1921, when the archaeologist urged him to finance just one more season, if only to clear the area which had hitherto been untouched. Carter knew that the funerary cache had been found near by, and suspected that the tomb—almost certainly robbed like all the others—must exist in the area.

Digging into the heap of rock-chippings left by the workmen who had made the Ramesside tomb, Carter came upon a flight of steps cut out of the rock beneath, leading to a sealed doorway bearing the sign of the Necropolis priests who were responsible for guarding the cemetery. The rubble filling, covered with plaster, had, he noticed, been breached at one point, certainly by robbers, but had been re-sealed. This raised his hopes and he sent a telegram to Carnarvon, who was then in England, saying that he intended to re-cover the entrance and await his patron's arrival.

Even at this stage it is doubtful if Carter believed that anything would lie beyond that sealed door but a ransacked sepulchre. Admittedly it had been re-closed by the priests, but thieves might have entered and plundered it by another route. The Ancient Egyptian tomb-robbers were masters of their craft, as are their descendants, the genial rascals of Sheikh abd el Gournah. But when, a few weeks later, Carnarvon arrived, with his daughter Lady Evelyn Herbert, and the entrance was again cleared, the archaeologists found that beyond the sealed doorway was a corridor packed with rubble, and beyond that lay another sealed doorway. The moment when the little party, Carter, Carnarvon, Lady Evelyn Herbert and a few others, stood in the cleared space, waiting for Carter to break down the second door, has been frequently described; but nothing can equal Carter's own account.

> With trembling hands I made a tiny breach in the left-hand corner ... widening the hole a little, I inserted a candle and peered in, Lord Carnarvon, Lady Herbert and Callender standing anxiously beside me to hear the verdict. At first I could see nothing, the hot air escaping from the chamber causing the candle flame to flicker. But presently, as my eyes grew accustomed to the light, details of the room emerged slowly from the mist, strange animals, statues, and gold—everywhere the glint of gold. For a moment—an eternity it must have seemed to the others standing by, I was struck dumb; then Lord Carnarvon inquired anxiously—'Can you see anything?'
>
> 'Yes,' I replied, ... 'wonderful things. . . .'[4]

Imagine that, 3,000 years hence, the whole of England or the United States with their towns, cities, and villages had been so thoroughly pulverized that, apart from a few battered stumps of buildings and a few isolated, unscathed public monuments, nothing remained to tell our successors how we lived in the twentieth century. Add, perhaps, a few magazines with coloured pictures, accompanied by a text which could only be read by experts, and with difficulty. Imagine that these specialists, dedicated to their mystery and largely indifferent to the layman, had thrown out a few crumbs of information, e.g. that there had once lived, circa 1966, an English Queen and her husband and family, and that the site of their palace was known, though nothing existed save the bare foundations. Then, suddenly, in a tiny suite of rooms buried under the rubble of London they discovered, intact, perfectly preserved furniture, pictures and domestic objects which had once stood in Buckingham Palace. That is the significance of the discovery, in 1922, of the tomb of Tutankhamun.

Throughout this book, perhaps in reaction against the often over-sentimental, over-speculative descriptions of life in Ancient Egypt, I have adhered rigidly to known facts. But in the case of Tutankhamun's tomb there is no need to embellish. Until its discovery, the King and his young Queen had been nothing but names attached to a few formal statues and inscriptions. Now it was possible to see not only more intimate portraits, but the beds, chairs, clothes, jewellery, ornaments and personal possessions of two human beings, rulers of what was still, even in decline, the greatest power on earth.

There were the King's chariots, richly embellished with gold, in which he had been driven through the streets of Akhetaten and Thebes. In its casket lay one of his beautiful ostrich-feather fans, the feathers, as Gardiner commented, 'fluffing out in the slight breeze which entered the tomb, looking as if they had been recently plucked.' And in a tiny golden box lay a lock of auburn hair, with the name of its owner, Queen Tiye. It may have had some funerary significance, or it could have been a 'keepsake,' a memento of someone the boy-king had dearly loved. It is even possible, as Madame Desroches-Noblecourt suggests, that he was Tiye's son, born to her in her forties.

If this theory is correct then Ankhesnamun was not only

Tutankhamun's wife but his niece and sister-in-law as well. [See "Family Tree," p. 227.] But she was, first and foremost, his 'Chief Wife,' his favourite, his lover. The fact that, on objects placed in the tomb, she is always represented looking her most seductive is not an accident. She is performing, in a more exalted fashion, the same function as the statuettes of naked concubines, lying on model beds, which were buried in the tombs of ordinary men. These were intended to restore the vital functions of the dead, to arouse the newborn soul to acts of procreation. In the case of the resurrected Pharaoh this was even more essential, because the fertility of the god-king was linked with the renewal of all life in Egypt, in man, animal and plant.

If this sounds far-fetched, we have the authority of the distinguished scholar Madame Desroches-Noblecourt, Chief Curator of the National Museums of France and a noted Egyptologist.

In the depths of his tomb, Tutankhamun prepared for the *agapes* (love feast) but Ankhesnamun, though left among the living, did not desert him, and remained, wherever he was, his 'favourite concubine.' ... On a sublimated level, where the poetic elegance of the objects disguise the religious and magical aspects of the scenes depicted, the annexe of Tutankhamun's tomb contained everything to favour this birth. Thus the gilt shrine on its sled, found in the antechamber ... had an essential role to play. A ritualistic shelter for the royal couple, it should have contained statuettes of the king and queen ... but the statuettes, probably of solid gold, had been stolen. On the doors, as on the sides of the shrine, the decoration consists of scenes in which only two characters, Tutankhamun and Ankhesnamun, appeared, in a variety of episodes centred upon their relationship as lovers. ...

Fondly the devoted wife heaps delicate attentions upon her husband. Dressed as a favourite she brings him the homage of the essential act, expressed by offering the symbols of the goddess Hathor; scent, flowers, and necklaces, presented by a woman who is at the same time presenting herself. And in order that no evil spirit should sap the king's renewed virility or abate the fecundity of his spouse, Tutankhamun is shown seated on a stool, escorted by his tame lion, showering arrows upon the evil wild duck in the papyrus thickets to put the evil birds to flight. . . The queen is shown in most seductive apparel and is wearing the pendant ear-rings owned by the king as a child. . . . Every variation on this single theme is present, and repeated so often as to appear obsessive.[5]

We do not know whether in fact Tutankhamun fathered any children. The mummified bodies of two stillborn infants, one of six and the other of seven months, were found in the chamber adjoining the burial-hall. Gardiner says they must have been his by Ankhesnamun and this seems probable. But Madame Noblecourt throws doubts on this theory, because in a number of burials of other women, the bodies of stillborn infants have been placed beside that of the mother inside her coffin. It could be argued, of course, that as Ankhesnamun survived Tutankhamun to marry yet again, she would not wish to take with her to the grave the products of her former union.

In any case, why should two infants who died before their father be buried in his tomb? The answer is to be found in Egyptian magico-religious beliefs, which resemble those found in the more primitive parts of Africa to this day. First it must be borne in mind where these two foetuses were laid—in the so-called 'Treasury'—a small chamber opening off that in which the King's body rested in its nest of coffins surrounded by four golden shrines. Above all one must avoid thinking of this royal tomb as little more than a furniture store, with the contents placed in no particular order. Allowing for the confusion produced by the robbers who tried to plunder the sepulchre, and the priests who tidied-up after they had left, there is high significance in the *way* the objects were placed, e.g. their orientation. This may be partially understood by referring to Egyptian religious beliefs, though some speculation is inevitable.

Even here the words 'religion' and 'magic' are both misleading. We think of religion essentially as a communication with God through worship, and the observance of certain rules of moral behaviour. 'Magic' suggests only superstitious mumbo-jumbo, or conjuring-tricks. At the risk of sounding materialistic and mundane, I would suggest that the best—indeed the only way—to find any point of contact with the Ancient Egyptian mind is to think of their temples not as churches but as power-houses, and their priests not as clergymen but as technicians. Even this is only an approximation of the truth, but it is, in my view, more accurate than equating the High Priest of Amun with a Christian archbishop or an Egyptian temple with a Christian cathedral.

Today the ordinary man or woman usually takes for granted the scientific explanation of 'natural forces,' e.g. sunshine, rainfall, flooding, thunder, and the 'natural processes' of generation, birth, growth and death. He or she also makes use of, without necessarily understanding, the powers which science has placed in our hands, e.g. electricity and radio-communication. One may be able to replace a fuse, attach the correct wires to a plug, or adjust a television receiver, but if the electricity supply is cut off one rings up the power station, or if the TV set refuses to work one sends for an expert. But in the pre-scientific age 'natural forces' were gods or goddesses, and the 'experts' were the priests, or rather magicians. There was very little moral content in primitive religion, which consisted almost entirely of complex and elaborate ritual observances which only the priests understood, or claimed to understand.

An example of this can be seen in the 'magic bricks' placed in the 'Tomb of Tiye' described earlier. Aldred comments that though these were still in their correct positions, and one bore the name of the King whose body it was supposed to guard from intruders, two had the name erased, and all of them were without the amulets which normally accompanied them. To our way of thinking it seems illogical that the desecrators who entered the tomb and mutilated the inscriptions on the mummy did not destroy or remove all the bricks. But to the Ancient Egyptian 'experts' it was probably perfectly logical; if one brick was defaced and so rendered inoperative the rest could be left undisturbed, just as today an electrician 'breaks the circuit' at one point and can then handle wires which, if connected, would electrocute him.

What we call 'magic,' meaning harmless superstition or conjuring, was as real to the Ancient Egyptian layman as electricity is to us. And he respected those who claimed to understand it, as we respect the specialised knowledge of the trained technician.

If this seems too prosaic, one may remember that rites of exorcism are still occasionally practised by the Christian clergy, whether or not one believes in their efficacy. In 1966, in a certain Sussex village, a woman of my acquaintance was worried because her young child persistently claimed to have been disturbed by a white figure which appeared in her bedroom. The local priest was called in to perform the rites of exorcism, just as, in 1366 BC, a priest of Amun might have been asked to perform a similar function. But the ghost, alas, refuses to be laid.

With this background in mind we may return to the tomb of Tutankhamun, and Ankhesnamun's place in it. Although she outlived the king and was therefore not buried with him, her spirit played a necessary part in his rejuvenation. As Madame Noblecourt states, 'every variation on this single theme' (i.e. the amorous relationship of the king with his Queen) 'is present, and repeated so often as to appear obsessive.'

The whole purpose of the elaborate burial, the interment of the royal body, with its scintillating funerary equipment, was essentially functional and practical. Here were no mere vague hopes of heavenly bliss, as expressed on many a Victorian tombstone. Every object, every detail of painting and inscription, even the placing of the furniture and equipment was carried out by specialists to ensure that the young Pharaoh would awaken from the sleep of death, would pass through the stages of birth, childhood, adolescence and maturity, renew his potency and, in the arms of his wife, become a man again.

This renewed life-cycle begins in the burial-chamber where the mummified body lies, within its nest of three coffins and four golden shrines, all inscribed with magical texts spoken by the ancient gods and goddesses of Egypt.

> *My beloved son,* says Geb, god of the earth, *inheritor of the throne of Osiris, the King Nebkheprure* (Tutankhamun); *thy nobility is perfect; thy royal palace is powerful; thy name is in the mouth of the common folk, thy stability in the mouth of the living, O Osiris, King Tutankhamun!*[6]

And the Divine Mother, Nūt, on the coffin inscriptions, cries:

> *Thy member is firm; thou smellest the air and goest out as a God, going out as Atum, O Osiris Tutankhamun!*

For far too long people observing the Ancient Egyptian customs of embalmment, mummification, endless care lavished on tombs and tomb-furnishings have imagined these ancient people to be death-obsessed. The very reverse is true. Sentimentality poured out over the 'pathetic body of the boy-king, imprisoned in his gold-and-jewelled coffins, loaded with funerary regalia' is wasted. The King was not lying, patiently, waiting for the Last Trump which would awaken him to a more spiritual form of existence. What he and every other Ancient Egyptian of rank wished for was a renewal of Life, here and now; life as he had known and loved it, with all the delights of flesh and spirit; the heat of the sun at midday, the cool north wind in the evening, the pleasure of the palate, good wine and food, the sight and touch of lovely things, the excitement of the hunt, the feel of fine linen on his body, and above all the highest of all sensual pleasures, love.

A fact not often mentioned in descriptions of Tutankhamun's mummy was that the penis had been replaced bandaged in an erect stance.

This, and the text 'thy member is firm' (often coyly translated 'thy members are firm'), shows the importance which was placed on the ability to procreate.

It is only the prudishness of Victorian and Edwardian scholars, on whose works most students depend for their introduction to Egyptology, which has obscured the essential earthiness of the Egyptian concept of the good life. If further proof is needed, one has only to consult Gardiner's translation of an Egyptian 'dream-book' in his *Hieratic Papyri Vol. 1*. This extraordinary document, which anticipates Freud by some 3,000 years, contains interpretations of dreams, both good and bad. Among these are the following:

IF A MAN SEES HIMSELF IN A DREAM —

— with his mouth split open	Good; it means something he was afraid of will be opened up by the god.
— his penis becoming large	Good; it means his possessions will multiply.
— seeing a serpent has entered into his beer.	Good; it means his heart overflows.
— copulating with his mother	Good; his clansmen will cleave fast to him.
— drinking wine	Good; it means living in righteousness.
— seeing a large cat	Good; it means a large harvest will come to him.
— sitting in an orchard in the sun	Good; it means pleasure
— capturing a female slave	Good; it means something from which he will derive satisfaction.
— drinking warm beer	Bad; it means suffering will come upon him.
— seeing his face in a mirror	Bad; it means another wife.[7]

And there are many other interpretations which are even more fundamental.

Besides the physical protection provided by the three coffins —the innermost of solid gold—the quartzite sarcophagus, and the four huge wood-and-gilt shrines which enclosed them, the royal body was also protected by masses of sacred amulets, on head, breast, arms and legs; even the toenails wore golden sheaths. One of the shrines was incised with a lovely figure of the goddess Isis with outstretched wings, but the face is that of Ankhesnamun, and she wears the slim-fitting, diaphanous dress of the 'Amarna' court lady, with one breast bare.

In the 'Treasury' opening of the burial chamber, its door guarded by a figure of Anubis resting on a shrine, stands another tall, rectangular wood and gold structure enclosing the king's canopic chest, of alabaster, each cavity of which holds a miniature golden coffin containing the royal viscera. The entrails, liver, and other organs have been removed from the corpse during embalmment, but they will obviously be needed by the reanimated king. So the golden chest is guarded by four golden goddesses, each facing one side of the chest with arms outstretched in protection. Their names are Isis, Nephthys, Neith and Serket, but the face, in each case, is that of Ankhesnamun.

One of the magical rites performed at the funeral was intended to reunite the various elements of the body, which is why there was no door between the burial-chamber and the 'Treasury.' In this room Tutankhamun would 're-make' himself, and the objects placed in it, including the two foetuses, were intended to assist this process. For instance, the model boats, of various kinds, 'would carry the dead man, once again a foetus, to the different stages in the aquatic region of the mother-goddess's womb. Like the son of Osiris, he would encounter attacking demons.' So in the chamber were placed various statues of the king, in wood covered with gold leaf, showing him launching a harpoon at the evil god Seth, being borne on the back of a benevolent cheetah, and being carried, wrapped in a shroud, on the head of a friendly spirit Menkheret. And to show how completely the king had returned to the old cult there were, besides the figure of the jackal-headed god Anubis, others of the cow-headed Hathor, and, lying on the floor, a wooden tray made in the shape of the mummified Osiris and filled with Nile mud in which corn had been sown and had sprouted in the darkness of the tomb: a symbol of resurrection and a re-minder of the Pharaoh's ancestral role as fertility-god.

He was, of course, also provided with everything he would need in the form of clothing, shoes, armour, weapons, and jewellery in such quantity that it now fills numerous cases in the Cairo Museum; and yet, according to Carter, who examined the many empty or half-empty boxes, more than 60 per cent of the golden jewellery which had been buried with the body must have been stolen. One can only imagine what the original collection was like, and this was one of the smallest royal tombs in the Valley of the Kings. Even the jewellery, however, had a magical purpose. There was the *wedjet*-eye which promised a reconstitution of being, scarabs with the royal name, the *djed*-pillar, symbolising stability, also images of Nephthys and Isis and the two goddesses of Upper and Lower Egypt.

In brief, the so-called 'Treasury' contained all the equip-ment needed by the body to achieve the first stage of its resur-rection and reconstitution. The next chamber, separated by a blocked doorway from the burial hall, seems originally to have been stacked with all the objects connected with the king's powers as a Pharaoh: his thrones, couches, parade-sticks, a scep-tre, travelling-cases, more jewel-boxes, a hunting-corselet, and the royal chariots used in hunting and warfare.

However, it was within the small room opening from the ante-chamber, its entrance orientated east to face the rising sun, that Ankhesnamun comes into her own. Within this room, which Carter called the Annexe, were found nearly all the objects connected with childhood and adolescence. Madame Noblecourt suggests that this was the Chamber of Rebirth. We know from wall-paintings in other royal tombs that after pass-ing the portals of death the king was reborn again as a child;

sometimes, as in the tomb of Ramesses VI, he is shown as a boy wearing the side-lock of youth. There were no wall-paintings in Tutankhamun's small, roughly finished sepulchre apart from those in the burial-chamber, but instead the Annexe was furnished with many things he must have used when a small boy.

It is easy to become sentimental over these, and they are, indeed, touching. There is a wooden device for making fire by rubbing a bow along the serrations of a wooden spindle which thus revolves in a hole, generating heat—rather like a Boy Scout's fire-making outfit. There are several slings, and a toy-box containing games, fitted with an ingenious secret lock which would delight any boy. Three ebony boxes bore hieratic inscriptions which read 'his majesty's linen chests when he was a young being'; a large bow-shaped chest contained bow, arrows and boomerangs; there was a large collection of sticks, some of them gold-plated, and archer's gloves made to protect the left wrist. Among the scores of other objects stacked in this small room were a child's chair of ebony and ivory, and folding stools, probably used on duck-shooting expeditions.

There can be little doubt that these things, too, were put there for magical reasons, to enable the reborn king to relive his childhood and adolescence. Very full provision was made for the King's delight when he crossed the threshold into manhood. Now he has his Queen, shown idling with him beside the reed-marshes of the Nile, languidly handing him an arrow which he seems almost too lazy to take from her. These delicate, sensuous reliefs, incised and embossed in gold, have a languorous warmth which suggests that Ankhesnamun is well aware that her husband's attention is not entirely on his shooting. Her half-parted lips, the indolent curves of her body under its pleated robe, are charged with an eroticism implied rather than stated. The scenes on the other sides of this small shrine are more openly sexual. Ankhesnamun is the Oriental Queen waiting upon her lord's pleasure, sitting on the floor beside him, her arm resting negligently on his knee, anointing him with perfumed unguents, or leaning provocatively forward, her left hand on his shoulder while with the other she fastens a necklace around his neck.

Again and again such scenes are repeated. On the backrest of the magnificent golden throne the King lolls on a deep-cushioned chair, while the Queen, dressed in a full-skirted transparent robe, repeats the anointing scene, her left hand holding the unguent-bowl. Above the royal couple the Aten sends down its rays, suggesting that this may have formed part of the palace furniture from Amarna. An interesting point is that the couple is shown wearing floral necklaces; actual necklaces of this kind were found in and near the tomb. One lay on the coffin, and the others, in excellent condition though the flowers had naturally dried, were those discovered by Davis among the remains of the funeral banquet buried near the sepulchre.

As chief mourner, Ankhesnamun must have worn one of these, and it is not unlikely that it was she who laid the necklace on the coffin, a last gesture before the great lid of the sarcophagus was lowered. The funerary banquet itself was also an essential part of the ritual which was to renew the life and vigour of the King. 'It is probable,' writes Madame Noblecourt, 'that the funeral banquet was primarily intended to induce scenes of procreation' and 'automatically led to a Dionysiac conclusion.' . . . The opposite poles of the Egyptian attitude to death—grief at the loss of the beloved, joy at his rebirth—are vividly expressed in the two poems which she quotes. The first is spoken by the Queen:

> *I am thy wife, O great one — do not leave me!*
> *Is it thy good pleasure, O my brother, that I should*
> *go far from thee!*
> *How can it be that I go away alone!*
> *I say; 'I accompany thee, O thou who didst like to*
> *converse with me,'*
> *But thou remainest silent and speakest not.*

And the second, probably recited by a priest, speaks of the rebirth:

> *Awaken, O sick one, thou who hast slept,*
> *They have lifted thine head toward the horizon.*

*Appear! Thou art justified against him who sought to
harm thee;
Ptah has overthrown thine enemies and has ordered
Him who stood against thee to be pursued.
Thou art Horus, son of Hathor,
He whose head was restored to him
After it had been cut off;
Never again shall thine head be taken from thee;
In the future never again for all eternity shall thine
head be taken from thee.*[8]

[1] Gardiner, Sir Alan, *Egypt of the Pharaohs,* Oxford University Press, New York, 1961

[2] Gardiner, Sir Alan, op. cit.

[3] Hayes, W. C., *The Scepter of Egypt,* Volume II, New York Graphic Society for the Metropolitan Museum of Art, Greenwich, Conn., 1959

[4] Carter, Howard, and Mace, A. C., *The Tomb of Tut-ankh-amen,* Cooper Square Publishers, New York

[5] Desroches-Noblecourt, C., *Tutankhamen,* New York Graphic Society, Greenwich, Conn., 1963

[6] Carter, Howard, op. cit.

[7] Gardiner, Sir Alan, *Hieratic Papyri in the British Museum,* Volume I (Third Series), British Museum, London, 1935

[8] Desroches-Noblecourt, C., op. cit.

14

'Send Me One of Your Sons!'

TUTANKHAMUN REIGNED FOR BETWEEN NINE AND TEN YEARS, and was nineteen, or at the most twenty, when he died. It is ironical that practically all we know of this, the most widely-publicised of all Pharaohs, was that he died and was buried. His relative unimportance and the fact that he belonged to an unpopular dynasty are two reasons why his small, obscure tomb was overlooked by the robbers who plundered every one of the thirty-odd other royal sepulchres in the Valley of the Kings. Another reason was the fortunate chance that the tomb of Ramesses VI was dug immediately over his, and the stone chippings from its excavation hid the entrance to Tutankhamun's modest mausoleum. Even so, two previous attempts had been made to rob it before the larger tomb was built, but fortunately the plunderers got away with only some of the more portable objects, including more than half the jewellery and a number of small gold statues. Then the guardian priests resealed the entrance and it remained undisturbed for over 3,000 years.

As for Ankhesnamun, we do not know when she died or where she was buried, and the same applies to all other members of the Amarna family except possibly Smenkhkare. But by a most extraordinary chance we do possess a number of letters addressed by the Egyptian Queen to King Suppiluliumas of the Hittites, and from the known dates of these letters there can be no doubt that Ankhesnamun was the Queen. From the beginnings of Egyptian history down to Ptolemaic times—for some 3,000 years—these are the only personal letters of a Queen of Egypt ever to be found.

They are among the most moving documents which have survived from the ancient world, but in order to appreciate the drama underlying them it is necessary to know something more about Egyptian funerary customs. The process of embalmment and mummification took a long time. First the contents of the skull were removed; then an incision was made in the side of the abdomen, and the embalmers took out the internal organs, which, except for the heart, were embalmed separately and placed in the canopic jars. The heart was replaced in the body before it was sewn up, since the Ancient Egyptians regarded it as the seat of intelligence. The eviscerated corpse was then allowed to lie in natron crystals for about two months, to dry it out. Then it was stuffed with bandages, aromatic herbs, and the flesh padded out to give the appearance of life. The final stage was the careful wrapping of the body in its mummy-bandages after the necessary jewellery, charms and amulets had been placed in the correct position. In Tutankhamun's case, a mask of solid gold, a masterpiece of portraiture worthy of Cellini, was placed over the head before the mummy was put in its solid gold coffin. The whole process took about seventy days.

The next point to remember is that Ankhesnamun, widow of the Pharaoh, was the heiress; whoever married her became the next king. But she could not be married until her husband's body had been ceremonially buried in his 'House of Eternity.' If Fairman and others are right, and the inscriptions found at Hermopolis and elsewhere can be relied on, she was no 'pathetic girl-queen' but a woman with considerable marital experience, even at twenty-one or twenty-two, which was her probable age at Tutankhamun's death. Before her marriage to him she had been married to her father Akhenaten and possibly to Smenkhkare as well. Now she was again a widow.

There are two versions of what may then have happened, depending on how one interprets the very meagre Egyptian evidence. But fortunately the main evidence comes from outside Egypt, in the form of a series of letters quoted by Mursilis, king of the Hittites, in a brief biography of his father Suppiluliumas, and there can be no doubt concerning their authenticity. Like the famous Amarna tablets, they were found, with hundreds of other documents, in the archive-room of a buried city, Hattusas, in Asia Minor. The story of their discovery, even more astonishing than that of the Amarna letters, deserves a mention.

In 1906, a German archaeologist named Hugo Winckler found the hitherto-unknown capital of the Hittite Empire. The existence of these formidable people was known from numerous sources. The Ancient Egyptian records refer to them as the Kheta (sometimes 'the abominable Kheta') and they are also mentioned in the Bible, e.g. 'Uriah the Hittite.' Their monuments and inscriptions, in an unknown language, had been observed at a number of places in Syria, e.g. Carchemish, but until Winckler dug at Boghaz-koy, a remote village in the high tableland of central Turkey, their place of origin was unknown.

Between 1906 and 1912 Winckler excavated the great Hittite capital, originally called Hattusas. He came upon over 10,000 tablets, most of them in Babylonian cuneiform writing, which could be translated. This was the same script used by the writers of the Amarna letters and some of them could be dated to the same period. Thus the existence of King Suppiluliumas, who wrote congratulating Akhenaten on his accession, was confirmed in numerous documents, among which was a lengthy account of the King's achievements by his son Mursilis. This is a fascinating example of how archaeological discoveries in one country can link up with those in another. We already know, from the

Amarna letters, of the plight of Ribbadi and his fellow-vassals, some fighting each other, others swearing loyalty to the Pharaoh, all asking for aid. But these were only the pawns in the power-game. The most powerful pieces on the board were far to the north, out of the Pharaoh's range: the Hittite King Suppilu-liumas and his generals. But in the letters found at Boghaz-koy we see them at closer range. Mursilis describes how his father, whose armies had advanced to 'the country of Carchemish' (northern Syria), attacked and took the country of Amka, an Egyptian vassal-state.

When the people of Misra (Egypt) learned of the de-struction of Amka, they were afraid, for to make matters worse their master *Bibhuria* (the Hittite rendering of *Nebkheprure,* one of Tutankhamun's names) had just died and the widowed Queen of Egypt sent an ambassador to my father and wrote to him in these terms; 'My husband is dead and I have no son. People say that you have many sons. If you send me one of your sons he will become my husband, for it is repugnant to me to take one of my servants (subjects) to husband.'

Mursilis continues:

When my father learned this he called together the coun-cil of the great and said to them 'Since the most ancient times such a thing has never happened before.' He decided to send Hattu-Zittish, the chamberlain, saying 'Go, bring me informa-tion worthy of belief; they may try to deceive me; and as to the possibility that they may have a prince, bring me back in-formation worthy of belief.' While Hattu-Zittish was absent on the soil of Egypt, my father vanquished the city of Carchem-ish . . . The ambassador of Egypt, the lord Hanis, came to him. Because my father had instructed Hattu-Zittish when he went to the country of Egypt as follows: 'Perhaps they have a prince, they may be trying to deceive me and do not really want one of my sons to reign over them.'

The Egyptian Queen answered my father in a letter in these words: 'Why do you say "they are trying to deceive me"?

If I had a son, should I write to a foreign country in a manner humiliating to me and to my country? You do not believe me and you even say so to me! He who was my husband is dead and I have no son. Should I then perhaps take one of my servants and make him my husband? I have written to no other country. I have written only to you. They say that you have many sons. Send me one of your sons and he will be my husband and lord of the land of Egypt!'

Mursilis continues:

Because my father was generous, he granted the lady's request and decided to send his son.[1]

The rest of the story is tragic. The Hittite records tell us that one of the king's sons, Prince Zannanza, set out for Egypt with an armed escort, but on the way he was murdered 'by the men and horses of Egypt.'

The questions are: Who sent those men? And how was Ankhesnamun's desperate stratagem revealed? All we know for certain is that the next Pharaoh was Ay, Akhenaten's former counsellor and Tutankhamun's Vizier of the South. After a short reign he was followed by another of Akhenaten's former followers, the general Horemhab. It is also known that Ay reigned for a time with Ankhenamun as co-regent, but there is no proof of marriage. The only evidence that they shared the throne is a scarab bearing both their cartouches. On the other hand Ay was not of the blood royal, so one would have thought he would have sought to legalise his accession by marriage to the heiress. So the much married Queen *could* have been married to her sixty-year-old great-uncle.

Was it Ay, then, who became aware of the plot to put a foreign prince on the throne of Egypt, and was it he who sent soldiers to ambush and kill Prince Zannanza? This is the generally-accepted view and one which the present writer has supported in previous books. Or, as Madame Noblecourt persuasively argues, was Ay privy to the plot in the first place, and encouraged Ankhesnamun to seek a foreign alliance to counter-balance the power of someone nearer home? And if this theory is correct who could that someone be but Horemhab? Was he the 'servant' whom Ankhesnamun found it 'repugnant' to 'take as husband'? And was it he who ordered the ambush?

We cannot know for certain, but on balance I am inclined to accept Madame Noblecourt's view. Let us look at the few fragments of information which are all we have by which to judge the characters of these two men. Ay was probably the son of Yuya and Thuya, the two nobles who were highly honoured by Amenophis III who married their daughter Tiye. He would therefore be Akhenaten's uncle and Ankhesnamun's great-uncle.* Whatever her parentage there is no doubt that he was one of Akhenaten's most highly trusted advisers, and when Tutankhamun came to the throne he guided the young monarch during the difficult period when the royal family had to effect a reconciliation with the priests of Amun.

He had been a devoted Atenist, judging from the inscriptions and reliefs on his Amarna tomb, and though, on returning to Thebes, he clearly advised and encouraged the young king to make his peace with the older gods, there is no evidence that he took part in any active persecution of the Atenists. Also, living, as he did, first at El Amarna and then at Thebes he must have been in close and intimate touch with the royal family and it is tempting to see him as the wise, tolerant, fatherly adviser.

But, being human, he would also have a very natural and tender regard for the safety of his own skin.

Now let us look at Horemhab. He was, throughout his life, a soldier. He did not live at Amarna, but at Memphis, far to the north, where he had a splendid tomb made with inscriptions which tell us practically all that we know about his career. He was not of royal blood, though his wife, Mutnodjme, may have been (some scholars suggest that she was Nefertiti's sister, but this is unproven). His tomb-inscriptions describe him as

---

* If as has been conjectured Nefertiti was Ay's daughter, then Ankhesn-amun would have been his grand-daughter.

'Great Commander of the Army of the Lord of the Two Lands' and 'Envoy of the King in front of the Army to the Southern and Northern Lands.' A most curious passage relates how he was summoned to the royal presence when 'the Palace fell into a rage,' which Gardiner suggests 'seems to hint that he faced the wrath of Akhenaten successfully.' But does it only mean this, one wonders? Had the king had a *crise de nerves* and had Horemhab been called in to calm him down?

There is no evidence of the close and affectionate relationship such as existed, apparently, between Ay and the royal family. Horemhab prepared no tomb at El Amarna, as the other officials did. He was a northerner, born in the unimportant town of Hnes about 100 miles from Cairo, and no doubt he chose to live at Memphis because there he was in a better position to control the northern frontier and maintain contact with Egypt's Asiatic dependencies. Considering Akhenaten's indifference to military affairs it must have been a frustrating life for a soldier, and it is clear from the scenes and inscriptions in Horemhab's tomb that he was an active military commander. He also acted as Vice-regent of the North and, after the death of Akhenaten and Smenkhkare, served Tutankhamun mainly as an administrator. There is a portrait of him as a scribe writing down his sovereign's commands. He has a powerful, somewhat ruthless face.

He was also a stern disciplinarian. When he discovered that some of his troops had got out of hand and had been robbing honest citizens of their boats and cattle, the penalties were severe. The mildest was 'one hundred strokes and five open wounds' while the worst malefactors lost their noses and were banished to the fortress-town of Tjel on the Asiatic frontier. Such severity was unusual in Ancient Egypt and may point to the character of the man. But I would not go as far as some writers on the Amarna period who, having cast Akhenaten in the role of gentle pacifist and Ay as his kindly mentor, have represented Horemhab as a brutal dictator. Most likely he was a brusque, somewhat impatient military commander, a lover of order and discipline, and a man who had scant patience with those who permitted foreign rulers to filch Egyptian possessions, or intrigue with them.

If General Horemhab was such a man, as I believe he was, perhaps one may be permitted a little 'imaginative reconstruction' of the events leading to the death of the Hittite prince. During the seventy days during which Tutankamun's body was being prepared for burial, messengers could have passed between Thebes and the Hittite headquarters at Carchemish several times. The messengers would almost certainly have to pass through Memphis on their way to the desert road, guarded by watch-towers and frontier-posts which would come under Horemhab's command. The longer the negotiations went on the more likely it would be that news of the plot would leak out. Or Horemhab may have had his spies in Thebes; an able commander would be sure to have an intelligence service.

The desperation in Ankhesnamun's letters when the cautious Hittite king at first refuses to believe her could be partly due to apprehension that Horemhab would learn about her plan. One can only conjecture what may have happened. Perhaps one of the letters was secretly opened, read and re-sealed. Perhaps one of Horemhab's agents in Thebes obtained a copy from the Queen's personal scribe (for a suitable remuneration). There are a dozen ways by which the general, who may already have had his eyes on the throne, may have learned of Ankhesnamun's plan to marry the son of Egypt's most powerful rival. It does not necessarily follow that Horemhab, at this time, was aiming at supreme power, but he would know that with a Hittite monarch on the throne of Egypt his own career, and possibly life, would be in jeopardy. So he formulates his plans.

The letters pass to and fro, the messengers clatter through the streets of Memphis and out by the northern gate, armed, no doubt, with the essential credentials which would enable them to pass the frontier-posts. Eventually news reaches Horemhab that Suppiluliumas has decided to send one of his sons to Egypt under escort, no doubt provided with safe-conduct passes signed by the Queen or by Ay. To stop and apprehend them at the frontier would be treason. No, that is not the way.

And so, one day, as Prince Zannanza, richly dressed and bearing gifts, rides with his picked bodyguard beside the banks of the Orontes, or perhaps across the Sinai desert near the Egyptian frontier, a squadron of Egyptian charioteers is seen approaching in a cloud of dust. Just a desert patrol, of course, looking for marauding Bedouins. But as they draw nearer their pace does not slacken, their bowstrings are taut and the young officer in the foremost chariot has his spear raised. Too late, the Hittite warriors grasp their weapons, the Prince's driver lashes the horses and Zannanza hurriedly draws a spear from its rest.

A second later he pitches from his chariot, pierced by several arrows. The driver is wounded, the horses run, whinnying in terror, while those of the Prince's escort who are still alive hurry to his aid. In the distance the Egyptian chariot-squadron wheels in a great curve and then gallops away until it is only a cloud of red dust which drifts slowly across the hot, stony plain.

At Thebes Ankhesnamun waits in vain. Prince Zannanza will not share her bed, or her throne.

It was all most unfortunate, of course, as Horemhab, at his Memphis HQ, states in the report he may have made to Thebes. The squadron exceeded its order. They should have halted the Prince's cavalcade and examined its credentials, and not have attacked without warning. Their commander has been severely disciplined.

'Severely disciplined . . .' The young officer seated opposite Horemhab hands back the report which he has just read. The General's eyes meet his but do not smile. 'I'm posting you to Tjel, Hori,' he says sharply. 'The beer's undrinkable, the women about as attractive as goats. You won't like it, but a bit of frontier experience will do you good.'

And he adds, as they both rise:

'But I'll let you keep your nose.'

---

[1] Desroches-Noblecourt, C., *Tutankhamen,* New York Graphic Society, Greenwich, Conn., 1963

15

Great Wife of Ramesses

Since, in the foregoing dramatic vignette, I have broken my self-imposed rule of never indulging in speculative reconstruction, it is only fair to the reader to give the grounds on which my fragile theory is based.

There is no doubt that Ankhesnamun wrote to Suppiluliumas; there is no doubt that the Hittite Prince was murdered on his way to Egypt; the written records state this. I have given reasons why I think Horemhab, and not Ay, ordered the killing. It remains to show why the attack may have been carried out in this particular way. Let us first examine the alternatives.

(a) The Prince and his escort were set upon by a band of marauding Bedouins, which most fortunately did Horemhab's work for him. Highly unlikely, since, apart from the coincidence that certain high-placed Egyptians were very anxious that Zannanza should not reach Egypt, the Prince was bound to have a well-armed escort, and the Hittites were redoubtable soldiers, well able to cope with such an attack. Again, Mursilis specifically states that it was carried out by 'the men and horses of Egypt'; in fact so certain was Suppiluliumas that Egyptian troops were responsible that he afterwards declared war on Egypt.

(b) The attack was carried out by Egyptian troops, but it was a genuine mistake; again highly unlikely in view of the importance of the Prince and his mission.

(c) The attack was launched under Horemhab's orders without any pretence that it was a mistake. This is improbable, because, to be effective, it would be necessary to wipe out every member of the Prince's escort besides Zannanza himself. This would have been risky, as in close combat some of the Egyptians might have been captured and taken prisoner; under interrogation they might have revealed the source of their orders and Horemhab would have been directly implicated.

My theory is that to achieve success it was necessary for the attackers to kill the Prince and then retreat as swiftly as possible; it would not then matter so much if some of the escort survived to carry the news to Suppiluliumas, since no one could prove that the onslaught was made under Horemhab's orders. The best way to do this would be a lightning attack by fast chariots in open country. Although Mursilis does not mention chariots, but only 'men and horses,' I believe that chariots would be used for the following reasons. The Egyptians were trained to fire accurately from a moving platform; e.g., Amenophis III is described as firing at a fixed target from his chariot as it 'circled like the sun' and this would be a standard manoeuvre. Thus, without having to come into close range, Hori's squadron could approach at a fast pace, wheel so that they passed alongside the Hittite cavalcade, firing as they went, then retreat. Their orders would be to dispatch the Prince—he would be the main target— and some of his escort, and then without pausing, gallop out of range, relying on the resultant confusion in the Hittite ranks to prevent their pursuing.

It is unlikely to have been a cavalry charge because (a) a close engagement would run the risk of some of the riders being brought down and captured, and (b) the small, light horses used by the Egyptians, though they could be harnessed in pairs to pull chariots, were not strong enough to carry men on their backs for any distance.

It was a disreputable piece of work, of which Horemhab —if he was not the black villain of modern Egyptological fiction—may well have been slightly ashamed. But if he felt that the safety of Egypt, and possibly his own life, was at stake, this would be sufficient to overcome any scruples. On the other hand, not being a gentleman, he may not have had any.

We hear no more of Queen Ankhesnamun, except for her brief co-regency with Ay, who became the next Pharaoh. After her death, and that of Tutankhamun, the blood of the fighting Tuthmosids no longer flowed in the veins of Egypt's rulers. The Eighteenth Dynasty was at an end. What had begun like the sun in splendour ended in a sordid struggle for power among the astute politicians who shuffled the royal children like pawns. We can regard Ankhesnamun's last gesture in a number of ways: as one of naked self-interest by a woman prepared to sacrifice her country's independence for the sake of personal power; revulsion at the thought of marrying an elderly courtier thrice her age, who may have been her grandfather. Or could it have been that—possibly with Ay's encouragement—she was trying to break the circle of continued inbreeding which had enfeebled the royal strain and introduce a new, healthier stock?

Whatever her motives may have been she failed. Ay became Pharaoh after presiding at Tutankhamun's obsequies, as we can see from the wall-paintings in the latter's tomb, where, wearing the leopardskin of a priest, he performs the ceremony of 'Opening the Mouth.' It has even been argued that the tomb in which Tutankhamun was buried had originally been made for Ay when he was merely a nobleman, and that the much larger sepulchre in which Ay was buried had originally been made for Tutankhamun. It is interesting that Ankhesnamun's name is not mentioned in Ay's tomb-inscriptions, which it surely would have been had he married her.

After a short reign Ay was succeeded by Horemhab,

though by what right we do not know, unless his wife Mutnodjme had royal blood. Horemhab stands between the end of the Eighteenth and the beginning of the Nineteenth Dynasty, belonging to neither. It was during his reign that Egypt was re-orientated along the line followed by the Tuthmosids: adherence to the ancestral religion dominated by Amun-Re, and a policy of expansion. He inherited a country burdened by corrupt and inefficient administrators, its people resentful against unjust taxation, its foreign dependencies almost lost, and a watchful enemy on its frontiers. When the Pharaoh died, Egypt had re-gained internal stability and consolidated her military strength in order to re-establish her influence in Asia.

His reign was marked by two other important changes. Every effort was made to stamp out what remained of the 'Aten-heresy.' It was at this time that Akhenaten became 'that crim-inal,' his name was obliterated wherever it could be found, e.g. in the 'tomb of Tiye,' and Horemhab's agents went to El Am-arna, destroyed the Aten-temples, mutilated the tomb-inscrip-tions wherever the name of the heretic appeared, and carried away stone from the royal palace for building operations at Hermopolis on the opposite bank. The other change is also sig-nificant. Except for Cleopatra, never again did the Queens of Egypt enjoy the power and influence which had been theirs un-der Amenophis iii, Akhenaten, and their two short-lived suc-cessors. The feminine encroachment was halted.

Horemhab's military leanings are shown in several ways. He chose his priests, he tells us, from 'the pick of the army,' and appointed as his Vizier or chief minister a man of obscure birth named Pramesse, whose father had been a simple 'captain of troops.' It was this man who came to the throne on the death of Horemhab, dropping the definite article 'P' at the beginning of his name and reigning as Ramesses i. Although he was the first King of the Nineteenth Dynasty (1304–1195 bc) he was already old when he came to the throne and reigned for about twenty months. The real founder of this glorious dynasty, the restorer of Egypt's greatness, was Sethi i, his son, who had also served under

Horemhab. Although his reign lasted only twelve years it was brilliant. It was as if Tuthmosis III, the great Menkheperre, had been restored to the Egyptians. Like that king Sethi was a great military leader; in the first year of his reign he led the reorganised army out of the border fortress of Tjel, across the Sinai peninsula and into the Lebanon. Towns which had slipped from Egypt's grasp, territory lost under the inept leadership of Akhenaten, returned to her when the Pharaoh appeared once again at the head of his armies.

The forts along the strategic route were regarrisoned, wells reopened, and the King returned to Thebes with droves of prisoners and rich plunder. Soon he was campaigning again, leading a successful attack against the walled city of Gaza, advancing up the coast, capturing Kadesh on the Orontes as Tuthmosis III had done, and eventually confronting the armies of the Hittite King Muwatallis. Although he was unable to defeat Muwatallis, he came to terms with him, the Hittites agreeing to cede to Egypt the whole of Palestine and all the coastal region of Syria as far north as the river Litany.

Next he turned westwards to deal with the Libyans, and later, in the far south, built a powerful fortress at Amareh West to hold the Nubians in check. As the face of his well-preserved mummy shows, he was a man of powerful physique, and due to his conquests Thebes became rich again; much wealth was expended on enlarging and beautifying the temples, particularly at Karnak. There, in collaboration with his son and co-regent Ramesses II, he built the enormous Hypostyle Hall with its 134 columns, of which the 12 nave columns are 69 feet high and 12 feet thick; it is the largest single chamber of any temple in the world, almost equal to the whole of Canterbury Cathedral. The walls and column-surfaces are covered with six acres of sculpted reliefs depicting Sethi or Ramesses sacrificing to the gods, slaying enemies from their war-chariots, or bringing back troops of prisoners and loads of booty to the capital city, once more the most powerful in the world.

Naturally the tombs of this period are equally grandiose.

That of Horemhab is splendid enough by the standards of his time, but it cannot compare in grandeur with that of Sethi i. Descending in a series of sloping corridors over 300 feet into the mountain, its walls adorned with delicately sculpted and painted reliefs, it is the most magnificent funerary monument in Egypt. From as far back as Greek and Roman times it has been visited and admired by successive generations, and though its walls and ceilings are grimed with the smoke of their torches it remains the supreme Pharaonic tomb, compared with which that of Tutankhamun is a rabbit-hutch.

At a time when the energies of Egypt's rulers were once again devoted to military conquest and self-aggrandisement, it is not surprising that women no longer figure prominently on the royal monuments. And yet, during the long reign of Ramesses ii, Sethi's successor, there is one woman whose figure rarely fails to appear—albeit on a much-reduced scale—beside his. She is Queen Nefertari, his Chief Wife, to whom he must have been devoted. She can claim the unique distinction of having had one of the two splendid rock-cut temples of Abu Simbel dedicated entirely to her.

No Pharaoh—not even Sethi i—ever built on the scale of Ramesses ii. Huge granite colossi were hewn from the rock of Assuan, carved in an idealised representation of the King, inscribed with hieroglyphs two inches deep, and set up throughout the kingdom. The one which now lies in fragments near his funerary temple, the Ramesseum, must have been one of the largest sculptured figures of a human being ever made. Each arm was $17\frac{1}{2}$ feet in circumference at the shoulder; each ear is $3\frac{1}{2}$ feet long; the nail on the middle finger is a talon $7\frac{1}{2}$ inches in length. Imagine every other feature in proportion, a height of nearly 60 feet and a weight of 1,000 tons, and one gets a slight idea of the size of Ramesses' ego.

This is borne out in his inscriptions, proudly vaunting his victories, especially that at the battle of Kadesh, where, according to his own account, he engaged a large part of the Hittite army single-handed.

Then His Majesty arose like his father Mont and took the accoutrements of battle, and girt himself with his corselet; he was like Baal in his hour, and the great pair of horses which bore His Majesty, belonging to the great stable of Usimare-setpenre . . . were named Victory-in-Thebes. Then His Majesty started forth at a gallop, and entered into the host of the fallen ones of Khatti, being alone by himself, none other with him. And His Majesty went to look about him, and found surrounding him on his outer side 2,500 pairs of horse with all the champions of the fallen ones of Khatti and of the many countries who were with them . . . whereas there was no captain with me, no charioteer, no soldier of the army, no shield-bearer; my infantry and chariotry melted away before them, not one of them stood firm to fight with them . . . etc., etc.[1]

Smaller but still enormous statues of the egocentric Pharaoh still stand at Karnak, Luxor, Abu Simbel and elsewhere; but in nearly every case the slim, high-breasted body of Nefertari in her tight-fitting robe, her small proud chin held high, her delicate features framed in her enormous curled wig, stands beside his. Hardly ever do we see any other Queen or favourite, although Ramesses had many wives and a legion of concubines. He liked to enumerate his many sons and daughters on the walls of his temples. At Wady es Sebua in Lower Nubia there is a list of over a hundred princes and princesses, all sired by Ramesses, who, having the good fortune to live to a great age, had plenty of opportunity to procreate. But Nefertari-mery-enmut, to give her full name, always takes precedence on his monuments, although he boasts of having children by Queen Isinofre and a succession of King's Great Wives.

It could be, as some have suggested, that the prominence given to Nefertari may be due to his having inherited his right to the throne through her, but there is no proof of this. It is just as likely that he loved and wished to honour her before his subjects, and she was certainly beautiful, to judge from her portraits. Unhappily the written records tell us hardly anything about her, save that, when Ramesses concluded a treaty with the Hittite king, the latter wrote letters of congratulation not only to the Pharaoh but to Nefertari. We know this from the Boghaz-koy tablets.

She looks down at us from the plinth of her husband's colossal statue at Abu Simbel, her slim hand resting on his shin (as high as she can reach due to the comparative scale of her fig-ure and his), unable to answer any of the questions we would like to have asked. Did she envy the privileges enjoyed by her predecessors, Nefertiti and Tiye, who on their husband's monu-ments enjoy equality both of honour and of size? Probably not. She had grown up in a male-dominated society and was ac-customed to it. Yet there is something in her expression, proud, self-confident, slightly disdainful, which suggests that the great Ramesses was not as colossal to her as he liked to appear to the world.

She must have been a remarkable woman to have held her husband's love against such multifarious competition, for Ramesses II was as ardent a collector of women as his great predecessor Amenophis III. Many foreign princesses came to his harem, including a daughter of Khattusilis, King of the Hittites. Ramesses was so proud of this acquisition that he caused large stelae to be set up at Karnak, Elephantine, Abu Simbel and else-where, stressing the difficulty the escort encountered in bringing the princess back to Egypt. The inscriptions go into great de-tail, describing the many mountains to be crossed and defiles to be passed, and, as it was winter, the Pharaoh, fearing snow and rain, offered up prayers and made a great feast for the god Sutekh to ensure favourable weather.

His prayers were answered, the winter was mild, and the Hittite princess arrived safely at Thebes amid great rejoicing. Her beauty was such that she was soon raised to the status of King's Great Wife. Gardiner comments that:

> if the wonderful statue of her royal husband in the Turin Museum tells the truth they must have been a handsome pair.

By a strange chance we have evidence that this alien spouse was sometimes taken to the harem kept by the sovereign at Miwer, a town at the entrance to the Fayyum; a scrap of papyrus found by Petrie lists garments and linen belonging to her wardrobe.[2]

This princess was given the Egyptian name Manefrure, but despite her high rank, and the importance of this dynastic marriage with the daughter of a king whose power rivalled that of Egypt, she was not honoured with burial in the Valley of the Queens. But Nerfertari was, and her much-visited tomb is one of the most beautiful in the Theban Necropolis. She was in fact the first Queen to be buried in this valley set apart for the burial of the Great Wives of the King. Her tomb is one of the largest and most elaborate in this valley and the vividly-coloured paintings on its walls reinforce the impression of charm, intelligence and regal dignity one receives from Nefertari's sculptured figures. They also tell us something about the current fashions in dress and ornament.

Her name means 'Beautiful Companion,' and she was married to Ramesses in the first year of his reign. Her tomb does not disappoint, though parts of it have been badly damaged, and it was of course despoiled of its treasures thousands of years ago. But it has a palatial atmosphere, even now, with its grand staircase leading down to a hall, probably meant for the reception of offerings. Here we see the Queen adoring Osiris, together with Anubis and the four 'children of Horus.' More intriguing is the scene on the left of the entrance, where Nefertari is shown playing a game with pieces on a squared board, rather like chess. One hopes she was good at it and occasionally beat her vain spouse.

The Queen is no longer the nubile girl sculpted on the colossi, but still elegant, despite the folds of flesh around her neck. She wears the gold vulture-head-dress surmounted by the two plumes, with the sun-disk between, and around her neck and shoulders is an enormous gold collar made up of hundreds of tiny gold beads. Each slender wrist wears a bracelet, and her white gown has wide pleated sleeves, drawn in at the waist by a coloured girdle with long pendant ribbons, and instead of the clinging, narrow skirt favoured by the ladies of Amenophis III's court, she prefers one which bells out from the narrow waist to fall in graceful folds around her gold-sandalled feet. But her still-comely legs are visible beneath it. Naturally other ladies of this period imitated the royal fashion, and most Ramesside tombs show women wearing this style of dress. Sandals turned up at the toe had also come into fashion, and the white gowns are often enlivened by coloured embroidery or coloured sashes.

She looks especially elegant in the scene on the walls of the staircase descending to the burial-hall, where Nefertari, again wearing the long, full, pleated white gown with coloured sash, makes offerings to the goddesses Hathor, Selquet and Maat, all of whom wear close-fitting dresses of the traditional pattern, with tight skirts, two shoulder-straps which support a dress ending below the breasts, and head-dresses which enable us to identify them, e.g. Hathor wears the sun-disk between cow's horns. By contrast the Queen is modestly attired in a flowing, full-skirted dress which reveals nothing save her outstretched arms.

It is a curious fact that, although so little is known concerning Nefertari, her personality imposes itself on one with every repeated visit to the Necropolis; I imagine a worldly-wise woman with a quick wit, high intelligence and strong character, well able to cope with the vagaries of her experienced and sophisticated husband. One would like to have known her.

---

[1] Gardiner, Sir Alan, *Egypt of the Pharaohs,* Oxford University Press, New York, 1961
[2] Gardiner, Sir Alan, op. cit.

16

'The Eddy in Deep Water'

IT WAS ADMITTED IN THE FIRST CHAPTER THAT THIS WOULD BE A deliberately discursive book in which the interest would lie as much in the journey as in the destination. Looking over the notes which have accumulated during its writing I notice many references which have so far been omitted lest the book become too digressive. One is rather in the position of the archaeologist who, having cleared a site down to its essential foundations, is left with a number of curious objects which he has decided to reserve for further study. I have also become aware of something missing from my sketch of Ancient Egyptian women. With the possible exception of Hashepsowe—of whom the worst that can be said is that she may have been over-fond of power—all my Queens and the lesser ladies have been most estimable women. But there were others, including a namesake of Queen Tiye, who were not.

Turning first to the *miscellanea*, little has been said so far about children, apart from certain objects found in Tutankhamun's tomb, and Pendlebury's intriguing suggestion that the paint-marks daubed on a wall of the Amarna palace may have been made by Nefertiti's infant daughters. But something can be learned about Egyptian children, mainly from objects found in tombs and on town-sites. Many toys, including dolls, have been discovered. In the tomb of Tutankhamun, besides the child's chair, there were slings and sling-stones, a collection of walking-sticks, bows and arrows in great numbers, and games played with pieces on a squared board.

Children of less exalted parents had to be content with home-made toys, some of which they modelled themselves. Petrie says about Ancient Egyptian children that:

> one of the favourite amusements, as they developed, was the modelling of clay toys on the canal banks, like modern African children. The best of these were brought home to play with, and are found in the houses—crocodiles, pigs, sheep, men, boats, and even a sarcophagus and mummy. . . . Beside the children's own toys, there were others made for them of wood, sometimes working figures; but these are of less interest than what children made for themselves. Wooden tops and tip-cats were in constant use as well as balls of leather stuffed.[1]

Other toys which have been found are rattles, crocodiles with moving jaws, and miniature battle-axes. Little girls played with dolls some of which were provided with cradles. Some of the games played by the boys recall those of a modern fairground: shooting at a target and fishing with a stick. Among sports were running, jumping and wrestling—all conducted according to accepted rules. The Ancient Greeks were certainly not the first to indulge in organised, competitive athletics. But for Egyptians of royal and noble blood, archery, including shooting from a moving chariot, seems to have been a favourite pastime. And judging from some of the tomb-scenes, the harem-girls were expert at ball-games both for the diversion of their masters as well as themselves. Women of rank also played a game like chess, as we know from the tomb of Queen Nefertari and other examples.

Egyptian women married at a very early age, often shortly after puberty, and had several children while still in their 'teens. Mid-wives assisted at the birth, and there were physicians who specialised in gynaecology. Despite this, infant mortality seems to have been high, and mummies have been found of women who had evidently died in childbirth, with their stillborn infants beside them in the coffin. Of medicine and surgery in general, one may say that provided an Egyptian woman did not contract a serious illness she had a good chance of remaining healthy, since Egyptian medical science, though it used magic a great deal, contained a very substantial body of sound doctrine.

Several medical papyri have come to us which give the diagnosis and prognosis of a number of diseases, and the therapy used. Among the illnesses treated were migraine, afflictions of the respiratory organs such as bronchitis and laryngitis—for which honey, cream and milk were prescribed for soothing the throat—digestive disorders, including constipation and other bowel complaints, and gastric upsets. Castor oil was used for the relief of the intestines, and Egyptian doctors were familiar with the use of the enema, herbal dressings and suppositories. Although a great many of the prescriptions were obviously based on the idea of driving out an evil spirit by administering some revolting concoction, others made use of substances which still form part of the modern pharmacopoeia, e.g. anise, cumin, poppy, cassia, sodium bicarbonate, sulphur, arsenic and nitre (the name of the latter is Egyptian).

> The various prescriptions [writes an Egyptian doctor who is also an Egyptologist] seem to be quite rational and natural applications to the alleviation of symptoms—complexes of knowledge of general physiological properties and actions of plant, animal and mineral medica. Notice, for example, the drugs cited to kill intestinal worms and those to purge or stop diarrhoeas.

There were specialists, too, in Ancient Egypt, e.g. in eye diseases such as trachoma, in disorders of the stomach, in pulmonary diseases, and in gynaecology. In fact one document, the Kahun Papyrus, is devoted entirely to gynaecological matters. There were also dentists; mummies have been found showing evidence of extraction and filling of teeth, and the draining of abscesses. Then there were bone surgeons; the Edwin Smith Papyrus gives instructions on how to treat bruises of the vertebrae, fractures of the ribs, clavicle and humerus, dislocation of the jaw, and so on. Fifty-eight cases are methodically and scientifically examined. There is no evidence, however, that any form of anaesthetic was known and used.

Aphrodisiacs are described in certain papyri, and in others there are spells for the restoration of flagging potency, e.g.:

> Hail to thee, thou (great) god, who created the patricians, thou Khnum [the creator-god] who established the plebs, mayst thou test the mouth of every vulva. . . . Be stiff, be not soft. Be strong, be not weak, [followed by the words] the member is to be annointed therewith.[2]

Marriage was a civil contract and among the wealthier classes, at least, a woman could marry more or less whom she pleased, with the exception, of course, of dynastic marriages between members of the royal family. Feudal patrons were expected, in the words of one document, 'to introduce young girls to the bachelors,' and the goddess Hathor is entreated to 'give a husband to the widow and a hearth to the virgin.' Egyptian husbands seem to have been kind to their wives and there are passages in the 'Wisdom Literature' which point to this.

> Love your wife in the intimacy of your home, as is your duty. Feed her, dress her . . . seek to please her as long as you live.

This intimacy and the implied comradeship extended even to Kings and Queens at times, as is shown in a charming passage in which the Pharaoh Amosis is described as sitting with his wife Queen Ahmose-Nefertari and pondering on what shall be done to confer funerary benefits on his ancestors.

His wife spoke and answered him; 'Why have these things been recalled? what has come into thy heart?'

The King's own person said to her; 'I have recalled the mother of my mother and the mother of my father, king's great wife and king's mother, Tetisheri, deceased. A tomb-chamber and a sepulchre of hers are at this moment upon the soil of the Theban and Abydene nomes, but I have said this to thee because My Majesty has wished to make for her a pyramid and a chapel in the Sacred Land close to the monument of My Majesty' ... His Majesty spoke thus, and these things were accomplished at once.[3]

The mere fact that the founder of the Eighteenth Dynasty should bother to record, on an inscribed stela, that he consulted his wife on this important matter of transferring the royal bodies of his grandmothers to a more suitable burial place indicates the respect in which the women of Egypt were usually held by their husbands.

No doubt there were family dissensions from time to time. One scribe adjures his readers to treat their wives courteously:

Be not rude to a woman in her house if you know her thoroughly. Do not say 'where is that? bring it to me!' when she has put it in the right place and your eye has not seen it. When you are silent you know her qualities and it is a joy for your hand to be with her.[4]

If a couple decided to separate, divorce was easy. It was merely a matter of stating one's intention before witnesses. But the woman's rights were safeguarded. The husband had to pay compensation to the divorced spouse, and, although the legal evidence is not clear on this point, it would appear that concubines with children also were protected by law. Reasons for divorce were various; adultery, of course—and this in the case of a woman could be punishable by death—but incompatibility could also provide grounds for breaking the union. But such ruptures were probably rare, because the Ancient Egyptians seemed to cherish family life in a manner reminiscent of the Victorians. As one writer expresses it:

> On the whole the biographies, wisdom literature, letters to the dead, the family groups in cemeteries, and statues of married couples side by side, their children at their feet, proclaim the devotion of the average Egyptian to his home—a narrow circle, quiet, respectable, and a shade dull. The regular characteristics were devoted respect for mamas, regard for the mother of a large family, adored children, concern about the sons' future, concern for women's needs and respect for the wisdom of the sage.[5]

There was, of course, another kind of woman. Egyptian literature abounds in warnings about her wiles.

> Beware of a woman from strange parts, whose city is not known. When she comes do not look at her or know her. She is the eddy in deep water, the depth of which is unknown. The woman whose husband is far off writes to thee every day. If no witness is near her she stands up and spreads out her net. O fearful crime to listen to her![6]

The harem system which prevailed throughout Egyptian history must at times have fostered intrigue, especially when an ambitious and unscrupulous Queen or concubine schemed to supplant the legitimate heir or heiress by her own offspring. No doubt this happened on more than one occasion, but the only record of such a conspiracy which has survived dates from the reign of Ramesses III, the great and long-lived monarch who is to the Twentieth Dynasty what Ramesses II was to the Nineteenth.

The plot was hatched in the harem, and the woman on whom it centred was a secondary Queen who bore the same name as her illustrious predecessor of the Eighteenth Dynasty—Tiye. In the Turin Museum a magnificent papyrus, written, as Gardiner comments, 'in large hieratic majuscules befitting a state document of the highest importance,' records the trial of the conspirators, one of whom was the Queen's major-domo, Paibekkamun.

> The great enemy Paibekkamun who had been major-domo. He was brought on account of his having attached himself to Tiye and the women of the harem. He made common cause with them and proceeded to carry their words outside to their mothers and brothers and sisters who were there, saying 'Collect people and foment hostility' so as to make rebellion against their lord. And they set him in the presence of the great officials of the Place of Examination and they examined his crimes and found that he had committed them. And his crimes took hold of him, and the officials who examined him caused his punishment to cleave to him.[7]

Six other wives were also arraigned, and twenty-nine officials, including a certain royal butler, the overseer and deputy-overseer of the harem, two scribes, six inspectors, and the wives of the doorkeepers. Among those arrested was a 'troop commander from Cush' (in Nubia) whose sister, one of the harem-women, had evidently persuaded him to stir up rebellion in Nubia.

The plot, so far as one can gather from the obscure, obliquely-worded document, was evidently hatched in the harem by Queen Tiye, who wanted to place her son Pentawere on the throne, after disposing of the Pharaoh. At the same time, other conspirators in positions of trust throughout the kingdom were to 'stir up rebellion' when the King was killed. This and other information we can glean from the Turin Judicial Papyrus. But there is another document, the Papyrus Rollin, which contains intriguing statements about 'making people of wax,' and these have been subjected to a variety of interpretations. In most translations it is assumed that this obscure passage refers to the use of magic, images of wax being introduced into the palace for the purpose of doing harm to the King. The passage reads:

> It happened because writings were made for enchanting, for confusing—because some 'gods' were made into wax and

some men (also)—and (furthermore) for enfeebling the limb(s) of men, and which (writings) were placed in the hand of Paibekkamun—that Re had not allowed that he act as chief of the chamber—and (of) the other capital offenders, saying 'Let them come close!' And one let them come close. And when he caused the doers of crimes to enter, he—that Re had not allowed that he grow up—acted along with them.[8]

The above translation is a recent one (1963) by Hans Goedicke and differs in some respects from earlier translations, e.g. that of Breasted. Egyptian philology advances at a slow but steady pace, and new interpretations of well-known texts may follow as a result of re-assessing the meaning of even a single word. Goedicke, in a fascinating but involved dissertation in the *Journal of Egyptian Archaeology* for December 1963, challenges the long-established belief that magic was used, and argues that the phrases 'because some "gods" were made into wax and some men also' really mean that certain priests ('gods') and officials of the palace were made malleable by the persuasiveness of the plotters, and by the use of faked documents permitting them to enter the royal apartments. He also argues that one of the plotters, though un-named, was probably the young Prince Pentawere, son of Tiye.

It would be impertinent to attempt to summarise this long and learned analysis of the documents, but some of Goedicke's conclusions, which I now quote, are stimulating:

> First of all we have the answer to the initial question about the use of magical practices or superstitions, in the plot against Ramesses III. The answer is definitely negative; i.e. there is no trace of any supernatural actions in the entire account; on the contrary, the people who hatched the plot show a remarkable ingenuity in order to arrive at their goal. *The alleged references to magical practices in the text are due to misinterpretation.* (Our italics.)[9]

Now there is a certain high tower in the great palace and temple of Medinet Habu which every visitor to Thebes is shown,

because on the walls of one of its upper rooms are scenes showing Ramesses III disporting himself with the girls of his harem.
This tower, according to Goedicke, was probably the scene of
the drama. One of the passages in the papyrus refers to the conspirators going up to 'a high place.' Here Goedicke describes
what he believes may have happened, and this is not the romantic
speculation of a novelist but the serious conclusions of a distinguished scholar supported by a wealth of philological argument.

> From what we can see, each participant in the conspiracy
> had a particular role assigned. We still have no specifications
> about the activities of the two main figures in the plot, namely
> those of the Queen Tiye and Paibekkamun. The texts discussed
> furnish us with detailed information about the two other main
> figures, namely Pentawere, apparently the son of Queen Tiye,
> for whom Ramesses should give way, and *Pn-hwy-bin* who
> was 'overseer of the herds,' presumably in the service of Amun.
> The two worked hand in hand. . . . While Pentawere was active
> in the immediate vicinity of the King, preparing the way for the
> conspirators, *Pn-hwy-bin* was the one who arranged the entry
> of the plotters into the place where the King was.[10]

Goedicke suggests that the plotters chose the beginning of the
Feast of the Valley as the time of their projected *coup*, relying on
the inevitable confusion which accompanied, and still accom-
panies, any Egyptian religious celebration.

> *Pn-hwy-bin,* presumably accompanied by a few others,
> made the advance to the place where the King was at the time.
> Possibly to avoid the bustle, or just to pursue his pleasures, the
> King left his official palace and retreated to the suite of rooms
> in the upper floors of the western High-Gate. This place, far
> removed from the commotion of the feast, was not much
> guarded on the occasion. Still, the sentries had to be passed, for
> which the faked royal document was used at the side entrance
> of the building. Once inside it was necessary to reach the King,

a point where Pentawere again came into action. Being in league with the advancing plotters he gave orders to let them in to the King.[11]

The evidence for this is contained in another papyrus, the Papyrus Lee, of which the following is part of Goedicke's translation, abridged.

When *Pn-hwy-bin,* who was (formerly) overseer of cattle, said to him 'Give me a piece of writing for giving me power (and) authority' he gave him a piece of official paper of *Usima-re-meramun* (Ramesses III) . . . the great god, his lord. And it happened because of (the feast of) the Arrival of the God and the excitement of the people that he reached the harem side of that other very high place. It happened because the people were made into wax (and) because of the writings of demand that one allowed that they were taken in. . . .[12]

But the conspiracy failed, bringing about the arrest of the plotters and their trial and punishment. Some merely suffered mutilation, their noses and ears being cut off; others probably were allowed to commit suicide. The records contain the cryptic phrase 'he brought his death to himself' repeated in the case of most of the culprits. But nothing is known of the fate of Queen Tiye herself, though her son certainly died. There is a gruesome theory, quite unsupported by positive evidence, that he was mummified and buried alive, perhaps after taking a narcotic. It is said that among the royal mummies found at Deir el Bahri was one without any name. It was that of a young man whose body had not been eviscerated and embalmed but merely swathed in mummy-cloths; on the face was an expression of extreme agony. I repeat this story for what it is worth.

Although it is sometimes stated that Ramesses III did perish by assassination there is no proof of this. His well-preserved mummy is that of an elderly man and shows no signs of wounds. He could, of course, have been poisoned, though this seems unlikely, judging from the nature of the attack. He keeps his secret, and we shall probably never know what happened to him, or to his treacherous Queen.

And while on this subject of feminine treachery there is an absorbing narrative preserved in the Papyrus d'Orbiney in the British Museum and called 'The Tale of the Two Brothers.' It dates from the New Kingdom and has, as its central female character, a woman totally unlike the devoted wives and mothers of conventional Egyptian morality. Her name is not given. She is just 'the wife of Anubis,' one of the two brothers, and she belongs to a clearly-recognisable type of whom Potiphar's wife is another example. She is sensual, unfaithful and quite ruthless.

The younger brother, whose name was Bata, worked in the fields for his elder brother Anubis. During the season of sowing, while the two brothers were working in the fields, Anubis sent Bata back to the farmhouse to obtain more seed. . . .

> And his younger brother found the wife of his elder brother as she sat having her hair done. And he said to her 'Up, and give me seed, that I may go to the field, for mine elder brother waiteth for me. Tarry not.'

—which was a little brusque, to say the least. Not surprisingly the wife, interrupted in her hairdressing, replies:

> 'Go, open the bin thyself, and take away what thou willest; but don't expect me to leave unfinished the dressing of my hair.'

The storyteller continues:

> And the lad went into his stall and took a great vessel, with the intent to take away much seed. And he loaded himself with barley and wheat and went out with it. And she said unto him 'How much is that thou hast upon thy shoulder?' And he said unto her 'Three sacks of wheat and two of barley, five in all, have I upon my shoulder.' And she said . . . 'Then thou hast great strength. Yes, I see daily how strong thou art.' And her desire was to know him as one knows a youth.

And she arose and took hold of him and said 'Come, we will take our pleasure and sleep. It will also be for thine advantage, for I will make thee goodly garments.'

And the lad became enraged like a leopard . . . at this wicked thing which she said unto him, and she was sore afraid. And he spake unto her, saying 'Lo, thou art unto me as a mother, and thine husband is unto me as a father, for as the elder hath he brought me up. What is this great abomination that thou hast spoken? Say it not again unto me. But I will tell it to no man, and will not suffer it to come forth from my mouth to any man.' And he took his burden and went into the fields.

The powerful simplicity of this description, the terse clarity of the dialogue, the absence of literary flourishes, recalls some of the finest passages in the Old Testament. It shows beyond any doubt the high degree of literary excellence which had been attained by the scribes and storytellers of the New Kingdom and the quality of the civilisation which produced it. This is a story which could well have been familiar to Tiye, Nefertiti and Nefertari, whether they read it in the original or heard it recited at court. Although mingled with the supernatural happenings which the Ancient Egyptians loved—such as animals which warn the young man of the treachery plotted by the wife—the story moves remorselessly along its allotted psychological path.

When Anubis returns to his home he finds his wife had made preparations for his deception:

. . . she took fat and . . . and made as though she had been cruelly beaten [probably she ate fat to make her vomit] desiring to say to her husband 'It was thy younger brother that did beat me.' And her husband came home at even as was his daily wont. He came to his house and found his wife lying down and made cruelly sick. She poured no water upon his hands according to his wont; she kindled no light on his return, and his house was in darkness; and she lay there and vomited. And her husband said unto her; 'Who hath spoken with thee?' And she said unto him 'no one hath spoken to me save thy younger brother. When he came to fetch the seed and found me sitting all alone, he said unto me "Come, we will take our pleasure and sleep. Put on thy ringlets" [i.e. her great wig]. 'So spake he, but I heeded him not. Then he was afraid and he beat me so that I might not report it unto thee. If, therefore, thou suffereth him to live, I will take mine own life; for behold, when he cometh home at even and I tell this evil tale he will make it look white.'

There is no space to tell the story in full and to abbreviate it would spoil it. In Erman and Blackman's translation you may read how Anubis pursued Bata, determined to kill him, of how Bata, warned by the animals, took refuge, and how Re, taking pity on the boy, caused a great stretch of crocodile-infested water to appear between the two brothers, so that Bata could tell Anubis the truth.

And he swore by Re-Harakhti, saying 'Alas, that thou desiredst to slay me by guile, and didst take thy lance on the word of a dirty strumpet!' And he took a reed knife and cut off his privy member and cast it into the water and the shad (fish) swallowed it . . . And his elder brother was exceeding sorrowful, and stood and wept loudly over him, yet he could not cross over to where his younger brother was because of the crocodiles. . . . And he came unto his house, and he slew his wife, cast her to the dogs, and sat mourning for his younger brother.

But this being Ancient Egypt and not Palestine of the Hebrews, the story does not end thus. The gods take compassion on Bata, and despite his self-inflicted mutilation, decide to make a wife for him.

and Khnum made him a companion that had fairer limbs than any woman in the whole land, and every god was in her. And he was greatly enamoured of her, and she dwelt in his house. And he spent the day hunting the game of the desert and brought it and laid it before her.[13]

Later the Pharaoh himself enters the story, when a lock of hair from the head of Bata's wife got into the royal laundry, and so sweet was the unguent she used that its perfume filled the palace, so that the King also desired her. So the story continues, miracle piled on miracle, surprise on surprise, to its delightful ending, when, on the death of the King, Bata takes his place on the throne of Egypt and rules for thirty years.

The mingling of naivete with sophistication, of realism with magic, is characteristic of Ancient Egypt; and the character of the wicked wife provides a piquant and necessary contrast with the cosiness of Egyptian family life and the splendid but formal phrases which extol the virtues of the great Queens. Warmth, pathos, and humour (as in the case of Snofru and the maidens in fishnets) are all there to prove that, beneath the crust of royal and religious ritual, the rulers of Egypt and their womenfolk had human qualities very like our own.

Running like a golden thread through the fabric of Ancient Egyptian history is the fascination of women; it is made up of many strands—love, respect, fear, often bewilderment, occasionally exasperation. Of all the ancient civilisations saving only, perhaps, that of Minoan Crete, Egypt gave them the highest honour, dignity and status—even in death. An unknown Egyptian had inscribed on his coffin this charming, whimsical poem:

These winds are given to me by these maidens.
It is the north wind who encircles the Aegean isles,
Who stretches out her arms to the ends of the Two Lands,
Who at night with regularity brings the effects of her concern.
A living wind is the north wind; through her I am made to live.

These winds are given to me by these maidens.
It is the east wind who opens the windows of heaven,
Who traces the beautiful path of Re, along which he rises.
Re grasps my arm, setting me in the rush-bearing meadows,
Where I graze like the Apis bull, where I gorge like Set—
A living wind is the east wind, through her I am made to live.

These winds are given to me by these maidens.
A brother of the desert is the west wind,
An offspring of desolation,
Living on only one portion,
No second helping in his land.
A living wind is the west wind; through him I am made to live.

These winds are given to me by these maidens.
The south wind is a living wind,
(coming from) the southern Nubians,
Bringing the life-supporting waters.
A living wind is the south wind; through him I am made to live.[14]

---

[1] Petrie, W. M. F., *Social Life in Ancient Egypt*, Constable, London, 1923

[2] Gardiner, Sir Alan, *Hieratic Papyri in the British Museum*, Volume I (Third Series), British Museum, London, 1935

[3] Gardiner, Sir Alan, *Egypt of the Pharaohs*, Oxford University Press, New York, 1961

[4] Posener, Georges, ed., *A Dictionary of Egyptian Civilization*, Tudor Publishing Co., New York, 1961

[5] Posener, Georges, op. cit.

[6] Erman and Blackman, *Literature of the Ancient Egyptians*, University Books, Inc., New Hyde Park, N.Y., 1964

[7] Gardiner, Sir Alan, op. cit.

[8] Goedicke, Hans, *Journal of Egyptian Archaeology*, Vol. 49, London, 1963

[9] Goedicke, Hans, op. cit.

[10] Goedicke, Hans, op. cit.

[11] Goedicke, Hans, op. cit.

[12] Goedicke, Hans, op. cit.

[13] Erman and Blackman, op. cit.

[14] Nims, Charles F., *Thebes of the Pharaohs*, Stein and Day, New York, 1965

Family Tree of the Amarnan Royal Family

Bibliography

Aldred, Cyril, 'The Tomb of Akhenaten at Thebes,' *Journal of Egyptian Archaeology,* Vol. 47, London, 1961

Aldred, Cyril, NEW KINGDOM ART IN EGYPT, Transatlantic Arts, Inc., Hollywood by the Sea, Florida, 1951

Baikie, James, EGYPTIAN ANTIQUITIES IN THE NILE VALLEY, Methuen, London, 1932

Blackman, A. M., 'On the Position of Women in the Egyptian Hierarchy,' Journal of Egyptian Archaeology, Vol. 7, London

Breasted, James Henry, ANCIENT RECORDS OF EGYPT, Vol. II, University of Chicago Press, Chicago, Illinois, 1906-07; 1927

Breasted, James Henry, A HISTORY OF EGYPT, Charles Scribner's Sons, New York, 1921

Carter, Howard, 'A Tomb Prepared for Queen Hatshepsut,' *Journal of Egyptian Archaeology,* Vol. 4, London, 1917

Carter, Howard, and Mace, A. C., THE TOMB OF TUT-ANKH-AMEN, 3 vols., Cooper Square Publishers, New York

Davis, Theodore M., THE TOMB OF HATSHOPSITU, Constable, London, 1906

Desroches-Noblecourt, Christiane, TUTANKHAMEN, New York Graphic Society, Greenwich, Connecticut, 1963

Desroches-Noblecourt, Christiane, THE SCULPTURE OF ANCIENT EGYPT, Oldbourne Press, London, 1960

Emery, Walter Bryan, EGYPT IN NUBIA, Hutchinson, London, 1965

Erman, Adolf, and Blackman, A. M., LITERATURE OF THE ANCIENT EGYPTIANS, University Books, Inc., New Hyde Park, New York, 1964

Fairman, H. W., 'Once Again the So-Called Coffin of Akhenaten,' *Journal of Egyptian Archaeology,* Vol. 47, London, 1961

Gardiner, Sir Alan, EGYPT OF THE PHARAOHS, Oxford University Press, New York, 1961

Gardiner, Sir Alan, HIERATIC PAPYRI IN THE BRITISH MUSEUM (Third Series), British Museum, London, 1935

Gardiner, Sir Alan, 'The So-Called Tomb of Queen Tiye,' *Journal of Egyptian Archaeology,* Vol. 43, London, 1957

Gardiner, Sir Alan, TOPOGRAPHICAL CATALOGUE OF THE PRIVATE TOMBS OF THEBES, Bernard Quaritch, London, 1913

Goedicke, Hans, 'Was Magic Used in the Harem Conspiracy Against Ramesses III?' *Journal of Egyptian Archaeology,* Vol. 49, London, 1963

Hayes, W. C., THE SCEPTER OF EGYPT, Vol. II, New York Graphic Society for the Metropolitan Museum of Art, Greenwich, Conn., 1959

Lucas, Alfred, ANCIENT EGYPTIAN MATERIALS AND INDUSTRIES, St. Martin's Press, New York, 1962

Murray, Margaret A., THE SPLENDOUR THAT WAS EGYPT, Hawthorn Books, New York, 1963

Nims, Charles F., THEBES OF THE PHARAOHS, Stein and Day, New York, 1965

Pendlebury, J. D. S., THE CITY OF AKHETATEN, Egypt Exploration Society, London, 1951

Pendlebury, J. D. S., TELL EL AMARNA, Lovat Dickson and Thompson, Ltd., London, 1935

Petrie, W. M. F., SOCIAL LIFE IN ANCIENT EGYPT, Constable, London, 1923

Posener, Georges, ed., A DICTIONARY OF EGYPTIAN CIVILISATION, Tudor Publishing Co., New York, 1961

Pritchard, J. B. ed., ANCIENT NEAR EASTERN TEXTS, Princeton University Press, Princeton, New Jersey, 1958

Rachelwitz, Boris de, EGYPTIAN ART, Viking Press for Studio Books, New York, 1960

Weigall, Arthur, THE LIFE AND TIMES OF AKHENATEN, G. P. Putnam's Sons, New York, 1923

Winlock, H. E., MODELS OF DAILY LIFE IN ANCIENT EGYPT, Harvard University Press, Cambridge, Massachusetts, 1955

Index